Managing Sport Organizations

Rubén Acosta Hernández

Human Kinetics

796.069
A185d
2002

Library of Congress Cataloging-in-Publication Data

Acosta Hernández, Rubén, 1934-
[Dirección, gestión y administración de las organizaciones deportivas. English]
Managing sport organizations / Rubén Acosta Hernández.
   p. cm.
Includes bibliographical references and index.
ISBN 0-7360-3826-4
1. Sports administration. I. Title.
GV713 .A36 2002
796'.06'9--dc21

2001039263

ISBN: 0-7360-3826-4

This book is a revised edition of *Dirección, Gestión y Administración de las Organizaciones Deportivas*, published in 1999 by Editorial Paidotribo.

Acquisitions Editor: Amy N. Clocksin; **Developmental Editor:** Joanna Hatzopoulos Portman; **Assistant Editor:** Derek Campbell; **Copyeditor:** Anne Meyer Byler; **Proofreader:** Julie A. Marx; **Indexer:** Sharon Duffy; **Permission Manager:** Dalene Reeder; **Graphic Designer:** Nancy Rasmus; **Graphic Artist:** Kathleen Boudreau-Fuoss; **Photo Manager:** Leslie A. Woodrum; **Cover Designer:** Jack W. Davis; **Photographer (cover):** Mark Downey; **Art Managers:** Carl D. Johnson and Kelly Hendren; **Illustrator:** Mike Cox; **Printer:** Edwards Brothers, Inc.

Printed in the United States of America   10   9   8   7   6   5   4   3   2   1

Human Kinetics
Web site: www.HumanKinetics.com

United States: Human Kinetics, P.O. Box 5076, Champaign, IL 61825-5076
800-747-4457
e-mail: humank@hkusa.com

Canada: Human Kinetics, 475 Devonshire Road Unit 100, Windsor, ON N8Y 2L5
800-465-7301 (in Canada only)
e-mail: orders@hkcanada.com

Europe: Human Kinetics, 107 Bradford Road, Stanningly, Leeds
LS28 6AT, United Kingdom
+44 (0) 113 255 5665
e-mail: hk@hkeurope.com

Australia: Human Kinetics, 57A Price Avenue, Lower Mitcham, South Australia 5062
08 8277 1555
e-mail: liahka@senet.com.au

New Zealand: Human Kinetics, P.O. Box 105-231, Auckland Central
09-523-3462
e-mail: hkp@ihug.co.nz

CONTENTS

iii

Part III People Leading the Way

PREFACE

Even in highly developed countries, national sport organizations are rarely structured adequately enough to meet the new challenges of a professional sport environment influenced by sport entertainers, promoters, television networks, and newspapers, all of which are intent on taking control of the promotional and marketing activities of major sport events.

Indeed, most national sport organizations are today in the hands of technicians, school teachers, physical education instructors, sport fans, and so on. These people may generally understand how the systematic practice of sport may benefit the individual and the community at large, but they usually fail to recognize its importance for individuals wishing to reach a competitive sport level, develop athletic skills or sport techniques, acquire competitive experience, and learn from their personal failures or poor sport performances. Furthermore, these leaders have little or no experience in conceiving and developing plans aimed at promoting highly competitive sport events to the satisfaction of sport enthusiasts, media, sponsors, and spectators.

Be they multisport or sport specific, very few national sport organizations throughout the world have adequately defined their role or suitably identified their image, goals, or objectives. Nor have they clearly established their program of activities with a view to maximizing individual and group efficiency over a certain period of time. The ineffectiveness of today's sport organizations is due largely to the lack of a compelling vision and the absence of a driving force based on administrative competence. These are the only elements capable of ensuring that the problems of sport are tackled in the right place, at the right time, and with the right people, who must be highly motivated and well organized.

Any sport organization wishing to fulfill its mission and successfully coordinate the day-to-day activities of its sport must improve the working conditions of its employees, volunteers, and members. It must also facilitate grassroots sport participation; ensure the availability of high-tech sport material; and create the adequate organizational conditions for sport events to ensure that they are more competitive for athletes, more entertaining for spectators, more interesting for the media, and more fulfilling for sponsors.

However, they can only undertake these responsibilities when they have achieved adequate organization, efficient administration, and professional management.

In spite of their inadequacies, sport organizations are forced to operate under social and legal conditions presented by the people and government of their countries. These may include a constraining or nonconstraining national legal framework; favorable or unfavorable socio-educational structures; and supportive or nonsupportive commercial, industrial, and governmental organizations.

My purpose in this work is to offer sport organizations a broad view on a variety of subjects to facilitate their mission and provide know-how for overcoming internal shortcomings, surmounting environmental or political obstacles, and countering negative forces. It is also the intention to assist them in meeting the new challenges arising from the recent professionalization and commercialization of sport events, including the Olympic Games, and from the intervention of external forces that disrupt relations between such sport organizations and their athletes and marketing agents. These disruptive actions include the intrusion of intermediaries such as players' agents or representatives in the running of sport affairs and the increasingly hegemonic attitudes of multisport organizations and governmental agencies.

The real question that must be answered is not whether intermediaries are beneficial to the smooth running of sport activities, but how the national sport organizations, including the respective national governing bodies of sport—national federations (NFs)*—should deal with such intermediaries in a manner that allows the NFs to remain at the helm of organized sport activities and maintain the authority vested in them.

All too frequently, national and international sport structures follow self-serving interests and affect the work of NFs in an adverse manner by belittling the important role they play. Under such circumstances, worldwide sport organizations—such as the international federations (IFs) and the International Olympic Committee (IOC)—need to institute a novel, modern, worldwide sport structure in which everybody can play a role without cross-interference, either from the national or international level.

This potential new structure will only come into being if national sport organizations are prepared to acknowledge their shortcomings, take remedial measures, and meet some of the specific needs addressed in this book. These needs can be summarized as follows.

---

*Note: The term "National Federations" or "NFs" also applies to national governing bodies of sport, national sport organizations, or national associations.

1. **The need for more theoretical studies and educational resources** to provide the knowledge that will boost the efficiency and effectiveness of sport organizations directly involved in the running of regular sport events at the national and international levels. Most of today's texts on the sport environment are written largely to help the managers of commercial sport enterprises improve the profitability, industrial efficiency, and competitiveness of their companies.

2. **The need for greater personal expertise in sport management** to meet the demands for management seminars on sport organization, sport marketing relations, and sport media relations. The difficulty in finding experienced speakers on such subjects suggests a shortage of professional management in sport generally. It also underscores the need for teaching material and textbooks on the subject of administration and management of bodies governing sport at all levels: national, continental, and global.

3. **The need to be familiar with PR activities and media relations.** Professional sport managers, supported by competent staff, sufficient administrative resources, adequate facilities and equipment, and appropriate organizational structures, can improve the performance of national sport organizations through their ability to plan, organize, control, lead, motivate, direct, and make decisions. It is equally true that successful managers must be familiar with the ins and outs of successful public relations activities and the ways to nurture marketing and media relations.

4. **The need for guidance and tools to attain higher administrative levels.** Last, but not least, there is also an obvious need to provide the presidents, general secretaries, chief executive officers, and managing directors of sport organizations with the necessary guidance and tools to enable them to lead their organizations to higher administrative levels. This involves mastering the modern techniques and skills required to tackle the many problems relating to internal communication, media relations, sport marketing, public relations, fund-raising activities, and management of people, as well as the motivation of their employees, individual members, constituents, and volunteers.

This book is intended to provide management knowledge and practical tools in a simple manner, focusing on systematic aspects as well as practical situations and work routines related to organizational trends, administration principles, and management abilities.

This book has been organized in three parts and seven chapters. **Part I** deals with questions related to the world of sport organizations, with chapter 1 presenting today's social sport setting, with a view to placing the reader in the current sport environment. This underscores the need for new structures and explains as clearly as possible the operational obstacles that sport organizations are experiencing nowadays, both at the national and international level. It also examines the origins of sport conflicts and suggests ways to address them.

On the basis of studies carried out by Professors Kapferer and Bernard Catry (from Switzerland and France), I also describe in chapter 1 the difference between sport identity and sport image, two concepts often confused if not altogether ignored by sport organizations.

Chapter 2 of part I addresses issues involved in establishing a new sport organization. It is devoted in particular to describing the process by which a new organization is created and arranging the types of organization best suited to serve as the framework of sport activities. Most of this material can also be applied to already established organizations.

Chapters 3 and 4 of **part II** explain the essential concepts in the power of performance that could benefit national sport organizations, should they follow and take advantage of the keys to success. This power of performance depends on the organization's ability to use top quality public relations to improve the image of its sport, practitioners, and leaders, and ultimately of the organization as a whole.

As a prerequisite to success, the organization must enhance its general perception by the media, business world, and political or social organizations. This can be achieved through the adequate planning and implementation of strategic activities in public relations (PR), communication, sport promotion, fund-raising, media relations, and events marketing, all of which are essential components of the successful sale of the sport to the community at large.

Part III is dedicated to the people leading the way, namely sport managers, and the different concepts for improving results and increasing their organizations' power of performance. Chapter 5 presents some of the operational aspects of sport organizations, starting with a description of the basic knowledge that sport managers should possess. This knowledge includes information on the personal skills necessary to manage the organization and on their managerial duties. As discussed in chapter 6, sport managers must also master the fundamental abilities necessary to plan the work of the organization properly; the relations with the media; and PR, promotion, and fund-raising activities.

Chapter 7 provides a thorough description of budgetary preparation and organizational controls from a variety of standpoints. I also include my own perception of the conditions under which sport organizations will operate in the future, be they NFs, IFs, or part of the Olympic movement as a whole. I also describe several likely hurdles these organizations will have to overcome arising from the new professional sport environment, including spectators' and media expectations in regard to athletes' performance in the highly demanding area of sport as a form of show business.

The keen interest I have taken in management and administration over the years has been nurtured by an extensive involvement in courses, seminars, and conferences and by my ongoing study of subjects connected to PR, planning, organization, and communication. My participation in the leadership of various sport organizations, including national governing bodies of sport (NFs), multisport organizations, and the Mexican Olympic Committee, has been extremely valuable, most particularly my involvement in the staging of the 1968 Olympic Games in Mexico City in the capacity of Deputy Director General of Sport. Also worthy of mention is the management expertise and torrent of knowledge I acquired during my professional management career—10 years of hard work for General Electric in Mexico—where I had the opportunity to take part in administrative and accounting audits as well as in government credit and financing affairs.

Although my experience and knowledge of sport management have been put to the test on numerous occasions during a long career as president-manager of national and international sports federations, they have provided a foundation on which I have built a personal philosophy, concepts, and attitudes in regard to sport. They have also enabled me to overcome the many problems that, at one time or another, plague sport organizations, both at the national and international level.

Today, I feel compelled to call for an urgent change of attitude and behavior on the part of sport leaders and of all those people involved in the operation, administration, and management of sport. Sport managers need to be willing to acquire a greater knowledge and mastery of contemporary management skills that will increase operational performance. They need knowledge and skills that will help them do the following essential leadership tasks:

1. Establish a plan of activities and implement it.
2. Determine the structure of a sport organization and the departments, sections, or units that are necessary to fully implement the plans approved by the organization.
3. Manage and motivate people.
4. Deal with internal factors such as the strengths and weaknesses inherent in the sport itself; its employees, clubs, leagues, national teams, and members; and with situations arising within the organization.
5. Face external factors, including the opportunities and threats generated by situations outside the organization's control, the calendar

of other sports, the attitude of sponsors in regard to such sports, the social environment, and political support.

6. Control the organization.
7. Make decisions.
8. Improve communication and implement promotional and PR activities as well as fund-raising programs.
9. Work with the media.
10. Understand the meaning of leadership.

It is my sincere wish that this book will be a valuable contribution to small and large sport organizations striving to become a permanent bridge between the hard living and educational conditions of youth and their dreams of fame and glory through sport. Not only inner cities and public parks, but middle-class neighborhoods as well, need to find a nonprofit organization prepared to offer youngsters in their own community the opportunity to develop their athletic abilities and participate in sport competitions of their choice. Governments could better justify their involvement in sport activities by providing support and encouragement to these groups. They would recover the costs by the savings in medical care and security measures against juvenile delinquency, in addition to the gains in community productivity and safety.

ACKNOWLEDGMENTS

I want to praise my wife, Malu, and express my heartfelt appreciation for her invaluable support throughout every activity that I have undertaken, including the conclusion and publication of this book. During our life together, we have overcome obstacles of envy and jealousy, but also have been enriched by the most gratifying experiences in crucial moments of our professional careers. We have never given up or felt discouraged, and in the end our most rewarding victory has been to work our way through difficulties side by side and loving each other more than ever before.

I am most grateful for the wise advice and inspired remarks of Professor Bernard Catry, former lecturer in the new field of sport administration and management at the University of Lausanne. His astute observations and insight provided me with valuable guidance. I also express my appreciation to Joanna Hatzopoulos for her intervention, revision, and restructuring of the English edition.

When I was 17, the San Luis State University (UAP) and Normal School in San Luis Potosi where I attended offered me my first enriching experience of community involvement as I led groups in sport practice and even organized competitive sport events among my peers.

I have also been fortunate to rely on the tireless support and personal dedication of all my collaborators at the International Volleyball Federation (FIVB) office in Lausanne, particularly Mrs. Rosemary Duc, in the preparation of the English version. The day-to-day existence of our federation has provided me with some answers to the many problems raised in this book and helped me to define what I view as the best possible operational conditions under which to coordinate activities with diverse organizations such as the International Olympic Committee, continental organizations, international commissions, and national federations.

I have to recognize that my experience and knowledge have been further enriched by the study of several authors such as Kathleen A. Davis, whose excellent book titled *Sport Management* represents a wealth of knowledge for presidents, general secretaries, and directors of sport organizations; William F. Stier Jr., whose book *Successful Sport Fund-Raising* contributes significantly to a better understanding of this particular issue;

Peter J. Graham, who offers several solutions for a simple approach to sport marketing principles in *Sport Business: Operational and Theoretical Aspects;* and finally David Stevens' *Participatory Business Planning,* which provides a useful description of the way group planning has evolved.

The World of Sport Organizations

The mushrooming of professional events (leagues, professional circuits, and sports shows), professional sport organizations, private sport clubs, and resorts and health centers, combined with the worldwide explosion of satellite and cable television broadcasting, corporate sponsorship, sporting goods manufacturers, and an ever-growing media hunger for more entertainment opportunities, has turned sport into a major social phenomenon. Its strength has surpassed the limits of individuals and placed it in the realm of governmental power, creating in so doing a "marriage of mutual convenience" and a strategic alliance against drug abuse and violence in sport.

Governmental sport institutions have also flourished. Many countries today have sport ministries, commissions, and youth sport institutes at the national level as well as sport departments at regional and city levels. Together, they represent new challenges to the smooth operation of national governing bodies of sport, the national federations (NFs), whose work is already hampered by excessive meddling of multisport organizations. Their dominant tendencies impinge on the coordination of sport activities by the official sport organizations, such as the NFs.

one

SOCIAL CONTEXT FOR MODERN SPORT

Courtesy of Nuova Immagine.

> Young men by the thousands, attracted by jobs and the excitement of city life, came into the larger cities (under the hardships of the industrial revolution) seeking employment. They were crowded into cheap rooming houses and dormitories. Their working hours were tedious and enervating; their social life often consisted of drinking, gambling and other forms of vice.
>
> **Elmer L. Johnson, The History of YMCA Physical Education**

This was the social setting in the second half of the 19th century at the dawn of the greatest sport movement of modern history. This movement would revive the values of physical fitness, health, and personal well-being; and it would encourage youth to practice athletic activities according to the principles of physical education, gymnastics, competitive sport, and modern Olympic ideals.

Today, idealistic principles are in a state of crisis; materialism and financial profit have gained the upper hand. For lack of new ethical standards and fundamental beliefs, a philosophy of life based on actual material conditions is evolving in most countries, where social considerations are placed at the lowest level of governmental and individual priorities. Immersed in this materialistic environment, youth of today are searching for their own way and, in this pursuit, also are seeking a new kind of leadership. What they so badly need today are leaders with a sense of mission who, free from hypocrisy and pretense, loyally dedicate the better part of their lives to making good use of the power inherent in sport; who guarantee the primacy of ethical and legal values; who show respect for the principles of democracy and fair play; and who serve youth sport activities on the strength of the belief that "there is always a better way for a better human."

Need for New Structures in Sport Today

All conservatism is based upon the idea that if you leave things alone you leave them as they are. But you do not. If you leave a thing alone you leave it to a torrent of change.

G.K. Chesterton, Orthodoxy

From the earliest years of the revival of competitive sport as a means to improve individual social conditions, most sport clubs, leagues, unions, associations, and national federations (NFs) operated exclusively under the impulse of two major tendencies: the socialist approach under populist concepts on the one hand, and the approach focusing on individual rights

4

and support to private organizations on the other. The former pursued traditional concepts such as sport for all, sport as a social service, and sport as an educational vehicle. The latter emphasized freedom of choice and enabled youngsters deprived of social opportunities to attain physical and moral health and avoid antisocial behavior and criminal tendencies.

In the past, volunteers promoted sport through improvised sport activities. These offered enjoyment, free-time leisure, and community contact to the youth of the day. Later on, clubs, leagues, associations, NFs, and others provided competitors with an opportunity to become local heroes through sport competitions. Simple sport enjoyment, combined with the honor of defending the colors of a group, college, university, or club, would sometimes lead to the pleasure of becoming a recognized community idol. This is no longer the case, because every sport event today is shrouded in a new atmosphere, surrounded by a whole set of new relationships, attitudes, and behaviors, creating a commercial sport world peculiar to our times.

New Trends in Sport

Times have changed, as have individual attitudes and behavior. As a result, the social context of sport has undergone a profound change. Today, in addition to honor and public recognition, new rewards await winners: fame, glory, money, and social status. By now every layer of society is affected by this shift.

In purely professional sport, the winner's social, personal, legal, or financial status is quite irrelevant today. Winning is the name of the game, and winners have become the new gods glorified on the altar of commercial benefits and material gain, regardless of their legal status, educational principles, or socioethical values. During the first half of the 20th century, athletes such as Joe Louis, Jim Thorpe, and Jesse Owens embodied the image of great champions with values such as personal attitude, moral principles, and respect for the law. With the media as partners, the rulers of professional sport are today taking control of sport activities. Sport organizations—be they local, national, or international—are helping those who rule professional sport by continuing to commit to, and primarily focus on, grassroots sport, educational events, and free-time activities. Only a handful of these events are organized according to competitive sport principles, the professional managers' forte, and NFs and international federations (IFs) alike give little or no regard to the financial well-being and material conditions of individual athletes.

Sport organizations at the national and international levels are deserting the battlefields of competitive sport and leaving professional sport activities in the hands of businessmen and promoters. At the same time they are being pressured by political, commercial, and domineering attitudes. Sooner or later, all this turmoil threatens to destroy current sport structures and compels NFs either to abandon the sport scene or, in exchange for their subservience, remain as passive bystanders with no significant role.

Historical Responsibility of Sport Organizations

Today, it is incumbent on the NFs, the International Olympic Committee (IOC), and the IFs to set the moral limits of competitive sport and enforce them; theirs is a historic responsibility. However, these limits will only prove credible if national and international sport organizations are adequately organized and duly prepared to prevent undesirable individuals or hegemonic organizations involved in sport from imposing on them conditions that overstep those moral limits or flout their institutional rights.

Maintaining cooperation and understanding in sport will be possible only if sport leaders at the national, continental, and world levels are elected from among individuals whose ethical principles make them trustworthy guardians of the moral and legal integrity of sport and of its democratic institutions. These leaders must not be people driven by personal ambition and plutocratic interests.

Needs of Today's Athletes

People today require three major conditions for practicing sport and taking part in sport competitions: material support (opportunities and infrastructure), organizational support (planning and programming), and professional administration (smooth organizational information and clear-cut management).

Athletes naturally want to win. However, they often bear the brunt of their country's poor organizational structures. Then they rebel against their national sport organizations for being unsupportive, neglecting their duties, eluding their responsibilities, and shying away from accountability. In developing countries, many organizations conceal their incompetence behind political influence and sometimes a hesitant media's fear of retaliation. Athletes have needs—such as a place to practice sports, an event to compete in, an instructor to improve their skills and abilities, and a performance to achieve—that most sport organizations today are not truly satisfying. If these needs continue to be forgotten, athletes will feel compelled to break the inertia of their own sport organizations and look elsewhere for action, excitement, and the fulfillment of their dreams of glory.

6

A Sport Organization's Worst Enemy

The worst enemy of a sport organization today is neither another sport organization, nor another sport, nor the social environment, nor the athletes, nor even their critics or opponents; public enemy number one is the local organizational structure and the sport organization itself. Because of their inertia, sport organizations risk losing their practitioners to professional promoters who are willing to offer them better opportunities through a solid marketing structure.

Inertia, combined with a lack of organizational structure, the absence of administrative procedures, and the ineptitude of managers, will not only destroy the sport organization itself but also the sport movement as we know it today. In the end, it will seriously damage the very roots of the Olympic movement.

Most Reliable Driving Forces

Organization, administration, and management are today the most reliable driving forces of sport organizations in any country. Indeed these three elements must function well together for a sport association, club, league, event organizer, or regional sport organization to attain the highest level of efficiency and effectively solve problems that arise.

A good organization arranges a coherent structure of interdependent and interactive units, sections, or divisions into a whole system. In any country, sport activities need a good organizational structure so that athletes, clubs, teams, and others can participate easily in events. To achieve this goal, well-prepared units of a sport organization must all work together toward the achievement of clearly determined goals and objectives.

Administration is the timely allocation of human, material, and financial resources needed to maintain the smooth running of an organization and implement its strategic actions. Once a sport organization's structure is clearly defined, an efficient administration to support and follow up the various actions of the units, as well as to connect with those practicing the sport, must be foreseen.

Management creates and maintains a coherent system of decision-making procedures and motivates people to identify themselves with and strive toward the accomplishment of an organization's strategic plan. This involves an adequate flow of information; the determination of goals and objectives; the selection of activities required to pursue those objectives; and the motivation of members, employees, and volunteers alike to work together toward those goals. An organization needs to be run by professional and competent managers from its earliest to its ultimate stage of development.

International Sport Environment

The needs of an interdependent planet cannot be met by the independent activities of all the world's political units (states or organizations).

A. Le Roy Benett, International Organizations, Principles and Issues

To operate successfully, all sport organizations, whatever their nature, must have a professional understanding of legal, commercial, technical, and organizational principles so that they can properly approach the complex situations that arise from dealing with international organizations such as the IFs and the IOC. The previous section attempted to justify the need for new organizational, administrative, and managerial concepts in sport organizations. This section deals with questions relating to the international environment that affects the performance of any sport organization.

What follows are fundamental concepts that come into play for regional and national sport organizations as they deal with international organizations. Organizations must implement these concepts professionally because they affect the performance of the organization and the fulfillment of its responsibilities. A correct approach will depend on the organization's perception of the sport environment and its understanding of sport identity and image.

Relationships Within the Olympic Movement

The IFs and IOC have joined hands at the international level to ensure that sport is maintained within the scope of certain ethical values and organizational systems. Their goals are to implement the underlying principles of the Olympic movement in all sport and to safeguard the continuity of the Olympic Games and the principle of fair play.

In addition to the IOC and the IFs, the Olympic movement includes the national Olympic committees (NOCs); the organizing committees of the Olympic Games (OCOGs); and the NFs, associations, and clubs. It also includes anyone belonging to these groups, particularly the athletes whose interests constitute a fundamental element of the Olympic movement's activity, as well as the judges, referees, coaches, and other sport technicians. The Olympic movement also includes other organizations and institutions recognized by the IOC, as stated in the Olympic Charter, rule 3.1.

Nobody has ever tried to come up with a definition of the Olympic movement, but it is generally thought of as a national, continental, and world sport structure aiming to ensure that the principles laid down in 1894 with the founding of the IOC are duly implemented through the joint efforts of all those involved. Figure 1.1 is based on the Olympic Charter

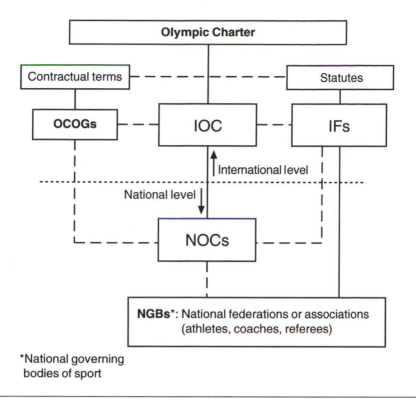

Figure 1.1   Theoretical structure of the Olympic movement.

and constitutes an attempt to reflect the relationships existing between the international organizations whose role is set out in the Olympic Charter.

There are three sport organizations with worldwide status: the IOC, the IFs, and the OCOGs of a given Olympiad (the four-year period between the end of a given Olympic Games and the end of the next ensuing Games). These are the only organizations operating with a role in worldwide sport.

Below these organizations, at the national level, we find all the NOCs recognized by the IOC in each country, such as the United States Olympic Committee (USOC), British Olympic Association (BOA), Australian Olympic Committee (AOC), and so on. Each is invested with authority in Olympic affairs within its respective country. The NOCs share the national level with the national sport governing bodies who are legally vested as NFs with the authority to administer and represent their sport as affiliated members and branches of the corresponding IF. At the same time, they are full-fledged members of the NOC of their country, which obliges the NOC to fully support their role and authority.

Olympic Sport Competition

Every four years, beginning in 776 B.C., the ancient Games were celebrated in Olympia, a city of ancient Greece. They were exclusively intended for Greek men and opened their doors to foreigners only in the latter part of their existence, first to Romans during the first century B.C. and then to other non-Greek athletes (cf. Ancient Olympics, edited 1985). With few exceptions (1916, 1940, 1944, which were times of war) the modern Games have been celebrated every four years since 1896 in many cities of the world. The Games prohibit discrimination of any kind and encourage the pursuit of human intellectual, physical, and moral improvement as one of their essential principles, in accordance with the principle of fair play.

The Olympic motto, *Citius, altius, fortius,* contains that competitive impulse to stretch beyond one's best efforts: faster, higher, and stronger. The Olympic Charter is the flagship of the Olympic movement, stating the underlying principle that intellectual, physical, and moral qualities of human beings should be developed. The Charter also underscores the need to blend together sport, culture, and education to promote peace and a way of life based on the enjoyment of effort, education through example, unequivocal respect for universal ethical principles, and mutual understanding through friendship and fair play. International sport organizations are very keen to promote understanding and reasoning by the athletes of how their performances are the result of a process in which mental concentration and attitude, together with a methodical training contrary to artificial methods, can prolong their athletic success. Mental power is often presented as the basis on which to develop physical strength, top-level performance, and excellent game situations, all claimed to be the expression of enjoyment through an intense mental activity.

International Olympic Committee

The IOC is the supreme authority of the Olympic movement. Its primary role is to promote Olympic ideals through the following activities, attitudes, and behaviors (summarized from the Olympic Charter):[1]

---

[1]From the Olympic Charter, 1997 edition, I have summarized these important concepts, quoted rules, and in the following paragraphs, made comments about recent changes. Therefore, I want to express my heartfelt thanks to H.E. Juan Antonio Marquis of Samaranch, former IOC president, and Dr. Jacques Rogge, who was recently elected the new IOC president, for their authorization to publish this section with my comments about the Olympic movement, the IFs, NOCs, and the IOC.

Adapted, by permission, from the International Olympic Committee. The Olympic Charter.

One of the roles of the IOC, NFs, and IFs is to promote sport at all levels.
Courtesy of Blaser Photography.

The role of the IOC includes the following:

1. To encourage the practice of sport at all levels and support any measure that provides for athletes' social and professional future and strengthens the unity of the Olympic movement
2. To place sport at the service of humanity, ensuring fair play, women's participation in sport, environmental and health protection, and the respect for ethical values
3. To act against all types of discrimination in sport as well as doping
4. To oppose political and commercial abuse of sport and athletes
5. To ensure the regular celebration of the Olympic Games during which individual and team competitions are staged between athletes rather than between countries (Olympic Charter, 1997, pp. 10-11)

Development of Sport Within the Olympic Movement

The Olympic Games began as a way to develop physical education and sport activities under the concept of competition. This brought new rules into existing sports, such as athletics, football, and gymnastics, and opened the door to the creation of new sports by prominent Americans involved in sport activities as the times changed. James Naismith gave birth to basketball and William G. Morgan created volleyball, to mention only two of the most successful sports today.

The modern Olympics were reborn in 1896 under educational and cultural principles intended to foster the harmonious and healthy development of the human body, mind, and spirit. Their explosive growth has forced the IOC to change course in certain areas and modify its attitude in others, essentially to ensure the inclusion of governments and private companies in the Olympic stream. To this end, several principles were revised to avoid apparent contradictions that could have diminished the credibility of the Olympic movement. For example, in previous versions, journalists and sporting goods manufacturers were not allowed to lead NOCs or become IOC members; government units were not welcomed in a NOC; and athletes were forbidden to sell their photographs, images, and the like. Today, government sport authorities and NOCs are one and the same unit, sporting goods business leaders and manufacturers are IOC members, and athletes are selling their photos and videos everywhere.

In the years to come, impassioned debates will take place on a wide range of hot topics including the professionalization of athletes, increased commercialization of sport, use of publicity and advertising during the Games, and the merger of governmental institutions with private organizations. It will be important, on such occasions, not to sacrifice the unity that surrounds yet unmodified principles of the Olympic Charter to the fractional unity centered on individual and group interests.

International Federations

The term *international federations* (IFs) designates the organizations responsible for administering and running worldwide day-to-day international sport activities. Each IF is the highest world authority of its respective sport. Within each country, a NF represents the IF's authority and the interests of the corresponding sport.

The IOC has recognized the IFs' authority and defined their role within the Olympic movement as follows.

Recognition of the IFs

When the International Olympic Committee came into being in 1894, the founders, headed by Pierre de Coubertin, made a clear distinction between organizing the Olympic Games as a multisport event and managing each sport at the world level with all its technical and specific organizational needs. Thus they agreed that such needs could be satisfied only by independent, international sport organizations that would have to obtain IOC recognition before their sport could be included in the Olympic program. These organizations were called the International Sports Federations (IFs).

The first IFs recognized by the IOC were those that governed the sports featured in the first Olympic Games held in Athens in 1896: athletics, cycling, fencing, gymnastics, shooting, swimming, tennis, weightlifting, and wrestling.

Today's Rule 29 of the Olympic Charter contains the conditions and procedure to be followed by an IF in order to obtain IOC recognition as the international organization governing a specific sport worldwide.

> **To promote the Olympic movement, the IOC may recognize as IFs international nongovernmental organizations administering one or several sports at the world level and organizations administering such sport at the national level. The recognition of IFs newly appointed by the IOC shall be provisional for a period of two years or any other period fixed by the IOC Executive Board. At the end of such period, the recognition shall automatically lapse in the absence of definitive confirmation given in writing by the IOC. As far as the role of the IFs within the Olympic movement is concerned, their statutes, practice, and activities must conform to the Olympic Charter. Subject to the foregoing, each IF maintains its independence and autonomy in the administration of its sport. (cf. Olympic Charter, 1997, p. 38)**

General Role of the IFs

The IFs are the worldwide authorities for any question related to their specific sport, and the IFs have accepted the following points regarding matters related to the Olympic Games:

(1)   The role of the IFs is to:

(1.1)   establish and enforce, in accordance with the Olympic spirit, the rules concerning the practice of their respective sport and to ensure their application;

(1.2)   ensure the development of their sport throughout the world;

(1.3)   contribute to the achievement of the goals set out in the Olympic Charter, in particular by way of the spread of Olympic ideals and education;

(1.4)   establish their criteria of eligibility to the competitions of the Olympic Games in conformity with the Olympic Charter, and submit these to the IOC for approval;

(1.5)   assume the responsibility for the technical control and direction of their sport at the Olympic Games and at the Games under the patronage of the IOC;

(1.6) provide technical assistance in the practical implementation of the Olympic solidarity programme. (cf. Olympic Charter, 1997, p. 39)

Olympic Sports

Olympic sports are those that are governed by specifically recognized IFs, grouped in sports of the Olympiad (including the summer Games) and winter sports as follows:

(1) Games of the Olympiad:

International Amateur Athletic Federation (IAAF)

International Rowing Federation (FISA)

International Badminton Federation (IBF)

International Baseball Association (IBA)

International Basketball Federation (FIBA)

International Amateur Boxing Association (AIBA)

International Canoeing Federation (FIC)

International Cycling Union (UCI)

International Equestrian Federation (FEI)

International Fencing Federation (FIE)

International Association Football Federation (FIFA)

International Gymnastics Federation (FIG)

International Weightlifting Federation (IWF)

International Handball Federation (IHF)

International Hockey Federation (FIH)

International Judo Federation (IJF)

International Federation of Associated Wrestling Styles (FILA)

International Amateur Swimming Federation (FINA)

International Modern Pentathlon and Biathlon Union (UIPMB)

International Softball Federation (ISF) (provisional)

World Taekwondo Federation (WTF) (provisional)

International Tennis Federation (ITF)

International Table Tennis Federation (ITTF)

International Shooting Union (UIT)

International Archery Federation (FITA)

International Triathlon Union (ITU) (provisional)

International Volleyball Federation (FIVB)

International Sailing Federation (ISAF)

(2) Olympic Winter Games:

International Bobsleigh and Tobogganing Federation (FIBT)

World Curling Federation (WCF)

International Ice Hockey Federation (IIHF)

International Luge Federation (FIL)

International Modern Pentathlon and Biathlon Union (UIPMB)

International Skating Union (ISU)

International Skiing Federation (FIS) (cf. Olympic Charter, 1997, p. 42
and p. 66)

The autonomy of the IFs is reflected by the fact that the IOC may not suspend an IF while it could suspend a NOC. Although it can decide to exclude one or all of the sport disciplines governed by an IF from the Olympic program, such a decision should be taken seven years prior to the Games in which it will apply.

Participation in the Olympic Games

The Games for all are not yet a reality. An athlete must enter a highly regulated system before a NF is able to propose a candidate to its NOC for participation in the Olympic Games.

The main conditions established for Olympic participation are to be declared eligible and qualified by the corresponding IF in accordance with the standards of each sport and afterward to be entered by a NOC. The following rules of the Olympic Charter determine the precise conditions to be fulfilled by any athlete wishing to take part in the Olympic Games.

Eligibility Code

The general principle is contained in this rule:

To be eligible for participation in the Olympic Games, a competitor must comply with the Olympic Charter as well as with the rules of the IF concerned as approved by the IOC and must be entered by his NOC. He must notably

- respect the spirit of fair play and nonviolence, and behave accordingly on the sport field;
- refrain from using substances and procedures prohibited by the rules of the IOC, the IFs, or the NOCs;
- respect and comply with all aspects in the IOC Medical Code. (cf. Olympic Charter, 1997, pp. 57-58)

The following rule represents a major change made by the IOC after 1980 to allow professionals to enter the Games:

(1) Each IF establishes its sport's own eligibility criteria in accordance with the Olympic Charter. Such criteria must be submitted to the IOC Executive Board for approval.

(2) The application of the eligibility criteria lies with the IFs, their affiliated National Federations, and the NOCs in the fields of their respective responsibilities. (cf. Olympic Charter, 1997, p. 58)

Entries to the Olympic Games

The basic principle of this rule is that the athlete's NF must propose him or her before his or her NOC can make its final decision.

(1) Only NOCs recognized by the IOC may enter competitors in the Olympic Games. The right of final acceptance of entries rests with the IOC Executive Board.

(2) An NOC shall only exercise such attributions upon the recommendations for entries given by National Federations. If the NOC approves thereof, it shall transmit such entries to the OCOG. The OCOG must acknowledge their receipt. NOCs must investigate the validity of the entries proposed by the National Federations and ensure that no one has been excluded for racial, religious or political reasons or by reason of other forms of discrimination. (cf. Olympic Charter, 1997, p. 60)

The following rule establishes the athletes' commitment to accept the IF's, NOC's, and IOC's antidoping tests at any time:

(3) As a condition precedent to participation in the Olympic Games, every competitor shall comply with all provisions contained in the Olympic Charter and the rules of the IF governing his sport. Such competitor must be duly qualified by such IF. The NOC which enters the competitor ensures under its own responsibility that such competitor is fully aware of and complies with the Olympic Charter and the Medical Code. (cf. Olympic Charter, 1997, p. 61)

Qualifying Events Organized by IFs

Qualifying events enable the allocation of available places in a given sport to athletes or competitors who win a place through a qualification process agreed on by the IF of his or her sport and the IOC.

(1)   For certain sports, the International Federations may organise qualifying events or otherwise establish a limited participation in order to designate the competitors, particularly teams in team sports, who will take part in the Olympic Games.

(2)   The systems of restrictions and of qualifying events are subject to the provisions of the Olympic Charter to the extent decided upon by the IOC Executive Board. The formula for qualification must be submitted to the IOC Executive Board for approval. The NOCs will be informed by the IOC of all matters relating to qualifying events organized by the IFs. (cf. Olympic Charter, 1997, p. 69)

Participants in the Olympic Games

It is important that there be an appropriate number of participants in the Olympic Games.

The number of entries is fixed by the IOC Executive Board, following consultation with the relevant IFs, two years before the Olympic Games. (cf. Olympic Charter, 1997, p. 69)

IFs' Technical Control

The organization of the Olympic Games requires a large number of services and essential support areas. These must be provided by the Organizing Committee of the Olympic Games in accordance with the Olympic Charter and an Organizational Agreement between the IOC and the OCOG. These services and support areas are made available under the supervision and control of the IOC.

A similar number of services and support areas must also be provided by the OCOG to each specific sport in accordance with the rules and regulations that govern the corresponding competitions. In this respect, the supervision and control of such services exercised by the competent IF must suffer no interference nor intermediation by any entity other than the IOC Executive Board should it be called upon to resolve a conflict of interest or opinion.

In recent years, the IOC and the IFs have outlined—and in some cases streamlined—those technical controls that the IFs are expected to apply in accordance with the by-law to Rule 57 as follows:

(1.1)   To establish the technical rules of their own sport, disciplines and events, including, but not limited to, results standards, technical specifications of equipment, installations and facilities, rules of technical movements, exercises or games, rules of technical disqualification and rules of judging and timing.

17

(1.2)   To establish the final results and ranking of Olympic competitions.

(1.7)   To enforce, under the authority of the IOC and the NOCs, the IOC's rules in regard to the eligibility of the participants before the Olympic Games (preliminaries) and during the Olympic Games. (cf. Olympic Charter, 1997, pp. 71 and 72)

Evolution of Competitive Sport and the Olympics

Sport competitions have evolved from entertainment and festive shows of different natures to religious ceremonies and finally to a highly regulated physical performance of athletes whose abilities and strengths are measured individually or collectively in accordance with specific rules aimed at declaring a winner.

First Entertainment, Then a Religious Act

The practice of sport has not always been conceived according to the same principles. Around the third millennium B.C., sport activities initially evolved as games to entertain the nobles of Egypt. Then the games moved to Crete, where they went from being acts of entertainment to religious celebrations. Later, they came to the Aegean Islands and took the form of boxing, wrestling, tumbling, bull leaping, and so on. In the 14th century B.C., the ancient sport festivals had already become grandiose celebrations where each athlete tried to surpass his opponents in a truly competitive spirit. These activities further developed in Mycenaean Greece and Crete between the 13th and 12th centuries B.C.; competitive events in running, chariot racing, boxing, and wrestling were staged, all of which required long and hard training even in those early days.

Competitive Concept

The first ancient competitive Games took place at Olympia, Greece, in 776 B.C. In 80 B.C., the CLXXV Olympiad was held in Rome. However, a series of mistakes, cheating, and other mishaps tarnished the Games' reputation and they degenerated until they were finally abolished officially by Emperor Theodosius II in 393 A.D. (*The Olympic Games in Ancient Greece*, edited and copyrights Ekdotike Athenon, S.A.). After 15 centuries, Pierre de Coubertin and the Greeks created a new version in 1896 based on modern principles.

Educational Concept

As previously explained, the Games were reborn under educational and cultural principles intended to foster the harmonious and healthy development of the human body, mind, and spirit. Pierre de Coubertin himself explained this: "Why did I restore the Olympic Games? To ennoble and strengthen sport, to ensure their independence and duration, and thus to enable them better to fulfil the educational role incumbent upon them in the modern world" (cf. *The Olympic Movement* published by IOC, 1984). Such an educational role is evident through activities such as the cultural program, Youth Camps, and antidoping and fair play campaigns.

Amateur Concept

Fifty years later, Avery Brundage said this: "The Olympic movement today is perhaps the greatest social force in the world. It is a revolt against twentieth century materialism—a devotion to the cause and not to the reward. It is a revolt against discrimination, racial, religious or political. It is a glorious living demonstration of that hopefully felicitous maxim 'The world is one'" (cf. *The Olympic Movement* published by IOC, 1984).

Open Concept

More recently, Juan Antonio Samaranch Marqués de Samaranch firmly stated the following: "The Olympic movement must no longer be a nice theme for declarations and conferences but a galvanising reality capable of defeating the challenges of bad politics, ambition, and hatred. Throughout its history, the International Olympic Committee has struggled to spread its ideals of fraternity, friendship, peace and universal understanding" (cf. *The Olympic Movement* published by IOC, 1984).

Starting in Barcelona in 1992, professional basketball and tennis players made their appearance at the Olympic Games. Later on other IFs were required to change their regulations to allow professional athletes to take part in the Olympic Games. Only soccer's FIFA has dared to impose an age limit and other conditions on professionals having participated in previous World Cups.

National Sport Environment

The more harmony reigns in the assembly means that the opinions are closer to unanimity, and more is the dominance of the general will; but long discussions, dissidence and turmoil announce the awakening of personal interests and the decline of the state (organization).

J.-J. Rousseau, The Social Contract

The preceding sections presented the new demands of sport today at the request of youth for better sport organization and increased governmental protection of the international sport structure to be regulated by the IOC and by the IFs who administer international sport events. For countries taking part in the international sport scene, their national environment will necessarily be influenced by the international environment.

This section takes a look at those countries in which NFs have joined other organizations and individuals to form a NOC to develop and protect sport in general and the Olympic movement in particular, in accordance with the principles of the Olympic Charter.

National Olympic Committees (NOCs)

To facilitate Olympic participation and promote sport under Olympic principles, a national sport organization geared to implementing Olympic regulations and programs must exist in each country (Olympic Charter, rule 4).

The creation of such NOCs must follow a procedure described by the Olympic Charter. This essentially establishes that any five NFs in a given territory, each affiliated to its respective IF, can create a NOC and request recognition from the IOC. The IOC will ensure criteria are met before recognizing the organization as a NOC. In several rules the Olympic Charter establishes the essential requirements for a NOC to be recognized by the IOC. The most important conditions may be summarized as follows:

> **(1) In order to promote the Olympic movement throughout the world, the IOC may recognize NOCs. Such organizations shall have, where possible, the status of legal persons in their countries. They must be established in accordance with the Olympic Charter and their statutes must be approved by the IOC. The Olympic Charter takes precedence over the statutes of an NOC in cases of conflict. (cf. Olympic Charter, 1997, p. 40)**

Mission and Role of the NOCs

Pierre de Coubertin and his contemporaries envisaged a sport system that would leave each sport's technical questions in the hands of the organizations encompassing the athletes, such as the NFs and IFs, and their national sport representatives would also allow each country to have an IOC branch called a NOC. These NOCs should encompass the same NFs and coordinate their sport activities under Olympic principles, while promoting the dream of Olympic Games participation.

> (1)   The mission of the NOCs is to develop and protect the Olympic movement in their respective countries, in accordance with the Olympic Charter. (cf. Olympic Charter, 1997, p. 40)

Sanctions Against NOCs

Sanctions are a protection of the IOC's role against political and commercial interference:

(9)   Apart from the measures and sanctions provided in case of infringement of the Olympic Charter, the IOC may, after having heard an NOC, suspend it or withdraw its recognition from it:

(9.1)   if the activity of such NOC is hampered by the effect of legal provisions or regulations in force in the country concerned or by acts of other entities within such country, whether sporting or otherwise;

(9.2)   if the making or expression of the will of the National Federations or other entities belonging to such NOC or represented within it is hampered by the effect of legal provisions or regulations in force in the country concerned or by acts of other entities within such country, whether sporting or otherwise. (cf. Olympic Charter, 1997, p. 42)

Composition of the NOCs

The Charter helps maintain NOCs within the sport structure established by the IOC and at the same time allows them to obtain much needed support of wealthy, famous, or political individuals, with the following provisions:

(1)   Whatever their composition, NOCs must include:

(1.2)   all National Federations affiliated to the IFs governing sport included in the programme of the Olympic Games or the representatives designated by them (with a minimum of five such National Federations). Proof must be adduced that these National Federations exercise a specific and real sport activity in their country and internationally, in particular by organising and participating in competitions and implementing training programmes for athletes. An NOC shall not recognise more than one National Federation for each sport governed by such IF. Furthermore, such National Federations or the representatives chosen by them must constitute the voting majority of the NOC and of its executive organ.

(2)   The NOCs may include as members:

(2.1)   National Federations affiliated to IFs recognised by the IOC, the sport of which are not included in the programme of the Olympic Games;

(2.2)   Multisport groups and other sport-oriented organizations or their representatives, as well as nationals of the country liable to reinforce the effectiveness of the NOC or who have rendered distinguished services to the cause of sport and Olympism.

(3)   When dealing with questions relating to the Olympic Games, only the votes cast by the executive organ of the NOC and by the National Federations affiliated to IFs governing sport included in the programme of the Olympic Games are taken into consideration. (cf. Olympic Charter, 1997, p. 43)

NFs As National Governing Bodies

National federations are central to the NOCs and represent the IF and its sport in their country. When adequately organized, efficiently administered, and professionally managed, NFs are the driving force of sport in their respective countries. As such, they are able to carry out day-to-day operations such as the following:

* Recruiting athletes and organizing groups of teams in clubs or other sport organizations capable of providing training and regular sport activities
* Organizing and promoting local, regional, national, and international competitions
* Being in charge of the preparation, selection, and entry of athletes for international competitions held under the authority of the respective IF
* Proposing to their NOC, in the case of regional, continental, and Olympic multisport competitions recognized by the IOC, those athletes that it considers to be prepared and eligible to represent their country, on the understanding that the NOC is the only competent body to enter the athletes in such games
* Providing technical assistance for implementing organizational programs to develop grassroots, educational, or free-time sport
* Facilitating the formation of leagues or events circuits (professional, semi-pro, national, regional, or local) under their umbrella that are run by affiliated organizations

Relationship Between NOCs and NFs

The Olympic Charter mentions some of the duties and prerogatives of the NFs as members of NOCs. The work of the NOCs and NFs is closely connected, and together they can do much to strengthen sport in their countries.

Legal Framework

The Olympic Charter establishes the functioning of NFs and NOCs and instructs all NOCs to fully cooperate with the NFs, respect their autonomy, and take the necessary measures to provide them with all possible support in their task of administering and governing their respective sport on behalf of their IF.

NFs have been given the difficult task of representing, promoting, and administering their sport at the national level, whereas NOCs are required to "encourage the development of high performance sports, as well as sport for all" and "contribute effectively to the establishment of programs for the promotion of sports at all levels" (cf. Olympic Charter, 1997, pp. 40-41).

True Mission of the NOCs

It is by supporting the tasks of the NFs that NOCs fulfill their true mission. The latter's contribution is measured by the economic or material means made available to the programs of the NFs on a regular basis and not sporadically or restrictively—such as only for multisport games. NFs have a daily duty; so do the NOCs.

NOCs' Duties Toward NFs

The duties of a NOC toward the NFs are a regular and permanent obligation, just as the NFs constantly promote, organize, and manage their particular sport. From the moment a NOC is recognized by the IOC, the Olympic Charter determines the former's duties, which become the responsibility of whoever is elected to conduct its activities. Obligations toward the NFs do not begin when they enter the race to obtain Olympic qualification and certainly do not end with the extinction of the Games' flame.

When NOCs Neglect Their Duties

When the fundamental obligation of a NOC is not fulfilled or is only fulfilled on the occasion of multisport games, the relation between the NOC and its NFs is jeopardized. This creates sport problems and turns the rights of NFs as constituent members of NOCs into pure rhetoric.

Such problems often become a nightmare for a NF wishing to exert its constituent powers within its NOC by dismissing unwanted NOC executives. This is particularly the case in countries where executives succeed in establishing strong ties with corrupt politicians. Such executives can then manipulate the credibility of the NF and the image of the sport they represent so that they remain in position for an unreasonable amount of time.

Consequences for Sport

The nonfulfillment of the fundamental duties of a NOC has severe consequences for sport in general and for the Olympic movement in particular. First, the NFs will be attracted to the governmental sphere, where they will obtain economic and material support. The government will then channel all financial support through the competent body with the consequence that it will start playing a major role in NOC affairs. The end result will be governmental bodies and NOCs merging into one, with the autonomy of NFs eventually coming to an end, thus forcing the Olympic movement to submit to the political interest of governments.

Consequences Within the Olympic Movement

The most damaging consequence to the Olympic movement is when, because of the breakdown of the national link between the NOC and the NFs, the latter are unable to perform their duties in the international arena, minimizing their sport participation and losing all opportunities to compete internationally against any country. Without financial support, a NF might even need to limit that country's international presence in sport events governed by its IF.

When NFs cease their activities, the role of the NOCs in the Olympic structure remains empty because NOCs do not have any direct sport responsibility without NFs. Indeed, the former's role is neither to arrange national competitions for a given sport nor to select national athletes or team members by themselves.

Governmental and Quasi-Governmental Organizations

Governments today consider their own units the ideal structures for addressing the need for sport facilities, training programs, and international participation. They are creating both governmental and quasi-governmental organizations for this purpose. The existing private organizations are left without the necessary material and financial means to fulfill their function, thus becoming marginalized and sometimes destroyed.

Sport Ministries, Institutes, and National Commissions

Through governmental agencies of this kind, governments attempt to protect the practice of sport by legislating their obligations and even sometimes establishing electoral constraints that national laws do not impose on other similar organizations also created as an expression of civil rights. Such a legal framework may be beneficial for sport as long as it does not restrict the freedom of association and expression that modern states are obliged to respect. Unfortunately, paternalistic politicians can use these sport organizations as political fiefdoms, and unscrupulous leaders can find there new avenues for their selfish satisfaction and a way to nurture their frustrated dreams of political power.

Multisport Organizations

Confederations, associations, and unions of NFs are other types of organizations that sometimes give a small amount of financial support to the programs of national sport organizations. However, they frequently do not find a useful place within the national sport environment. If they are inefficient and incapable of helping other sport organizations, they become parasites of the budget allocated to sport by governmental agencies.

Regardless of whether they are governmental units (ministries of youth and sport, departments of sport and leisure) or quasi-governmental organizations (sport commissions, sport confederations, or unions), all these organizations converge in the field of sport events and try to justify their own existence by joining their action to that of the recognized sport associations (NFs, NOCs), thus duplicating their programming and becoming parallel organizations. It is also common to see these multisport organizations, through political or financial pressure, become deeply involved in the affairs of regular sport associations and adopt a "big brother" attitude.

External Interference in NF Affairs

In extreme cases or when NFs, mainly sport organizations, oppose being mediatized, they are subjected to tricky legal accusations and their leaders even ousted to impose more lenient representatives. This manipulation is known as *external interference.*

These situations may seriously damage the credibility of local or national sport organizations, such as NFs, by interfering in their activities and jeopardizing their function. Unfortunately this interference may not only come from governmental organizations (as in the case of the Cameroon Football Association in 2000) but also from NOCs (as in the case of the Italian Volleyball Federation in 1993).

By Governmental Organizations

External interference in the administration of a NF by governmental or other sport organizations jeopardizes the NF's capacity for action and limits its possibilities of establishing successful sport programs of its own. Any interference creates administrative uncertainty and seriously damages the credibility of both the sport and the NF, regardless of whether such interference comes from a governmental sport agency or from the NOC itself.

By a NOC

If a NOC ever overrides the authority of the NFs with the intention of controlling their administration or the participation of athletes in international competitions, then it is considered to have breached the principles of the Olympic movement, compelling the IFs to use their sovereign international powers to support and protect the NFs' rights.

Duties and Responsibilities of NFs

NFs duly recognized by the law of their country are obliged to assume certain responsibilities assigned to national sport governing bodies; they are also full-fledged members of their NOC and affiliated members of the IF of their respective sport. Their function entails a series of responsibilities, duties, and rights that place them at the center of the problems arising when personal hierarchic status or financial interests clash in their sport.

Their overall duties stemming from their legal recognition as national sport governing bodies and those arising from their role as NOC members are explained here. Their duties and responsibilities as representatives of the corresponding IF of their sport are contained in the statutes of the latter and have priority over the statutes of the NF.

Overall Duties

NFs should be at the helm of the sport movement. Through the motivation and interest they can generate in the youth of their countries for the practice of sport and by integrating youth into their sport organizations, NFs are making a substantial contribution to the fight against drugs, crime, and social disintegration. They are the national branches of IFs. For this reason, they are responsible for administering their sport and enforcing the relevant rules and international decisions at the national level, while the corresponding IF they are affiliated with governs that sport at the global level.

When a NF is created subsequent to the recognition, in a given country, of its NOC by the IOC, such a NF must in turn be recognized by that NOC and be accepted as a member. However, the NF must exercise a specific and real sport activity, be affiliated to an IF recognized by the IOC, and conduct its activities in compliance with both the Olympic Charter and the rules of its IF (cf. Olympic Charter, 1997, p. 47). The statutes of an IF as well as those of a NF apply at the national level and take precedence if a contradiction arises. A NF can be suspended or lose its affiliation by decision of the IF concerned, in which case the NF ceases to be a member of its NOC.

NFs' Role As NOC Members

With respect to their NOCs, NFs have the right

1. to constitute the voting majority in any decisions made by the NOC,
2. to be the one and only national governing body of their sport recognized by their NOC if the NF is affiliated to the IF governing their sport worldwide, and
3. to propose to the NOC those athletes or team players to participate in regional multisport events and the Olympic Games. Without the NF's consent the NOC may not enter any athlete or player of their sport in the Olympic Games.

NFs' Essential Tools

The most important elements needed to accomplish their tasks are organization, administration, and management. (See page 7 for the discussion of these aspects.) To date, NFs have not properly seized the notion of these concepts, and by failing to establish groups or associations responsible for the local and national promotion of their sport, they are not adequately performing their role.

Governmental authorities and NOCs claim that NFs are responsible for promoting their sport, but these authorities rarely provide them with the necessary support and guidance to develop an organization that best suits the country's political and social conditions. Furthermore, administration is typically neglected, leaving NFs to operate under subjective or externally imposed decisions. This fuels poor management resulting in poor performance and the adoption of bureaucratically entangled systems imposed by governmental organizations, personal or group interests of influential members, or even by foreign organizations.

The most damaging consequence of such poor organization, administration, and management is a lack of timely actions: slow decision making, delays in servicing the members of the organization or providing medical treatment for athletes, and the absence of training facilities. And to think that all these adverse situations can easily be avoided through professional management, efficient administration, and adequate organizational structures!

NF As a Sport Authority

In regard to a specific sport, the only legitimate international speaker for a country is the respective NF. Once recognized by its government authorities and invested by its constituency with such power, the NF can request affiliation to the respective IF, which requires producing evidence that it has been legally recognized as the only national organization for that specific sport within its territory. The affiliation to its respective IF under such conditions grants the NF the title of "national governing body of (its) sport" (NGB) along with all the rights stated in the Olympic Charter, whose rules become national law when the IOC recognizes the country's NOC.

Financing NFs

NFs and IFs are the only sport organizations directly involved in the day-to-day operations of sport activities. Together with their affiliated sport clubs (whether professional or not), NFs have to deal with the daily struggle of financing sport activities in a country. The same could be said for sport-oriented governmental agencies, although they are usually dependent on governmental funding priorities or subjective preferences, due to political affiliation or personal objectives, and most of them normally use sport for educational, occupational, and sometimes political purposes.

Certain corporate sponsors with political concerns might sponsor governmental sport programs, but too cautiously and on a limited scale because of the possible notoriety of the government. In addition, in their situation as taxpayers they consider they have already made a contribution to the national budget.

Government Funds A limited amount of government funds are made available to NOCs and NFs through direct governmental allocations or national sport lotteries. However, they also have a political price. Such funds often influence the nominations of NF and NOC leaders, either in accordance with local regulations or in violation of them, in certain countries where democratic principles are not commonly practiced. However, whatever the real purpose for allocating government funds to sport, such funds are public and their availability will depend on political priorities, personal contacts, honest and capable management, and most of all, each country's economic stability. Each country's NFs should attempt to find their own way of taking advantage of public funds allocated directly (national budget) or indirectly (lotteries) by governmental agencies or through the NOC and sport confederations. Unfortunately, by operating *only* with governmental funds, a NF will always depend on the goodwill of third parties and most probably on their mood and political persuasions. For these reasons NFs are better off becoming self-sufficient and not relying on government funds for sport promotion. This should therefore be a goal of NFs, even if it demands the strategic framework of a sport marketing plan (as described further on p. 141) that is carefully drafted by professional personnel or marketing agencies.

Generating Funds The modern approach to financing sport activities is through the marriage of a corporate brand or image with the image of a top sport event, a phenomenon known as *sport marketing*. From the standpoint of a sport organization, this approach consists of the development of a marketing plan aimed at selling publicity, promotional activities, logos, and the general image of the event as well as its entertainment value for television audiences and spectators. This helps secure financial resources for the organizational and administrative expenditures of the event, the NF, and its program, while satisfying the goals and needs of the sponsor with regard to its corporate brand or image.

Sport event marketing should not be taken to mean sport commercialization, because the two are totally different. Commercialization means to manage or exploit sport for profit, whereas *sport marketing, sport event marketing,* or *marketing of sport events* means to buy or sell the image of an event, a sport organization, or an athlete in order to finance the event, the organization, the athlete, or other sport activities, with the purpose of promoting a sound image of the sponsor and its product.

NFs are nonprofit but should become organized in a businesslike manner, even though they are not looking for profit. Nevertheless, they should try to obtain sufficient funds through the sale of sport entertainment to serve the public interest of the community by facilitating or motivating sport participation. These are two reasons for NFs to resort to sport marketing. Furthermore, to meet these ends, NFs need sufficient funds to purchase or produce teaching material, sport equipment, and administrative facilities. NFs also need funds for engaging professional personnel to organize courses, clinics, seminars, and sport meetings to update their members on the most recent sport techniques, sport rules, and so on.

As previously stated, when governments are unable or unwilling to grant adequate funds to support the NFs' activities, the latter are obliged to generate enough resources to become socially productive and financially self-sufficient. However, this cannot be obtained by levying high fees on athletes, particularly in countries where part of the population cannot even cover its basic needs. The only way for NFs to fund their own operations and subsistence is through fund-raising and marketing of sport events, the two latest and most important methods, which will be described in more detail in chapter 4.

Addressing Problems

The heavy and difficult tasks of coordinating grassroots sport, educational sport, and competitive sport oblige NFs to have recourse to all legal means available in their country to increase their revenue and at the same time address their sport's fundamental problems. Certain signs would indicate their need to pay special attention to setting up an appropriate organizational structure and administration and to improving their management, sport facilities, personnel, programs, and sponsors. These warning signs include the following:

- They are not conducting their promotion campaigns in an efficient manner and have not yet managed to organize professional leagues or run normal national leagues or event circuits in a professional way.

- Their overly bureaucratic system, particularly if operating in a developing country, is jeopardizing the development of adequate organizational structures, the independent administrators, and the recruitment of professional managers.

- Potentially jealous and politically biased authorities are eager to control the sport movement, thus hampering individual initiatives or belittling the genuine efforts of national sport organizations.

Professional Administration

Each NF should set up its own organization based on professional principles and obtain legal recognition as a noncommercial and nonprofit-oriented organization operating under the principles of private enterprise. It should then proceed to organize national competitions, national league tournaments, and international events using a businesslike approach. When organizing national or international tournaments or simply performing its daily activities, each NF should keep in mind the following basic principles:

- **Discipline at work:** Do your work, do it to the full, do your best, and do it now.

- **Efficient management:** Use professional, skilled personnel who know how to competently organize events and administer the area under their responsibility. These professionals will determine the programs and establish aggressive policies to transform a given sport into sport entertainment and awaken the interest of spectators through the use of marketing techniques and the media.

- **Methodical organization of events:** Carefully plan events, following a step-by-step approach for each phase, from the preparation to the conclusion of the event and production of the post-event reports. Give special attention to choosing the best possible dates, cities, and facilities; preparing the program best suited to the public interest; and selecting the most enthusiastic organizers, the best media coordinator or agency, and the marketing agency most interested in promoting the event appropriately.

- **Publicity:** Information must be distributed to all spheres of the community via newspapers, radio, television, printed material (pamphlets, posters, leaflets, programs), and through the sale of souvenirs and gadgets to create a favorable atmosphere and public awareness.

Need to Face New Priorities

It is obvious that the responsibilities of a NF today go beyond serving individuals who wish to practice a sport or follow suitable training programs. New priorities today force NFs to

- improve the availability of material and social conditions for the practice of their sport,
- offer elite athletes full-time professional training with frequent national and international sport experiences,
- offer all practitioners the opportunity to earn the social status that the community is willing to confer on winners, and
- provide sport enthusiasts with full satisfaction as spectators of professionally organized events.

Sport Conflicts

Submission to general will is the common bond of all societies without excepting criminal organizations. Alas! Virtue is so beautiful that thieves respect the image even at the bottom of their caves.

Denis Diderot, Encyclopaedia

Sport today is plagued by conflicts ranging from technical complaints to civil lawsuits, a result of national and international sport organizations' failures: inadequate organization, incompetent management, and poor administration. Many of these conflicts are also the consequence of athletes' feeling that they have been abused and their rights neglected or their fear of being found guilty of breaking fair play, antidoping, or game rules.

Sport organizations should be aware that sport means order and discipline under the law, especially in view of their recognition in many countries as private organizations responsible for a public service that the state supports by granting them disciplinary powers over their constituency (athletes and affiliated clubs). These powers require that the constituents themselves establish the penalties and that they be applied in full respect of individual rights. This section will seek to justify the inalienable right of organizations to exert such disciplinary powers.

Assumptions About Conflict in Sport

Competitive sport is freely chosen by individuals or groups and practiced in relation to other individuals or groups. This practice is made following the rules that regulate competition in that specific sport, including rules of conduct, restrictions, and disciplinary sanctions. Confrontation between individuals or groups takes place within the established rules that grant not only rights but also impose duties and responsibilities that are also part of the freely chosen sport. These rules are necessary to maintain its good order, prevent criminal behavior, and protect the physical and moral well-being of all persons involved.

The Need to Judge on Site

In the pursuit of that moral order, the NFs must invest referees and officials with the necessary power to judge the conduct and actions of participants on site, in the light of the rules governing the sport, and at the same time to apply the sanctions as foreseen in the rules. A legal dispute arises when a participant contests the legal ground of a sanction or decision that has been taken. Such disputes are numerous and vary widely depending on the sport concerned, the type of conduct penalized, and the subject on which the decision or sanction is applied.

As a private activity freely chosen by individuals and considering that each affiliated body must respect the obligations that were undertaken by its authorized representatives, sport activities cannot subsequently fall under the tutelage of local or supranational magistrates, judges, or courts of arbitration requested to intervene. This would conflict with the need for decisions to be taken on site and within the competition itself, which guarantees the particular freedom required for the judges, referees, and officials to assess technical and behavioral factors of the competitors.

Regulating Disputes

Sport conflicts involving athletes or sport organizations have to be judged among peers, and disputes must be solved in accordance with the regulations governing the subject in which they arise. To seek to impose on sport conflicts all the procedural formalities established to solve legal disputes arising from individual or group behavior in daily life would amount to maintaining the sport community in a permanent state of confrontation.

Sport is an individual expression of freedom of choice. Individuals who choose to practice a particular sport freely determine its organizational structure and establish its regulations. State affairs belong to governments, religious affairs belong to religious institutions, and sport affairs belong to sport organizations.

Disputes Related to Sport Performance

The rules governing sport must be *strictly* observed. No appeal is possible against the decisions of the judges or referees of the event who, considering the athletes' performance from the technical standpoint, have applied the rules of the sport. Only the acting judges, referees, and officials of the event or game are vested with jurisdictional powers. Their decisions are final and no appeal to external bodies is possible, be they civil courts or courts of arbitration.

Disputes Concerning Participation in Events

Regulations governing participation in a given event must also be strictly observed. Once those wanting to participate have accepted these regula-

The officials observing this match have the final say regarding rule violations. No appeal to a higher instance is possible unless the officials themselves break the rules.
Courtesy of Nuova Immagine.

tions, there can be no further appeal against them at the international level if the credibility of sport competitions is to be preserved and the relevant television and sponsorship contracts respected. If the rules governing participation seem to be unfair, the members of the IF should analyze them in the light of the general interest of the sport and, where necessary, modify them.

All the affiliated members (NFs) of the corresponding IF decide on the principles of international participation and eligibility. These principles apply to individuals and national or club teams, depending on the competition. An IF's affiliated NFs are vested with all the moral and legal powers to represent their respective countries and are authorized to subscribe to international undertakings in their sport. Decisions of NFs are governed by international rules and should never be the subject of an appeal to an external body or to any ordinary court of law, which cannot consider international rules of any sport.

Role of Sport Administration

Conflicts relating to the conditions of sport participation (eligibility, licensing, establishment of regulations governing qualification and selection, athletes' transfers, and so forth) fall under the administrative rules governing the sport concerned. Only the administrative authority of each NF should deal with them.

As already stated, participation in a given sport is a voluntary act and implies for each individual prior acceptance of the conditions governing such participation and of the rules governing that sport, including matters relating to the performance of the participants in competitions. To allow recourse to an external body for decisions made in this area by the competent administrative bodies of a NF would mean denying the authority of the NF and would open the door wide to appeals. NFs would lose their credibility and the recognition they were granted in the Olympic Charter and national law to solely govern and administrate their sport at the national level.

> **Sport federations, as organizations of public interest, are expected to act to some extent on behalf of and in the place of the state. (cf. Jean Morange, "Sport and Human Rights")**

This is one of the reasons NFs are obliged to follow the principles of secularity, neutrality, nondiscrimination, and respect for the rights of individuals that are in force in their respective countries. Essentially, NFs act on behalf of the free will of individuals who decide to solve their disputes within the structures of their sport and deal with them as an internal affair of the organization. Intervention by jurisdictional powers would constitute another interference by the state in the right of individuals to freely associate and would certainly be contrary to natural law.

Rights of the Athletes

The rights of the athletes must be guaranteed in the rules and regulations of the respective NFs and IFs. Whenever sanctions have to be applied, NFs and IFs must be careful to comply strictly with the procedural rules. Judging the behavior of athletes in light of the applicable rules and deciding whether or not to impose sanctions are part of the duties to be carried out by the competent officials of the federation governing the sport concerned (cf. Olympic Charter, 1997, p. 38).

Just as civil rights of individuals in local activities are guaranteed by national laws and in international activities by international laws and conventions, sport rights are guaranteed by the statutes and regulations approved by NFs, who considered the principles recognized by their countries. NFs and IFs alike must respect such principles in each sport. Civil activities fall under civil law and criminal activities under criminal law, but sport activities come under the law of the sport concerned.

Athletes are subject not only to the rules of their sport but also to the laws of their country. "The relationship between the athlete and the group which he has voluntarily joined is governed by the rules adopted by the latter" (Morange, ibid). These relations, regulated by private law, respect freedom of consent, commitments freely undertaken, the laws and legal system of the country concerned, and the general principles of law.

International Sport

To ensure the possibility of international participation for all national athletes practicing a given sport, each country makes the sovereign decision to submit its own sport organization to the principles and international conventions governing that sport activity at the time it decides to authorize the NF to affiliate to the corresponding IF.

In certain countries, there are different principles in force, which the NFs of these countries are compelled to follow. All NFs are obliged to observe certain universally accepted principles and abide strictly by the rules and regulations of each sport, among others nondiscrimination and respect for the rights of individuals as established and recognized internationally.

Internal Disputes Within Federations

The relationship between the IF and its affiliated member federations is not only contractual but also causal. Without the organs of the IF, the member federations could not organize their life in common, and without the latter the former would have no reason to exist. Indeed, the international character of an IF clearly implies a relationship between national organizations of several countries and territories.

Principle of Common Will

Respect for a federation's internal regulations by its own members is the key to its survival. The constitutions of federations stipulate the procedures to follow for settling internal conflicts and nominating competent panels of appeal. Those constitutions and their provisions fall under the concept of civil law for private federations at the national level and of private international law for international organizations. The individual right of free association is guaranteed not only for individuals but also for private associations, thus making their life in common possible, notwithstanding the fact that each member is in turn subject to different legal regimes in its own country. The constitutions of federations contain the common will of their members and represent the social contract formulated and reformulated on the occasion of each congress.

Principle of Authority

At national and international levels, the authority that the organs who represent the organization have over individual members of its constituency lies in the principle of inviolability of the organization's administrative and disciplinary powers exerted within established procedures, as it manages all sport matters; this is an essential principle that needs to be respected. An appeal from a NF to a civil court or court of arbitration against a decision of its IF would nullify the principle of authority that all NFs undertook when they joined the IF. Through such an act, a NF would be unilaterally disavowing the authority of its IF, thereby destroying its very structure and excluding itself from the organization. The same applies for the constituency of a NF.

Principle of Disciplinary Measures

Admittedly, judges have guaranteed the right of an organization, with which individuals have chosen to associate, to impose disciplinary measures. These measures are needed to guarantee adherence to its rules and decisions and include the exclusion of an individual by decision of the group.

Judges have also recognized the obligation to exhaust the jurisdictional appeals provided by the statutes of the sport organization before appealing to a civil court. As already described, such appeals are not acceptable in view of the restrictions and obstacles they represent for the positive development of sport life.

NFs and IFs have a dual objective of primary importance: to protect the rights of athletes while safeguarding the integrity of their sport. These two elements go hand in hand and entail not only rights and obligations but also some degree of power to enforce internal regulations and make final decisions. For this reason, it is essential that all the organization's activities in this regard should be internally valid, legally justifiable, and morally correct.

The responsibility for settling any of the above-mentioned legal disputes (which are essentially of a sport nature) lies exclusively within the administrative powers of the sport organization—IF or NF. This is so because the relevant congress, in the event of a final appeal, must decide and apply the law on behalf of all its affiliated federations in the case of an IF or of its own country's constituency in the case of a NF. In both instances, the respective congress is only exerting the authority of a sovereign assembly self-declared as the supreme organ of all the affiliated members of the federation. Allowing recourse in such cases to an external body, whether a civil court or a court of appeal for sport, would create obstacles to the smooth running of sport competitions. Even worse, this would destroy the very essence of any general assembly or congress originally recognized as the sport's constitutional and sovereign authority (excluding certain autocratic sport organizations).

Disputes Concerning Individual Rights or Obligations

Sport is expected to respect individual rights established by national labor laws, criminal or civil law, and so forth. When those rights are part of the conflict, national laws prevail over the decisions of the sport authority concerned, unless the said laws provide for an exception in favor of that sport authority, which is not the case today in most countries.

Unilateral Action by a Sport Organization

Disputes arising from labor laws and civil or criminal law in sport-related activities may not be the subject of that federation's arbitration because they fall under the terms of the local laws, a situation that excludes any intervention by arbitration courts.

Rights protected by national laws cannot be renounced outright or time-barred. Submitting to international arbitration a legal dispute over a disciplinary act in which the claimant asserts that individual rights have been neglected (including the right of work, security, defense, or procedure) in no way excludes the possibility of a subsequent intervention by a civil court, unless national law declares that disciplinary procedures by a sport organization in full respect of its own rules are lawful.

Cooperation between the IOC and NOCs to obtain professional legal advice for sport federations would diminish the intervention in sport affairs by a civil court. It would be even more effective if such advice provided guidance to the IFs and NFs on how to ensure that the rights of individuals are duly respected when disciplinary measures are applied.

Disciplinary Action Against Drug Abuse

Legal disputes over disciplinary actions taken against the use of forbidden methods and substances in sport normally culminate in a claim that the action violated the individual's rights as protected by the national laws of the individual.

In such disputes, the recourse to civil courts is always possible except when the state manifests a will to protect sport organizations by recognizing their right to impose disciplinary sanctions. This right is delegated to NFs for local competitions and conferred for international competitions on IFs, with the reservation that the rights and liberties of individuals be preserved throughout the disciplinary action, including procedural and defense rights. Conflicts arising from disciplinary actions against doping are not the exclusive concern of one or another federation. They may affect all IFs, in particular those that do not follow prescribed procedures or neglect the rights of individuals.

Conflicts Arising From Antidoping Tests

Doping is not only deceitful but also fraudulent conduct against the sport principles of fair play and fair competition. Doping includes any use of forbidden substances with the aim of improving personal performance in competitions of any sport.

An eventual conflict resulting from the analysis of samples as established by antidoping regulations or the IOC Medical Code should be decided by a judge. Only a judge should decide if attenuating circumstances or a just cause exists for use due to the right of the athlete to protect his or her health. A number of the forbidden substances are also medicinal and can be prescribed by a physician. If such substances are detected, it would not be fair to declare an athlete guilty of a crime that infers the intention to deceive other competitors. However, no athlete should be allowed to exceed legal limits and profit from exemption.

The IOC, NFs, IFs, and governmental authorities need to take concerted action to achieve effective results in the fight against the use of doping substances before and during sport events. This concerted action should be undertaken in several steps, some of which have already been initiated. Before such action it is essential that there be

- unity among the IFs and the IOC,
- general and individual commitment to enforce the unified antidoping rules,
- government support in each and every country involved in international sport competition for the legal recognition of the IFs' disciplinary powers in respect to doping, and
- the commitment to take part in a concerted action.

On the occasion of the Antidoping World Conference called by the IOC to unify action by all parties concerned in the fight against doping in sport, I presented a proposal aimed at bringing the authority of IFs to the forefront of the problem. The proposal was not submitted to debate, due as much to the conference organization itself as to the open opposition by governmental representatives to the idea of an IOC-controlled antidoping agency.

My proposal demanded that before any agreement for a unified war against doping in sport could be feasible, it is imperative to remove certain technical and legal obstacles that prevent IF actions and sanctions from being given legal recognition in every country.

It is important to recall the terms of that proposal neglected by the IOC Antidoping World Conference in 1998. For each of the four main prerequisites to unified action listed on page 38, possible solutions were given as follows:

1. **Satisfying the need to reach unity among the IFs and IOC.**

    a) Regulations may be unified around penalties, while respecting the specific needs for individual and team sport, as well as those of professional and nonprofessional sport.

    b) The sample-taking procedures need to be unified and strengthened in respect to the secrecy of identification and controls.

    c) The recognition and functioning of laboratories should include security measures aimed at protecting the identification of samples and containers, reliability of methods of analysis, and confidentiality of results.

2. **Demonstrating the general and individual will to enforce the unified antidoping rules.** This will should be expressed in the statutes of the NFs and IFs, as well as in the eligibility rules governing the Olympic Games, as follows:

    a) All athletes (male and female) wishing to take part in any international sport competition, including the Olympic Games, must state in an "Athlete's declaration," countersigned by his/her NF or NOC as the case may be, that "they declare under oath that they have not had recourse to any forbidden substance or training method to improve their physical or mental performance and do not intend to do so, whether during their preparation for the competition concerned or the competition itself."

    b) This "Athlete's declaration" constitutes the athletes' formal acceptance of the "Act for Drug-Free Sport," which commits them to

        i)   adhere voluntarily to the general antidoping rules approved by the world sport organizations and the IOC and willingly subject themselves to the control procedures provided for in these rules;

        ii)   freely submit any appeal regarding possible violations of individual rights, control procedures, or any of the anti-doping rules to the exclusive jurisdiction of the "International Court of Arbitration for Sport"; and

iii) appeal to the "International Court of Arbitration for Sport" before the jurisdiction of another court to which they may be entitled.

c) Competitions under the authority of NFs and regional events recognized by the IOC may be entered only by those athletes who sign the "Act for Drug-Free Sport" and adhere to it unreservedly.

3. **Asking for government support.** Sport organizations should strive to obtain, through the United Nations, a resolution by which each United Nations Organization (UNO) member country agrees to the following:

a) To adopt in its national legislation all measures needed to declare illicit the use of any forbidden substance or artificial method aimed at enhancing personal sport performance or the inducement of a third party to use such substances and/or methods with the purpose of taking part, under such advantageous artificial conditions, in any sport event.

b) To qualify as "fraudulent conduct" (or "fraud attempt" as the case may be) those illicit sport practices of the athlete and others involved of their own volition or by inducement when tests have proven positive. The IFs should penalize those sport practices using a scale of sanctions associated with specific aggravating or mitigating circumstances. The NFs should enforce the penalties imposed on individuals residing in their countries.

c) To grant legal recognition to official proceedings against one of its NFs, because of fraudulent sport conduct, started by the IF concerned when such legal proceedings are conducted in accordance with previously approved rules and procedures.

4. **Demonstrating the will to take part in this concerted action.** This can be expressed in an IOC-IF special meeting at which all participants will be requested to endorse the "Act for Drug-Free Sport."

Sport Identity and Image

When I start to conceive things that often seem to be true, they appear to be false when I want to put them on paper.

René Descartes, "Discours de la méthode"

Identity is the whole set of elements that, together, establish beyond any reasonable doubt that someone or something is who is claimed or what we assume. *Image* is the mental representation of someone or something resulting from the perception by the public of a whole set of elements or qualities emitted by that person or thing.

Brand Identity

For Professor Kapferer, the brand of a product is considered to have its own identity and image. Grouped under six different facets that constitute the *identity prism*, the identity of the brand (product or service) is the sum of values inherent in the product that can be emitted or projected to customers. The image is the reception or perception by the customer of the brand (product or service) or, alternatively, the state of mind produced in customers when they receive or perceive the brand (product or service). It is thus the way the public sees a product, a politician, an organization, or a sport. Therefore, brand identity comes from the brand itself and precedes the image created in the minds of customers on receiving or perceiving the brand as presented to them by the distributor.

Brand identity may be broken down into six dimensions:

1. **Physique (appearance):** the objective and prominent characteristics of the brand

2. **Personality:** the distinctive personal human character

3. **Relationship climate:** the sensorial relation that the brand creates and offers to the customer

4. **Cultural facet:** the "essential awareness" governing the brand

5. **Reflex produced by the brand:** this facet synthesizes an image of the customer to which the brand seems to be targeted. The target is the objective description of potential buyers of the brand, and the reflex of this target is produced by the brand. This image may be viewed as the outer mirror of the target produced by the brand as an "identification model."

6. **Mind-setting (mentalization):** the inside mirror of the brand. Customer adherence to a brand establishes a kind of spiritual community, with the effect that customers of a given brand feel strongly represented psychologically in that brand.

These six facets constitute the identity prism, which today has become the platform used to determine strategies for brand development. It may be considered as the starting point when drafting plans for sport development programs.

Sport's Identity

In this connection, it could be said that each sport is a brand (product or service) and as such possesses its own *identity* consisting of the values inherent in each sport. These values can be emitted or projected to potential customers (athletes, spectators, sponsors, and the media) from six different facets, all of which may be viewed together as the identity prism of the sport. The way in which potential customers perceive the brand (sport) or the state of mind created in them when they perceive the sport as presented to them by sport distributors (managers of associations, event organizers, sport clubs, leagues, and regions) constitutes the *image* they have of that sport.

To determine the identity of a given sport and define its image, its values must be identified to create a profile that is then used to present a credible, positive, and outstanding image in a convincing manner. Just as brands do, sport activities can attempt to define their own identity in relationship to the following facets: physique, personality, relationship climate, cultural, reflex, and mentalization (mind-setting).

Physique

This is the appearance of sport in its corporeal presence in the eyes of spectators, sponsors, media, and practitioners. This tangible presence of a sport is characterized by the following:

- **Practice environment (where to practice):** indoor, outdoor, or universal (any environment)
- **Participation required:** individual, collective, pairs, men, women, unisex, and so on
- **Medium required for its practice:** water, sand, aerial, or mixed; grass, ground, special ground, or universal; equipment; and individual efforts required

Personality

Personality is the profile of the sport consisting of its personal traits or characteristics, which include the following: popularity, sympathy, whether easily influenced or not, and the degree of aggressiveness in attitude or actions.

Relationship Climate

Sport also offers practitioners and spectators the possibility to develop a relationship climate. Sport is offered as a service to practitioners and as a product (brand) to the media, sponsors, and spectators. The distributor of the brand may be alternatively the sport manager; an event organizer; or a sport club, league, or regional organization, who carry out their jobs on the basis of all the elements available to them for the development and promotion of their sport activities. Athletes, media, sponsors, and spectators are the recipients of the product or service; they are the clients of the sport distributors who aim to develop intimate relations of affection, advice, protection, support, and complicity with them.

There is always a sense of complicity between actors. In this connection, there may also exist in sport a sense of protection and mutual support between distributors and customers (athletes, spectators, sponsors, and the media), which occasionally culminates in a form of complicity when they have the opportunity to share and experience exceptional events and sporting feats.

The relationship climate is very similar among different sports. However, some sports develop more positive relations and others more negative ones. Individual sport may create jealousy, rejection, sympathy, and even admiration among practitioners. Team sport may create a sense of complicity or mutual support, mostly creating relations such as partnership, self-sacrifice to reach a common goal, team spirit, and an individual sense of collective dependency. In golf, beach volleyball, tennis, and other individual sports, an interaction is created between the players and the public as well as a sense of self-sufficiency, independence, and freedom of mind.

Cultural

This facet comprises the general awareness of essential principles governing the sport when exhibited. A given exhibition becomes a manifestation of the sport's roots and origins and its refinement in regard to intellectual and artistic taste, with its titles indicating long-practiced activity. The facet of universal culture is often found in traditional sport events such as Wimbledon (grass and aristocracy) or Roland-Garros (clay and popular ambience), the Football World Cup (conquest and mass involvement), and Giro d'Italia (legend and gigantic effort).

Reflex

This facet synthesizes the idea of the sport fan, who either practices the sport or takes part in it as a spectator, and for whom the sport seems to have been made. Reflex also synthesizes the idea of the sport sponsor and the media, who decide whether the sport is suitable or not to reach their objectives or satisfy their needs. The target of the brand (sport) is the objective description of the practitioners or spectators of the sport. The reflection (reflex) is the image that sport produces of them as spectators or practitioners, thereby creating an "identification model" and generating a spirit of a community inasmuch as their own image is also reflected in other spectators or practitioners.

Professor Bernard Catry expresses a similar point of view in his article published in the *Revue Française du Marketing* (No. 159-1996/4) when he writes that "this sense of common image or perception is mostly determined by the communication of the sport concerned or on the contrary by the absence of communication," adding that "the spectator attending a sport event identifies the other spectators attending the same event with a group the profile of which he has outlined."

The same can be said of the way practitioners and sport managers react. Spectators also identify themselves with athletes in the sport arena. This explains why the reactions of a public attending boxing bouts or football matches are different from those of a public attending tennis or volleyball matches, which are considered sport for elder spectators in tennis and youngsters in volleyball, in both cases with college/high school or university backgrounds.

Mind-Setting (Mentalization)

Though largely linked to the presence of major stars on the playing field, this facet should not be considered as its only interpretation. When spectators attend a sport event, they live in the shadow of their favorite player, whose image is adopted by the spectators who follow that sport. Every sport fan experiences a transfiguration in the presence of a favorite sport star.

An Example of Sport Image (Volleyball)

Before trying to construct the anatomy of volleyball's identity, it must be ascertained how the sport is perceived, and this from two different standpoints: first from that of people who have seen major volleyball events and received direct information, and second from that of people who know little about volleyball because of a lack of information. The latter can come from the absence of major volleyball events in their country or from lack of a successful national team or national league. Frequently, a national team or league is not given proper media coverage because of the lack of resources of the sport organization or because it is not well enough prepared to promote the image of its properties because of insufficient funds, poor management, unfit administration, or inadequate organizational structures.

For People Who Have Seen Major Volleyball Events
Speaking of volleyball, Juan Antonio Samaranch Marqués de Samaranch said:

Volleyball has managed to have itself identified in the world's eyes as a sport that is youthful, athletic, universal, and democratic, a sport that has in its spectacularly telegenic nature and in its clear-cut heroes a new model that I do not hesitate to recommend to the youth of the world today. The image, behavior, athletic capability, and above all drug-free performance are of the highest class, and are the winning tools needed to perpetuate the Olympic spirit in the twenty-first century.

Mr. Adolf Oggi, former Federal Councillor of the Swiss Confederation, stated:

Volleyball has enhanced the value of all the qualities required of a man or a woman today: quick mind, prompt decision, hard training, self sacrifice, team spirit, tenacity and will, excellence in physical abilities, health, beauty, elegance, and refusal of violence and provocation in order to give a suitable place to physical and intellectual achievement.

Mr. Kurt Furgler, former Federal Councillor of the Swiss Confederation, declared:

The synthesis of volleyball cannot be grasped only from the mirrored reflection of an individual or from the elegance of a star. Technique, energy, and creativity are at the very heart of a group activity. Sport is community life "par excellence" and volleyball builds teams and is a catalyst for solidarity. On a volleyball court, everyone playing there learns the rules of community life because balance, performance, and success of the group are determined by the harmony and the behaviour of individuals. (cf. "100 Years of Global Link", Publieditor, 1995)

For Countries Where Volleyball Has Little Presence

People in these countries have a poor image or perception of volleyball because they receive information only from their limited environment and often do not see that sport on television, in films or photos, or through publicity. As a result, they do not have in their possession the elements to ensure a real perception and positive image of volleyball. Instead, theirs is the image described by Professor Bernard Catry in his excellent article on sport identity and image published by *Revue Française du Marketing*, which describes volleyball as a "family sport," little known and infrequently practiced. This is in spite of the fact that the International Volleyball Federation

(continued)

(continued)

(FIVB) is the largest sport organization in the world with 217 affiliated countries, 600,000 spectators attending World League matches every year, and over 100 countries broadcasting images of the 1994-1998 World Championships. It was also ranked among the top five sports with the largest worldwide TV coverage during the Barcelona, Atlanta, and Sydney Olympic Games.

The same magazine published a European survey that described volleyball in Europe as having less than average interest, far below football, swimming, and other sports. However, this survey did not mention which layers of Europe's population were polled on the subject. The validity of the survey is thus quite arguable with respect to its findings at the European level. In addition, only 11 countries were included in the survey, namely France, England, Luxembourg, Norway, Monaco, Iceland, Andorra, Ireland, Scotland, Wales, and to a lesser extent Switzerland, which by no means reflects the European situation as a whole.

The results of the French survey bear little significance in light of the fact that

• during the World League and Olympic Games, television broadcasting of volleyball in Italy and the Netherlands obtained ratings equivalent to those of Olympic football and sometimes even higher;

• in the Netherlands, Italy, Spain, Greece, and other European countries, the World League and several major events have set new records with large crowds attending the matches; and

• in Belgium and Germany, not to mention the Netherlands, Italy, Greece, Spain, Russia, and Poland, among others, national volleyball leagues are operating successfully.

The obvious conclusion that football occupies the number one spot did not require a survey. In any case, the number of practitioners is not that much greater than in other popular sports such as motorcycling. However, the NFs of the 11 above-mentioned European countries should seek to benefit from the survey's findings insofar as they can immediately start preparing plans to improve the disastrous image of volleyball in their respective countries, an accurate reflection of the image that the volleyball administration has created there. Other countries such as Italy, the Netherlands, Greece, Spain, Russia, and Bulgaria, not to mention Yugoslavia, Belgium, and Germany, cannot be put in the same basket considering that powerful national leagues have been successfully operating there for a number of years.

Identity Versus Image

It is worthwhile to remember that identity corresponds to the essence and values of the sport, while image is the collective perception of the sport by customers, athletes, spectators, sponsors, and the media. It should also be recalled that brand (sport) identity is born from the brand (sport) itself and that the image follows once the customer receives and perceives data relating to the sport.

Image may or may not coincide with brand (sport) identity because of a distorted perception by the customer of the brand (sport). There may be a perception of a badly formulated message or the poor presentation of the brand (sport), which leads customers to receive a distorted image of what is presented to them. This does not modify the brand (sport) identity as such; rather it produces a poor image. Identity contains the values of the brand (sport); its image, which is created by an accurate or distorted presentation, cannot influence or modify the brand (sport) identity in itself.

However, NFs can change the image or public perception of a sport in their respective countries by adopting strategic actions. In this context, NFs may draw some inspiration from the actions presented in the FIVB's "World Plan 2001." The poor image of a given sport could be the result of a perception stemming from the low technical level of local, national, and league teams or athletic representatives, inadequate publicity of that sport's events, lack of promotion, absence of top-level events, mismanagement of the sport from improper organizational structures, inefficient administration, or inappropriate management, as is the case in many NFs.

Beach Volleyball Identity

Professor Bernard Catry believes that beach volleyball was created to counter the lack of popularity of volleyball—which I prefer to call a lack of presence in the media and in television programs, or more precisely the lack of a positive image in certain countries, such as England and France, that shape European public opinion thanks to their important media environment. Furthermore, beach volleyball is not, I believe, adequately perceived by the previously mentioned article (Catry, *Revue Française du Marketing*) when it compares the sport to street basketball, which is more of a promotional tool than a competitive discipline.

Once again, this stems from the French image of beach volleyball as promoted by the NF of that country, which portrays the sport as a leisure

(continued)

activity in a program called "volley vacances" (holiday volleyball). In fact, this has nothing to do with competitive beach volleyball, whose true identity will be described later on. The FIVB does possess a promotional tool similar to street basketball, called park-volley, a four versus four open-air version of volleyball with rules similar to those of beach volleyball.

Volleyball is traditionally played outdoors. Indeed, from the very beginning of its competitive existence, volleyball was played outdoors with great success in socialist countries and some western European countries in the post-war era. When volleyball was introduced to IOC members for Olympic recognition in 1957, the presentation was made in a 1,500-seat hall. It was in those days that indoor volleyball events began overshadowing their outdoor counterparts. Today, European summers still play host to several huge outdoor volleyball events such as the Sandwell Tournament in England, the Saalo Tournament in Finland, and other events staged in Germany and in the Czech and Slovak Republics.

Establishing a Sport Identity

On the basis of Professor Kapferer's principles regarding brand identity, the identity of a sport—in this case volleyball—can be defined independently from the image of it that a person or a community perceives.

A list can be drawn up of the recognized values of volleyball that will assist in establishing its own identity, which may or may not correspond to the image that the public and practitioners have of it in their own countries. This image may not correspond to the value-based identity because of the varying degrees of organization of the national sport and more often to the varying quality of communication systems. Some of the values recognized in the game of volleyball are

alertness and rapidity of decision making,

loyalty and self-sacrifice,

the absence of deliberate violence,

cooperation and team spirit,

collective creativity,

solidarity,

sociability (communication),

harmonious conviviality,

athletic team synergy,

fair play model,

self-fulfillment,

generic participation (boys, girls, men, women, young, adult, and the elderly),

universal demography,

geographic versatility,

year-round practice,

simplicity of equipment,

scholarly character,

rotation of game positions,

practice on almost any surface, and

speedy reaction and flexibility.

The above values and others may be found in beach volleyball as well, the identity of which has also been established, as can be seen in table 1.1, which breaks down the six facets for each identity and compares them side by side.

CONCLUSION

In their early days, sport organizations assumed their social responsibility through improvised sport activities and volunteer work with which they were able to provide enjoyment, free-time leisure, and community contact to the youth. Today's national and international sport organizations, while still willing to render an effective service to the youth, must do more. They are compelled to operate in a professional manner, adopting adequate organizational structures and efficient administration under modern management principles. Above all, they have to be prepared to elect their sport leaders from among persons whose ethical principles and cultural level make them trustworthy guardians of the moral and legal integrity of sport and its democratic institutions.

Only through such measures will national and international federations be able to deliver the kind of services youth are expecting and successfully confront external interference that hampers proper coordination of sport activities with their own affiliated members, governmental or quasi-governmental units, and NOCs. Organizations unable to rely on efficient administration and professional management, particularly in developing countries, will feel the pressure from governmental and nongovernmental parallel sport organizations. Their political orientation and hegemonic attitudes will sooner or later make NFs an endangered species or push them to leave competitive and professional sport activities in the hands of businessmen and sport promoters.

Table 1.1   Volleyball and Beach Volleyball Identity Elements

Volleyball	Beach volleyball
Physique	
Universal environment and elements	Nature as playing ground
Collective and generic	Simplicity of equipment
Simplicity of equipment	Overall athleticism
Absence of violence	Absence of violence
Personality	
Athletic team synergy	Individual athletic energy
Alertness and rapid decision making	Alertness and rapid decision making
Explosive power	Glamorous youthful character
Self-control skills	Endurance
Relationship climate	
Harmonious conviviality	Mutual advice and understanding
Sociability	Identity between players and public
Solidarity	Collective interaction
Mutual recognition	Mutual support
Culture	
Universal demography	Elitist character
Gender accessibility	Gender accessibility
All-year practice	Summer atmosphere
Scholarly character	Relaxed attitude
Reflex	
Collective creativity	Romantic attractiveness
Self-fulfillment	Party celebration
Cooperation	Trusting partnership
Speedy reaction and flexibility	Speedy reaction and flexibility
Mind-setting (mentalization)	
Sense of group mission	Self-reliance
Loyalty and group identity	Self-esteem
Fair play prototype	Fair play prototype
Team spirit	Sense of freedom

It is now clear that Olympic competitors emerge from the constituency of the NFs. It is also a fact that NOCs can only justify their sport mission by providing day-to-day support to the NFs of their country. The NOCs' duties toward them do not begin on the eve of the Olympic Games and do not end with the extinction of the flame. The accountability of both these sport organizations, NFs and NOCs, is an ongoing matter and does not rest with their title or the fancy of their administrators, who could be brought to justice at any time.

It is about time that the world of sport took its responsibility for supporting and preparing national sport organizations seriously in order to better perform their duties. After all, these organizations are the front line in the fight against the doping of athletes, the commercialization of sport, the use of publicity on athletes' uniforms, and the merger of governmental institutions with NOCs or NFs.

It is about time to stop labeling the top athletes as those who represent sport, forgetting that behind their success an army of volunteers has sacrificed the best of their lives to provide them with the necessary facilities and support. A major injustice must be made known: The winners are placed at the heart of sport because of the much-publicized need (and it is a real need) of giving the youth role models that they can easily follow.

The problem is that in the process, the undervalued national sport governing bodies are neglected and do not get the support and care that they need. These organizations are made up of small and large groups of volunteers associated with sporting clubs, high schools, colleges, universities, and other groups that all together, united in a NF, are the silent heroes of the 20th century sport boom.

NFs nurture the needs of professional leagues of their sports and of businesspeople exploiting them, and, at the same time, provide us with the heroes of the Olympics. Yet, they are always in search of financial, material, and personnel support. It is they who go knocking on doors of the rich and famous. They lobby powerful politicians, privileged institutions, and indifferent media tycoons just to transfer all or most of the support obtained to a group of athletes, who later on compete at the national, continental, or world level. In the end, if those athletes lose, the NFs will be crucified for doing nothing for sport, but if the athletes win, the fame and glory will go to them while the NFs will be simply ignored!

two

A SUCCESSFUL SPORT ORGANIZATION

Courtesy of Nuova Immagine.

> **Sovereignty is the exercise of the general will and can never be alienated. The sovereign is a collective entity that can only be represented by itself; its power can be delegated but not its general will.**
>
> ***J.-J. Rousseau, The Social Contract***

Chapter 1 established the need for new organizational structures in sport to improve sport opportunities and facilitate the practice of sport within clubs, leagues, associations, and so on. In addition, it described the national and international environments in which sport organizations have to operate and examined the most important responsibilities and needs of NFs.

This chapter describes the operational conditions that a successful sport organization must develop in the pursuit of its goals. To have a better understanding of those conditions, it is important to be aware of the way an organization comes into being.

Origins and Operations of a Sport Organization

Nothing which potentially exists can be transformed into action other than through something which is already in action.

Aristotle, Nicomachian Ethics

People wishing to create a club, association, organizing committee, league, and so on must first outline the profile of its initial structure and further development, define its essential principles, and set up a system for communication with and between its members. Only then should it tackle the more detailed problems inherent to its chosen structures. Once the profile has been defined, certain basic constitutional and operational questions must be addressed:

- Who exactly are the potential members?
- What are the objectives of the organization?
- What are its priorities?
- What are its decision-making bodies and from where do they draw their power?
- What authority does each level hold?
- How does communication flow between different bodies?

Finally, you must decide which administrative structure will best enable these bodies to function.

Meetings

Very often, a small group of people meets to discuss the establishment of an organization and, on this occasion, they propose the objectives, priorities, and functions of the decision-making bodies. However, subsequent meetings should not neglect to define the channels of communication, future mechanisms to check whether the objectives and priorities have been attained, and those required to monitor the constitutional bodies. Make sure that these items are on the agenda of your organizational meetings.

Preliminary Organizational Meetings

Meetings prior to the constitution of a sport organization should take place in compliance with several fundamental principles to ensure successful meetings and the ultimate achievement of the organizational goals. These principles include a clear definition of objectives, a thorough knowledge of the objectives on the part of the person responsible for the presentation, previous general information regarding the purpose of the meeting, and prior acquaintance by the organizers of all participants.

It is also important that

- the meeting has a clearly defined objective or target,
- the person making contact with participants be perfectly aware of all details regarding its objectives and be capable of explaining them clearly,
- people invited to the meeting be well informed and understand the aim of the meeting, and
- the person who organizes the meeting know the names of all those who are to be invited to attend it.

Preparatory Meetings

Such meetings are intended for small groups of people who need to meet from time to time to prepare their proposals regarding operational and constitutional issues. Once preparatory meetings are concluded, a final meeting is called in which the members invited will decide whether to make public their agreement to create the organization and its basic principles, as well as to request legal registration and official recognition from the country's political and sport authorities.

Organizational Meetings

Once an organization has officially begun (whether as a sport club, association, or other), meetings can be held at different levels. This being said, the three most important levels of a sport organization that must meet

This International Volleyball Federation (FIVB) meeting of the general assembly takes place regularly to make decisions and ensure that those decisions are enforced.

Courtesy of Nuova Immagine.

regularly are the operational level, the executive level, and the decision-making level.

Operational Level   The group of volunteers or employees responsible for the day-to-day administration of programs; implementation of decisions; execution of policies; and actual performance of activities included in a program, project, or plan forms part of the operational structure. They are divided into several departments, sections, or administrative units.

Meetings at the operational level are held inside sections, departments, and administrative units to assess priorities, define work routines, and eventually to discuss small discrepancies or distribute tasks. These meetings must be called and conducted in a friendly atmosphere by the unit head.

Meetings are also held between heads of administrative units, departments, or sections to coordinate action on a project, receive information on new projects or evaluate current ones, and agree on sensitive issues affecting all their units. There should always be one or two important topics on the agenda. Good managers can streamline meetings so they need to happen less often and take less time.

Executive Level (Executive Committee)   The body responsible for the administration and coordination of activities, the attainment of objectives laid down in the constitution, and the implementation of general assembly decisions is generally called the executive committee. It meets to plan strategies for reaching goals, oversee the administrator, set up the operational structure, and maintain the necessary contact with the various governmental groups. When not in session, the executive committee acts through the intermediary of its president, who is entrusted with the management and administration of daily tasks.

The meetings of the executive committee take place either from time to time or on a systematic basis. Deciding to hold a routine, but unnecessary, meeting is just as detrimental as not holding a meeting that is necessary. For this reason, the president must usually be vested with the power to decide if an executive committee meeting is necessary or not. Even so, a minimum number of executives should be empowered to demand that such a meeting be held, taking care to define beforehand the business to be discussed.

The routine meetings of the executive committee will only be effective if they contribute to the progress of the objectives the committee has set. Do not hold meetings that are likely to be a waste of time. Without exception, participants in any executive committee meeting must be members of that body, although the president may call on any other person deemed suitable to provide information on specific subjects. The executive committee may also convene for an extraordinary meeting or meet outside the usual period.

Decision-Making Level (General Assembly) The body in charge of supervising the management tasks entrusted to the executive committee and to the president is called the general assembly. It confers all power and is thus vested with the highest function of decision making and must meet regularly to see that its decisions have been applied.

The general assembly is normally held periodically (every year or two), the constitution stipulating clearly who can attend and what business should be discussed. Regularly scheduled general assemblies are necessary. They must never be cancelled or postponed, as this could suggest serious trouble in executive coordination.

The general assembly can also convene for an extraordinary meeting or outside the usual period. In such cases, the president must

- fully justify calling the meeting and clearly stipulate its aims;
- be perfectly aware of expectations from this meeting;
- be sure that this meeting is the *only* (or the *best*) way of achieving the objective; and
- have evaluated other options for meeting the objectives, such as consultation by correspondence, conference call, telex, and teleconference.

Every organization must have its structure reflected in a chart showing the chain of command going from one level to the other and representing decision making in the organization. The structure must be clearly separate from a jurisdictional body in charge of solving conflicts. Figure 2.1 reproduces a chart model for a national sport organization.

Making Meetings Productive

To facilitate the paperwork and help the organization run smoothly and efficiently from the administrative standpoint, you should follow several

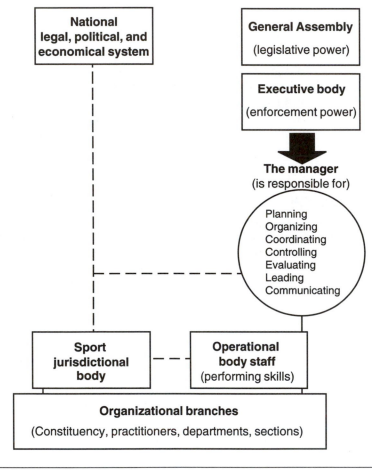

Figure 2.1 Example of the organizational structure of a national sport organization.

basic principles. These help organize productive working meetings and general assemblies that will help the organization determine a clear-cut direction for its activities and programs.

No meeting can reach its objectives if its respective president and secretary are not properly prepared—not only documented but also sharing objectives and having a common understanding of how to approach each item. Such preparation requires three things: personal preparation, material preparation, and knowledge of how to conduct a meeting.

Personal Preparation The president and secretary of the meeting must hold a prior working session in order to prepare for the upcoming meeting. Both of them must have the same objectives and share the same understanding of each item on the agenda, dispose of the same information, agree on the pros and cons, envisage potential replies to questions and eventual disagreements, and so on.

Material Preparation The secretary must ensure well in advance that the meeting facility is adequate and necessary equipment functions properly and should also inform members of the meeting and send them any preparatory documents. For their part, members due to make a presentation should check that they have delivered all the necessary documents and material in advance and that they know when on the agenda they will be presenting.

The secretary should check ahead of time with special guests or lecturers. Greet them again at the meeting and see if they have any documents for distribution available in sufficient quantity. Make sure all written reports submitted do not exceed the normal length. Each subject presented must be brief, clear, and concise.

Conducting a Meeting The president is responsible for chairing the meeting and ensuring that it runs smoothly. During the meeting, the president should proceed as follows:

1. Open and close the sessions and the discussions.
2. Introduce and present clearly and concisely each item on the agenda, in the order listed.
3. Open the debate on each subject once all members clearly know the discussion topic.
4. Ensure the strict application of the constitution, regulations, assembly rules, and decisions contained in the minutes of previous meetings.
5. Give the floor to those wishing to speak and discuss items in the order of the agenda.

6. Ensure that each speaker deals only with the item under discussion and keeps it brief.

7. Close the discussion of each item once the members have expressed their opinions, make a brief summary, and then suggest conclusions and/or proposals.

8. Ask members to agree to these conclusions or to propose modifications or additions.

9. Confirm the text of the proposals as agreed by the members and proceed to put such proposals to the vote after sufficient debate.

10. Announce the result of the vote and call on the secretary to read the action as approved.

Defining Legal Status

The representativeness of a sport organization is the right that allows the organization to act for, represent, and speak on behalf of its members (athletes, coaches, referees, officials, clubs, leagues, etc.). This right is based on the recognition received from its constituency, consisting of representatives of people practicing the same sport and established in previously recognized zones, regions, or even whole countries or territories. Those representatives are invested with legitimate authority through a mandate expressed in an accreditation letter received from the athletes or clubs based in those zones, regions, or territories in accordance with national laws, local practices, or customs.

NFs become affiliated members of the IF of their sport only upon producing evidence of having received governmental investiture as the only body with national authority to administer and govern the respective sport. Normally such evidence consists of a letter signed by the local city council, state authority, ministry of sports (if no NOC exists in the country), or National Olympic Committee in the case of NGBs of a given sport. A NF also must represent either local people or other organizations practicing or promoting the same sport within the country.

Structural Divisions of Power

Sport organizations, whatever their nature or socioeconomic situation, must develop an adequate structure in order to operate successfully within the local, regional, or national community. Every sport organization should establish a clear-cut division of power in three major bodies and one operational structure. This division of power has the effect of providing the best (or least damaging) harmonization of behavior and understanding, and balance between social and individual rights. Those four bodies are as follows:

1. **A legislative body** is made up of the members' delegated or elected representatives. It reflects the members' interests and has authority to make binding principles and decisions to achieve organizational objectives.

2. **An executive body** is in charge of abiding by and enforcing those principles and decisions. It acts as a guarantor of the organization's independence and sovereign powers.

3. **A jurisdictional body** is entrusted with legal powers to solve sport conflicts. It protects an individual's rights, including those of self-defense and due process, consisting of defense, audience, and procedure.

4. **The operational body** is responsible for implementing the programs, actions, and decisions throughout the organizational structure, by means of adequate administration and professional management. It is composed of the people directly working for the organization.

An Organization's Social Profile

The social profile of a sport organization delineates in chart form which individuals or groups could be interested in the sport, what are the main tasks of the organization, what basic actions are to be performed by paid or volunteer staff, and how other groups and individuals could be involved.

Profile of Newly Formed Sport Organizations

Emerging sport organizations are simple and do not have to solve major organizational, managerial, or administrative problems. They normally depend on the work of one or several people, mostly sport enthusiasts carrying out volunteer work.

Such volunteers and enthusiasts are the essential part of any emerging sport organization; they normally do all the work, such as preparing sport events and their venues; establishing rules; recruiting potential participants; and collecting funds, sport material, and equipment from public or private institutions. Frequently they also compete, organize, publicize, promote, and perform public relations activities. They are the authentic founding fathers of sport in many communities worldwide.

The social profile of an amateur association of any sport can be represented from its initial stage (see figure 2.2) to its most developed stage (see figure 2.3), showing the progressive growth of the organizational structure, administration, and management.

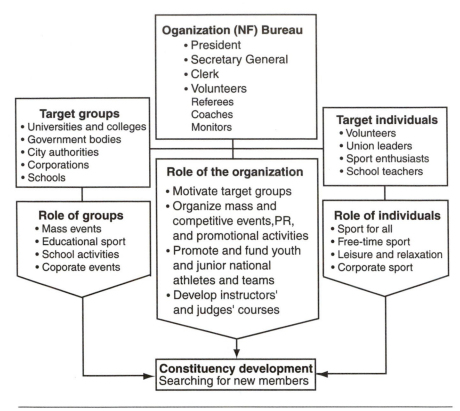

Figure 2.2 Social profile of an emerging sport organization.

Profile of Developed Sport Organizations

Different institutions and organizations, public and private, may participate in sport activities as a consequence of sport promotional campaigns, public relations activities, or social programs conducted by sport organizations or governmental agencies. These activities require adequate follow-up to convince those organizations to become permanent cells of sport participation and, eventually, full-fledged constituents of a sport organization.

Highly complex and sophisticated organizations may develop as shown in figure 2.3. For organizations to be successful, good managers must head the units and departments that plan activities. Managers, employees, members, and practitioners of the sport need to share the clear and compelling vision of the organization and be committed to reaching the same goals.

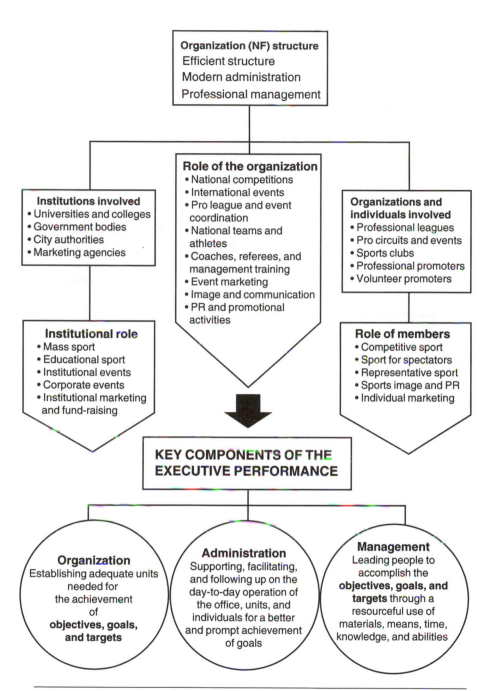

Figure 2.3 Social profile of a developed sport organization.

Choosing a Type of Organization

When society requires to be rebuilt, there is no use in attempting to rebuild it on the old plan.

John Stuart Mill,
Essay on Coleridge

The previous chapter addressed the social context in which sport organizations find themselves today, the responsibilities that national and international structures assign to certain sport organizations called NFs, and the concept of sport identity and sport image and their relationships to the public.

This chapter has so far dealt with the development of a successful organization from its informal beginnings. This section will introduce administrative, technical, and scientific principles necessary to develop a successful organizational sport structure—whether local, regional, or national. A new organization must be planned in accordance with its own objectives and needs, considering that, as John Stuart Mill said, we cannot duplicate the structure from another organization.

This section addresses what an organization is and the different forms it can take, as well as various principles likely to be of assistance in choosing the kind of organizational structure needed in a given country. Next follows a look at the human aspect of the organization in notions of authority and power, authority versus autonomy, delegation of authority, and finally responsibility in a chain of command. The chapter concludes by introducing the concept of short- and medium-term objectives and proposing some models of organizational charts both for emerging and highly professional and developed organizations.

Good Organization

Good organization maximizes efficiency, productivity, and employee performance. Job descriptions, adequate allocation of tasks in departments or units of reasonable size, definition of authority, delegation of power, and a good relationship between all units will substantially increase the level of performance.

Properly organized units with clear-cut lines of responsibility, good communication, and adequate equipment and resources will help ensure a smooth and continuous flow of activities and services. Clearly define responsibilities so there is no duplication of efforts. Establish healthy lines of communication between various levels and departments. Finally, nurture employee morale and job satisfaction carefully, in small as well as large departments, for this increases commitment to the overall organization.

Types of Organization

The economic, social, legal, and political conditions in each country will determine the environment in which sport organizations develop. Whether public, private, governmental, or nongovernmental, they are working to coordinate the practice of their sport. The organization is not isolated, but part of a community in which many other organizations are also active. Based on its objectives, each organization establishes its own structure to achieve the efficient and continuous flow of operations necessary to attain its objectives.

Private enterprises may follow many different forms of organization, but sport organizations should keep in mind the following forms: those distinguished by authority and responsibility assigned and those distinguished by different models of decision making.

Lineal Command- and Labor Division-Based Types

Organizational types distinguished by authority and responsibility assigned include those characterized by lineal command, functional (based on division of labor), and territorial structures.

Lineal Command   Under lineal command, authority and responsibility are centralized in one person, the manager or president. Orders emanate from that person with everyone below following those orders. Organizational failure is the failure of that person, who normally steps down. On the other hand, success brings the same person great recognition.

Small emerging organizations in developing countries are advised to follow this lineal system because of its reaction speed in regard to urgently required changes, decisions, and actions.

Functional   This type of organization is based on the division of labor and requires a careful analysis of the functions needed to carry out the tasks of the organization, so that those functions may be grouped by department with clearly defined levels of authority and responsibility. Orders may emanate from different levels of the organization.

This is a good method for major sport organizations because of the advantages of specialization, with experts in specific functions forming the different departments. However, this functional organization does hold dangers for sport managers.

Because of the various specialized activities involved, such as the organization of sport events, the preparation of marketing and development programs, and the implementation of promotional and public relations activities, each of these departments may have different goals. Each individual area represents a series of problems that may require sport managers' attention. In addition, the different departments must be properly coordinated and the contact between them adequately maintained, while ensuring that they remain connected to the organization as a whole, pursuing common objectives and operating under the administrative policies of the organization.

Territorial Territorial organization offers improved coordination and control of each zone considered a territory, with adequate administration of its own and delegated authority. However, the danger is that people in each different geographic zone gradually tend to identify only with their region and consequently neglect the general interest of the organization.

Control- and Power-Based Types

These organizational types are distinguished by the way in which they concentrate or distribute decision-making power and include central planning and control, decentralized competence by political region, and decentralized administration with locally held power.

Government or Central Planning and Control An organization subject to this kind of central planning enjoys the advantages offered by full governmental financing. However, effectiveness depends on the government scale of priorities and whether or not sport is considered part of national policy, be it under educational or health programs. Another disadvantage is that clubs, practitioners, and people involved in sport have no say with regard to the implementation of programs or events and so cannot engage in any international activity without prior governmental approval and support.

This type of organization is only feasible in countries where the sociopolitical structure is based on central planning. Typically in such countries, an individual's political affiliation rates higher than his or her ability. The other types of organization are better suited to countries where free association constitutes a fundamental part of the national political system.

Decentralization by Political Region This type of organization consists of having, in different regions, states, or provinces, a local committee with identical or similar functions to those of the central committee.

The disadvantage of this type of organization is that it is plagued with bureaucratic procedures in which the objectives and practical needs of clubs and practitioners are of little concern. In organizations based on the political geography of the country, decisions about associations, leagues, and practitioners are made according to the subjective interpretation of local and national leaders. Clubs and individuals are not involved in the decision-making process and their needs are totally neglected. Governments recognizing this type of organization (Argentina, Mexico, and most Latin and

African countries) are afraid to confront people's demands about what they can provide to organizations for the practice of sport. Therefore, people prefer to avoid government intervention and accept whatever they are given instead.

Decentralized Administration With Local Power This structure helps to obtain a wider participation of experts in the different areas of sport: technical aspects; coaching; refereeing; events organization; and the promotion of sport clubs, teams, and leagues. Often, self-elected leaders at the local level can direct club teams and local associations or leagues that have year-round activities.

Under this concept each region, institution, and local association of a given sport should have representation in a general assembly that is part of the decision-making process of the NF. A NF should not be expected to consciously reflect its country's political divisions within its structure. Instead, its structure should serve the teams, associations, and individual athletes, allowing them to express freely their will and be part of the decision-making process. They can then promote and practice their sport according to the set of rules approved by the NF, and perhaps the IF, with which they are affiliated.

Bureaucratic Organization

Bureaucratic indicates a more formal model of organization, which includes the following characteristics:

- Regular activities required for the achievement of the organizational objectives are listed as official fixed duties.
- Organization follows hierarchical principles.
- Operational activities are governed by a system of abstract rules applied to individual cases.
- Top-level managers operate with impersonal formality.
- Employment within the organization is based on technical aptitude and is less subject to arbitrary or selfish decisions.

Organization With Delegated Authority

This type of organization clearly recognizes that authority is vested in positions. The job descriptions then imply the authority to carry out the responsibilities of the position. Remember several key points when defining authority relations, such as the following:

- Employees must be willing to accept their supervisor's authority, otherwise they might refuse requests from that supervisor.

67

- Employees must clearly understand what is expected of them. If uncertain, they might ignore or not carry out the wishes of their supervisor.
- Supervisors must ask employees to perform tasks consistent with the goals of the organization.
- Employees must be physically and mentally capable of carrying out a work request.
- Flowcharts must be accurate and concise to avoid employees overstepping their delegated authority.

Environmental Indicators

When choosing an organizational style, one must consider the contextual factors discussed here:

- **Specific sport environment.** In any country, attitudes, as well as economic, political, and social forces, determine sport participation. Such factors are the best indicator when choosing the type of organization for promoting and coordinating a national sport. Suitable organizational structures are of great assistance to the management of any sport enterprise and the running of NFs. In the same vein, inadequate structures and poor organization impede the smooth running of the NFs and the timely execution of their programs. Favorable conditions require a functional organization; lineal command could be better in unfavorable conditions.

- **Geography and infrastructure.** The topography, means of transportation, and communication systems, as well as available equipment and technology, can facilitate or hinder the supervision and implementation of programs. In the case of favorable conditions, it is much easier to develop a consistent and flexible organization. In general, a territorial organization is more suitable in these conditions.

- **Area cultures and institutions.** Every well-founded sport organization must take into account regional or local factors: the multiplicity of cultural roots existing at local, provincial, and national levels and the need to maintain permanent contact with schools, universities, and other civil, governmental, and military organizations.

Careful study of how these organizations work will help you choose an appropriate style for your organization.

Authority Versus Autonomy of Branches

At every local, regional, and national level, individuals and organizations must have authority and enjoy autonomy. They must have free rein to originate ideas. The decision-making power for local and regional questions must belong to the local or regional organization, although that level must also remain and operate within the general rules and guidelines approved by the national organization.

Avoid administrative and bureaucratic delays that disrupt local and national programs. Programs should flow freely without neglecting the administrative controls and supervision needed to keep the central bodies informed at all times of local and regional activities.

For a national sport organization, the secret of success lies in the balance between the uninhibited progress of local and regional activities on one hand and, on the other, the control and supervision by its central bodies. Efficiency will depend on how well the central bodies have delegated authority down through the various levels of the organization, together with the quality of communication at all levels.

Keeping Objectives in Mind

From its very inception, the national sport organization's objectives must, in the short and possibly medium term, be feasible and easily achievable with a minimum of delays, interference, and effort.

A good organization requires a good structure, strategy, and operative system, along with competent managers and assistants. Everything and everyone has to be moving toward quality objectives that can be achieved in the not-too-distant future. The National Basketball Association (NBA) has gone through all these situations, and its phenomenal success was not attained before the arrival of David Stern, one of the greatest sport managers today. David had to draw a new strategy and, at the same time, convince the clubs to change their structure and show discipline while implementing a new operative system. The NBA is an example of good structure, excellent administration, and the best management in the world. Special care must be given to not oversizing departments, which may lead to bankruptcy or bureaucracy. The number of employees should correspond to the actual needs and programs underway.

Departmental Organization

When organizing departments, you must be aware that they will function as one of two types: externally focused departments and internally focused ones. Each department must be assigned only duties corresponding to its objectives, and the number of employees should be limited to the needs of the programs to be implemented.

Externally Focused Departments

A sport organization should include departments that address the following externally focused categories:

- **Product:** the specific sport activity
- **Customers:** including young people of several age groups, sponsors, spectators, television, and press
- **Territorial coordination:** among the states, regions, and provinces in the case of NFs; regions or zones in the case of confederations; zones or continents in the case of world organizations

Organizing solely on the basis of technical specifications of each sport—just as the International Amateur Swimming Federation (FINA) has done with its sections of diving, swimming, water polo, and synchronized swimming—restricts the organization to its own area. Organizing solely on the basis of specific groups or types of athlete (elite, university, or schoolchild) restricts the action of the organization because of a lack of technical or territorial reach. Organizing solely on the basis of geographic conditions makes no sense and will create a large but empty organization with nothing of its own to offer any group. Every element should be considered while defining the scope of the action. Open organizations may access more easily the different groups of individuals, institutions, and communities. Not even national boundaries should limit the reach of an organization giving attention to cooperation and understanding of the needs of the other similar organizations that could become affiliated members.

Strategies and objectives are relatively easy to determine once the mission statement or compelling vision of the organization has been drafted. Avoid the danger of departments focusing only on their own goals and neglecting the programs of other departments.

Internally Focused Departments

These departments carry out the internal operations and can be either processing departments or functional departments. Processing departments' organization is based on the specific activities required to complete a task; that of functional departments is based on specific functions.

Size of Departments

The size of departments depends on how many employees you would like one supervisor to oversee and how much money you have for staffing at different levels. Larger units place more people under one manager, which allows for less individual employee contact by the supervisor, even though communication may be more efficient. When determining the size of a department, a manager should consider the following:

- Highly specialized employees require less oversight.
- Highly experienced managers can oversee more employees.
- Seasoned veteran employees need less oversight.

Organizational Principles

In order to operate efficiently in its internal operations and external activities, every organization should pay attention to the following organizational principles:

- **Unity of command:** Each member of the organization reports to just one supervisor.
- **Principle of exception:** Low-level managers must routinely handle recurring decisions and high-level managers must handle unusual aspects. Decisions may be foreseen for specific cases and do not need to be explained due to their repetitive implementation.
- **Extent of control:** The number of people to be overseen by a superior is limited.
- **Numerical principle:** Authority and responsibility must have uninterrupted flow from the highest to the lowest executive level (managers are given a number). This principle simply establishes the organization as a hierarchy and follows the "chain of command." The highest manager is number 1, the next is number 2, and so forth.
- **Departmental division:** This is the way activities must be separated and integrated in specialized groups. The objective is to unify similar activities, simplify managers' tasks, and maintain oversight.
- **Decentralization:** This is a system of forcing low-level managers to make decisions. It is closely related to delegation of authority from high- to low-level managers. This decentralization is necessary when immediate decisions are essential to ensure the coordination of activities.
- **Chain of command:** The chain of command goes from the top to the bottom in organizational hierarchies. Employees and managers are aware of the person to whom they report and the people they must supervise. The chain of command has several rules:

  1. One person should report to one manager or one supervisor only.

(continued)

71

(continued)

2. Individuals at the top of the chart carry the most power and authority, while individuals at the bottom carry the least.

3. Individuals at the same horizontal level carry the same amount of power and responsibility and should only report to those above them but never to each other. (This communication ensures coordination).

4. Vertical lines stemming from a department or section usually indicate a staff position to support that department or individual.

When identifying and grouping activities, the organization should apply the following criteria:

- Group together activities that have similar requirements, common purposes, or uses (e.g., security and production).

- Assign functions to the manager most invested in their proper implementation.

- Consider grouping activities in ways that will stimulate competition or reduce friction between them.

- Group activities that cannot easily be attributed to one section or another into the same unit.

- Group together activities that require close coordination.

Power and Authority

Authority over people who assist an employee is granted within the job description for that position. But power also resides in the ability or capacity of people to take effective action, which gives them a position of control or dominion (competent secretaries have more power than poor ones). Delegated power duly balanced with authority gives supervisors and managers the right to make requests to subordinates and expect them to follow through. One term for this, when used appropriately, is *job position power*.

Other types of power, such as those in the following list, may become abusive within organizations:

- **Coercive power** causes fear and panic in others.

- **Reward power** is used to reward others for behaving or acting in a certain way.

72

- **Expert power** influences people by dispensing or withholding information from those who would benefit from such expertise.
- **Referent power** is the power of role models and heroes over people willing to emulate them.

Delegation of Responsibilities

Delegating responsibility necessarily hands over authority and power to someone else. It is therefore advisable to consider the advantages and disadvantages of such a step:

- **Advantages:** Delegation encourages decision making on the part of employees, which can lead to job satisfaction. It also helps create a productive working environment by increasing employee efforts and freeing managers of some tasks, allowing them to take on other responsibilities.
- **Disadvantages:** Delegation requires further training and oversight, which means more work for the manager. Oversight includes additional planning to ensure timely feedback from employees who are granted such delegation.

Organizational Charts

To make the organization suitable for the needs of a specific sport in a given country, national sport organizations or NFs must have adequately structured units so they can operate. They will need to be able to reach target groups they intend to integrate into the practice of their sport.

The organizational chart provides the description of the organization's internal working conditions. Different organizations will have different financial resources at their disposal. In addition, the external environment and social conditions will affect the kind of operational units that make sense in an organization as it develops from an informal structure to a highly complex and sophisticated one. For this reason, not every sport organization can operate the same units of the same chart.

Theoretical Model for an Emerging National Sport Organization

Governmental and private organizations, including the army, police and fire departments, factories, labor unions, sport clubs, and schools, are the potential targets of promotional activities to gain affiliates for a new sport organization. These activities, along with event promotion, instruction of coaches, judges, and referees, and technical coordination, are portrayed in the organizational chart in figure 2.4.

73

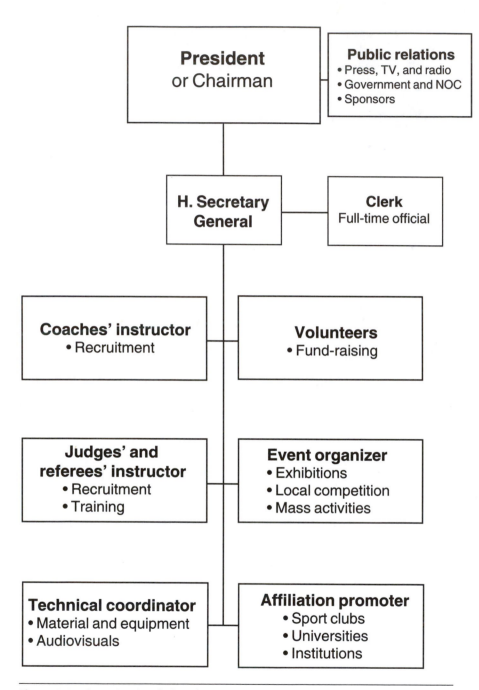

Figure 2.4 Organizational chart for emerging sport organizations.

Theoretical Model for a Fully Competitive Organization

Affiliated members of a developed sport organization include sport clubs, leagues, circuits, local sport associations, colleges, universities, and regional associations. Marketing, programming, membership, and general administration are possible operational units of such an organization as shown in the chart in figure 2.5.

CONCLUSION

Anyone wishing to create a club, association, organizing committee, or league must from the outset define its essential principles, set up a system for the flow of communication with and between its members, and outline its profile, prior to tackling the problem of its overall structure.

Once the profile has been defined, certain basic constitutional and operational questions must be addressed: Who exactly are the potential members? What are the objectives of the organization, its mission statement, priorities, decision-making ability, and operational bodies, as well as communication system? These are some of the essential elements to be established at the earliest stages of a newly created sport organization.

Preparatory meetings will enable you to draft responses to operational questions and definitively create the organization. The final meeting will serve to make known publicly the agreement of the constituent members, the organization's basic principles, and the decision to request legal registration and official recognition from the country's political and sport authorities. Organizers must keep in mind that no meeting can reach its objectives without adequate preparation by the president and secretary. This includes personal preparation, preparation of documents and the facility, and knowledge of how to conduct a meeting.

The organization in itself will not be an isolated island, but part of a community in which many other organizations also work. Based on its objectives, each organization establishes its own structure with a view to achieving an efficient and continuous flow of operations to pursue the goals in its mission statement.

A good organization requires a fit structure, a good operational system, competent managers, and motivated employees. Everything has to be moving toward quality objectives that can be achieved in the not-too-distant future. Everyone must be operating under policies aimed at maximizing efficiency, productivity, and employee performance. Clear job descriptions, adequate allocation of tasks in departments or units of reasonable size, definition of authority, delegation of power, and a good relationship between all units will substantially increase performance.

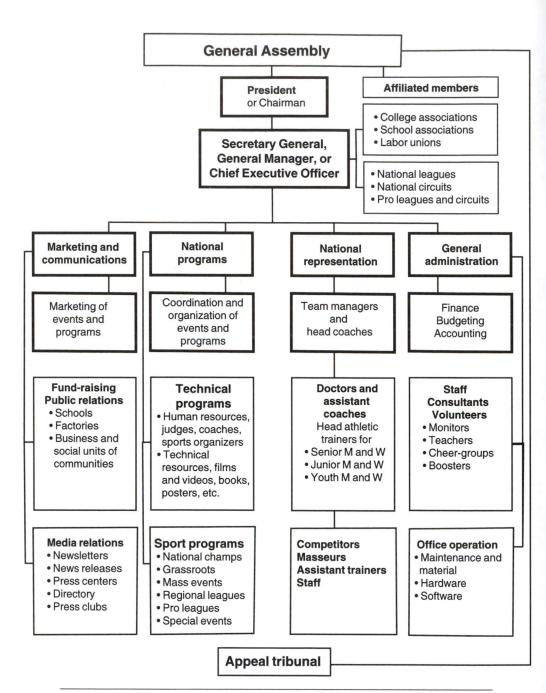

Figure 2.5 Organizational chart for competitive sport organizations.

When choosing the type of organization, remember that an organization subject to central planning enjoys the advantages offered by full governmental or corporate financing but is dependent on the government or corporation giving the sport high priority. In addition, the clubs and people involved in the sport have no say in the implementation of programs or events and so cannot engage in any international activity without prior governmental, or corporate, approval and support.

If the new organization is a NF, it should not reflect its country's political divisions but rather have a structure capable of serving the club teams and individual athletes, allowing them freely to express their will and be part of the decision-making process.

Concerning its general structure, every organization must have a clearly defined chain of command following the three classic levels: decision-making (or legislative), executive, and operational. These three should be separate from a jurisdictional body in charge of solving conflicts and keeping the organization in line with the decisions made by its constituency.

To operate its internal relations and external activities efficiently, every organization should pay attention to the basic organizational principles: unity of command, principle of exception, extent of control, numerical principle, departmental division, decentralization, and chain of command.

It will also be important to pay attention to the distinction between power and authority, both of which are required to maintain the chain of command. Authority over people is granted within the job description for that position. But power resides in the ability of people to influence others and involves delegated power to make decisions and take action. Job position power, duly balanced with authority, gives supervisors and managers the right to make requests of subordinates and expect obedience from them.

The Road to Success

Individuals or organizations that know where they are going will certainly trace the direction of their actions in order to keep them oriented toward the achievement of the chosen objective. The primary goal set in their mind is to reach success, but their major concern is to follow the right direction and not to miss the road leading to success.

The following chapters will provide you with guidance to help you use the keys to success properly and to lead the organization to improve its operational structure, dispose of an inefficient administration, and identify professional management, all of which will result in a highly productive executive performance.

In chapter 3 we will discover the meaning of executive performance, which together with the keys to success, make the primary tools of the organization. The keys to success to be studied are communication, public relations and media relations, public relations and sport marketing, public relations and promotional activities, and fund-raising.

three

THE POWER OF PERFORMANCE

Courtesy of Nuova Immagine.

> **Actions speak louder than words.**
>
> *Xenophon (428–354 B.C.)*

Sport organizations, just like athletes themselves, have different levels of executive performance that result from their own preparation, training, and commitment to success. Their respective levels of performance depend on the strength and power built into the administrative units that implement sport programs or events and, in the case of athletes, into the muscles and parts of the brain involved in the physical movements required by the sport activity.

The executive performance of sport organizations corresponds to the competitive performance of the athletes. For both of them, learning and understanding come from practice and experience. Learning and understanding are not two separate roads to knowledge; they complement each other and are both attainable only through constant practice and experience. "Try and fail, but try again" is the motto for learning and understanding the keys to organizational success.

The Keys to Success

> *The heights by great men reached and kept were not attained by sudden flight, but they, while their companions slept, were toiling upward in the night.*
>
> H.W. Longfellow, "The Ladder of Saint Augustine"

The most important key to success in any human activity is revealed by the American poet H.W. Longfellow in the previous quotation. Thus, successful sport administration requires the national sport organizations to be willing to work hard day and night, carrying out their duties and striving independently toward their fulfillment.

In addition, leaders and managers with organizational and managerial skills need to demonstrate professional know-how and be adequately prepared for the task. This means they should clearly understand their mission and have sufficient knowledge of the highly specialized theories and principles involved in basic areas, such as communication; working with the media; PR, promotion, and fund-raising; and sport marketing. The next chapter will deal with each of these areas in greater detail; this section will simply provide a few short definitions.

Communication

The term *communication,* for modern enterprises and sport organizations, includes the two essential meanings of organizational and external communication. These are the two pillars necessary to the success of any enterprise or sport organization because they improve the level of understanding inside the organization and between the organization and its external environment. In its traditional meaning, communication is the oral, written, or visual transmission of ideas in the form of messages through any possible means in a two-way process between a *sender* and a *recipient*.

Oral Communication

This is the most frequently used means of communication in conferences, meetings, and congresses involving speech from the sender to the recipient. Oral communication is the perfect vehicle to convey an idea to another person and the best method to negotiate contracts, conclude agreements, or win people over to a cause. It is very effective when dealing on a person-to-person basis, but very limited in its broad reach. It is not recommended for large audiences even if those attending the meeting, congress, or conference are doing so for the same purpose. In such settings, the attention span of individuals is often limited.

Written Communication

This covers a variety of means of communication and has long-lasting effects. The number of recipients is unlimited, and they are immediately attentive to the content of the message. Newspapers, magazines, and newsletters are very effective means of written communication when their form and content follow principles suggested by experts. Written or audiovisual communication is preferable when the targeted audience cannot be assembled.

Audio-Visual Communication

This means of communication has mushroomed with the rise of television, over-the-air, cable, and satellite networks. It is a very sophisticated and costly means of communication, the value and impact of which exceed those of any other means. Television and movies are great communicators because they are exciting and interesting. They have a direct impact on the minds of passive recipients and have great psychological impact. They represent the supreme means of publicity in today's world, with the widest instantaneous reach.

Electronic Communication

This is the latest means of communication and could one day become its most sophisticated form. Special hardware and software are required by the user—whether a person or organization—to take advantage of this modern form of communication. Electronic mail (e-mail) takes place on

Using television or movies to communicate can make the sender's message more exciting and interesting to the recipient.

the *Internet* when it occurs between separate organizations and *Intranet* when it occurs inside the same organization.

Working With the Media

Dealing with the media is only effective through PR activities aimed at creating a good impression among journalists, TV and radio commentators, and other media representatives. This requires that you have a good understanding of media needs and that PR activities take into account the following tips.

Different Types of Media

In today's society, the media is more powerful than any other means of communication when it comes to sending messages to the general public. Together with the visual and audio impact of television and radio, the written press is one of the three most powerful communications media with respect to its impact on the masses. NFs should be in close contact and develop personal relationships with reporters and editors and, whenever possible, the directors of television networks and radio stations.

The written press has the advantage of a lasting influence on mass opinion because the message remains once it has been printed. Newspapers and magazines are important vehicles of expression. Both are published daily or periodically and both usually print news or comments of general interest to the public at large.

All three means sell publicity. It is therefore in the best interest of NFs to motivate their sport's sponsors and promoters to buy space or time in order to advertise their products together with the event or activity they are sponsoring. Focus particularly on those television networks, radio stations, and newspapers that frequently broadcast or publish feature stories or news reports about such sport events or activities.

If the written press happens not to be publishing information on a given sport, every member of that NF should send in letters to the editors of a given publication claiming their right and need to be informed regarding the national and international events of the sport. Fans of that sport should impress on the editors that they represent a large portion of the press market and can have a significant impact on circulation figures. If they succeed in doing so, it will not be long before the publication starts covering that particular sport.

Making Media Relations a Priority

You must foster close relationships with the media. Eliminate anything that gets in the way, because developing and nurturing a truly professional relationship with the media needs to be a NF's top priority.

Sport managers must develop the knowledge and skills required to establish such a relationship and work with the media. First they must identify the NF's responsibilities toward the media and keep in mind the behavior and attitudes presented in "Facing the Media," on pages 86-87. Managers should not neglect any of the three powerful means of mass communication represented by television, press, and radio. Instead, they should make it a point to understand the media's duty toward the public, which is to report news on subjects of interest to the general public in an unbiased fashion. (Naturally, the media cannot guarantee extensive coverage of a given sport, whatever it may be.)

What Is News?

News happens when people do something significant or accomplish something of value. The size of the community has a considerable effect on the extent of the news coverage of particular events. In addition, small

organizations have to compete with major sport organizations and professional sport for space in the press and electronic media.

As detestable as it may seem, the media seems to find negative news to
be more newsworthy than other items. The public wants to read negative
news and for this reason buys newspapers where editors offer it to them,
keeping a number of journalists busy. Some people think that even negative public exposure is still exposure, but sport organizations need to maintain high profiles and good images if they want to be seen as reliable
and trustworthy. Negative reports should not be circulated through the
organization's channels.

Facing the Media

Sport managers should learn how to face the media, paying special attention to their behavior and attitude toward the press. Pay attention to the
following desirable and undesirable behaviors.

Desirable Behaviors in Dealing With the Press

Be cooperative and accessible by telephone.

Always make time for the press, even if you have a busy schedule.

Become personally acquainted with journalists.

Call and visit media representatives to find out what they need and when
they need it.

Treat journalists properly, honestly, and fairly.

Answer every question to the best of your ability.

Mention both the negative and positive aspects; do not only report good news.

Reporters need "hot news"; get the story out as quickly as possible.

Supply appropriate pictures, correct information, and current items for
stories; the media wants news rather than publicity or history.

Keep responses brief and to the point to avoid being misquoted.

With student reporters, tape interviews openly to encourage accuracy.

Deny false rumors as soon as they become known; share information.

Always keep in mind what might make good feature material.

Get to know the media deadlines; know when to send a press release.

Find out the lighter days for the media and take advantage to send releases on those days.

Say "thank you" for a good story on your sport or your organization.

Use ceremonies and special events to recognize media staff and to make
their acquaintance.

Provide free tickets and invite media representatives to all events.

Behaviors to Avoid With the Press

Careless and indiscreet statements

Favors or bribery with gifts and promises beyond accepted practice, as well as favoritism; don't give "scoops"

Taking it personally when nothing, or negative stories, are published

Aggressiveness and anger

Trouble-seeking or controversial actions

Making off-the-record statements

Begging or demanding someone to run a story

Threatening the press with a withdrawal of support

Asking that a story be withdrawn, except in the direst circumstances; you may ask that they run corrections

Using publicity tricks that mislead the press

Promoting unimportant items

Blocking news by evasion, censorship, pressure, or trickery

Enhancing Your Image With the Press

Admit mistakes rather than cover them up.

When controversial issues appear, provide written releases to the media.

Tell the truth, the whole truth, and nothing but the truth to maintain credibility.

Keep the public and media well informed about events in your sport programs.

Communicate precise information to the media representatives.

Consider strengthening press relations through trade-out of sport event exposure and publicity whenever it is permitted.

Seek personal involvement in the sport by asking reporters and radio or television commentators to reward players, make first-serve balls, become masters of ceremony, draw lots, speak at banquets, become members of an assessment committee, and so on.

A Case of Press Involvement in Sport Activities

Sport leaders in an ex-socialist country were trying to introduce baseball in a city where the sport had never been organized as a competitive sport.

(continued)

(continued)

Toward that end, a series of presentations of famous baseball stars, and even exhibitions, were organized with relatively good public attendance the opening day. The next day, no major press reports were published in spite of the presence of several journalists. That evening, only a few spectators showed up, and the people concerned were on the field looking at empty stands.

One week later, a new presentation was made, but this time the players were introduced to the journalists and autographed photos were presented. Several journalists were invited to catch and throw the ball from the infield to the catcher at home plate and vice versa. The next day, the newspapers were covered with information. More journalists attended the evening session of that second day, and the stands were crowded again.

Marketing

Fund-raising, PR, and *promotion* are not identical. Each one of these can make a difference in the quality of programming of a NF. The following section will explain each of these terms. The next section will focus particularly on several different aspects of *sport marketing.*

Marketing Terms

Fund-raising is to solicit donations from individuals, businesses, or organizations. This requires a specific plan with a defined strategy for reaching a reasonable goal. You must support fund-raising with promotional activities. Fund-raising can help the NF promote specific programs, such as the national team (junior, youth, or senior), athletes' training, participation in international competitions, or courses for coaches or officials.

Promotion creates public awareness or makes people clearly understand the importance of the sport program or sport event in order to motivate and obtain their participation and financial support.

Public relations (PR) is one of the most important activities. Its purpose is to influence, modify, or improve the attitude and behavior of the public, spectators, media, sponsors, sport leaders, governmental authorities, and others toward the sport, the sport organization, its leaders, members, and constituency. It also involves adequate communication, which helps to enhance the image of a given sport, sport program, organization, event, or the people involved with it. The aim is to create an honest, valuable, and credible image of the sport, sport organization, sport program or event, and the people involved, thus making all of them worthy of public sympathy and support.

Through PR activities, the NF projects positive attitudes and a "top quality" image with which the general public can easily identify. One such image would be of an honest, considerate organization, committed to working positively for the benefit and well-being of the community and particularly concerned with the physical, mental, and moral development of youth. Such an image must be compatible with the underlying values of the country in general and the community in particular.

Sport Marketing

Sport marketing is the technique used for selling or distributing sport services (use of the organization's image, logo, or space) or sport products (sport events, billboards, or titles) for cash or value-in-kind. During the 1998 Volleyball World Championships in Japan, the rights holder asked for permission to manufacture playing uniforms with the color of the countries and the name of the player. They were quickly sold out. Other gadgets like baseball caps, T-shirts, mascots with logos, key holders, and dolls were also very much appreciated by the public.

An in-depth knowledge of sport marketing is indispensable for sport leaders to enable them to understand better the needs of the specialized professionals handling the marketing of their events and also to learn how to keep control of their own sport. In the following section you will find descriptions of three different approaches in sport marketing that are based on similar principles but have different objectives.

Corporate Sponsorship Corporate sponsorship is an approach to sport marketing from a corporate standpoint. This approach involves the use of athletes, sport events, or programs in the marketing activities and publicity of a company. This approach is made from the company standpoint. For example, after 1988, the International Olympic Committee created a TOP PROGRAMME for Olympic corporate sponsorship. Only a few companies were given the opportunity, and it seems they satisfied their objectives and enhanced their image. They were allowed to call themselves Olympic sponsors, use the Olympic rings, and were given exposure in films, videos, and IOC publications.

Product Endorsement This occurs when the use of a product is recommended by athletes, teams, event organizers, and the sport organization (such as the National Basketball Association, National Football League, Fédération Internationale de Football Association, and International Volleyball Federation). Businesses find the public awareness of those sport images connected to their products beneficial to the promotion of the products. For example, Nike exchanged an eight-digit check for the Brazilian men's World Cup soccer team and all pro teams to wear the Nike logo on clothing and shoes for four years.

Event Marketing These are activities undertaken by the event organizers, marketing agencies, or sport organizations with the purpose of meeting specific groups of corporations in order to obtain cash or value-in-kind in exchange for joining the image of a sport event to the image of products or services. The aim is to expose both to the public through static publicity, cross-marketing, promotional activities, and product sampling carried out during the event.

A new activity in sport marketing, event marketing has led to the need for national sport organizations to modify their concepts, structures, strategies, and even their approach in the operation and administration of their sport.

Communicating Effectively

An organization is a collection of inert resources brought alive by communication.

Dave Francis, Unblocking Organizational Communication

Communication is any form of human expression—oral, written, or "body language." It is a process that starts with a need to communicate, continues with the formulation of a message, and ends its first stage with its transmission.

In the second stage, the recipient synthesizes the message while the sender seeks feedback that confirms understanding. This can include following the directions given, acknowledging the content, asking for additional information, or rejecting the content. Sport organizations need to pay close attention to the system of communication they adopt. They need to establish a flow of coherent information in two directions: internally, inside the organization and externally, toward their outside environment. Internally, all sport organizations need to closely monitor the communication between the different sections, departments and administrative units, employees, athletes, clubs, and affiliated organizations that form part of their structure. The external recipients include television, radio, and the press; other sport organizations; governmental agencies involved in sport activities or responsible for governmental funds; private organizations funding sport activities and companies interested in sponsoring sport events; and, finally, the general public through mass communication and publicity.

Organizational Communication

Today's concepts of communication provide managers with tools for achieving organizational objectives through a good communication system. Organizational communication keeps the members informed, motivated, and confident. As Dave Francis rightly puts it in his book entitled *Unblocking Organizational Communication,* good communication

- **shares the compelling vision** (mission) of the organization with its members;
- **integrates the efforts** of the members toward achieving common goals, with everybody working in the same direction;
- **sustains a healthy community** in which each member is valuable and each manager is trustworthy; and
- **makes intelligent decisions** allowing the organization to react wisely and efficiently to threats and opportunities.

All these values are inherent to effective communication, and each one of them helps to prompt the organization's management and employees to coordinate their efforts in search of success. When correctly applied by a sport organization, such communication will achieve maximum results in its operations. Such values can be visualized in figure 3.1.

After sections dealing with each of these four concepts, this part of the chapter that deals with an organization's internal communication will conclude with sections on specific aspects of communication: channels, elements and barriers of messages, communication styles, and dangers and solutions.

Sharing the Vision

Sharing the vision, or *mission statement,* of the sport organization means that all members, employees, and officials of the organization identify themselves with its goals, plans, identity, and intended image. This happens when the individuals emotionally identify with the organization, and their attitudes reflect the following:

- **Sensitivity** to detect any possible opportunity or threat from the external environment, which could be facilitated by a free flow of information
- **Concentration** on the plans to make them happen and keeping focus on them via follow-up reports
- **Willingness** to share part of the responsibility for the success of the organization by showing each person his or her own concern and readiness to take action

Integrating Efforts

This happens when all members and employees work together to pursue the organization's long-term goals. Such integration will be effective when the following factors are present:

Figure 3.1 Diagram of organizational communication.
Adapted, by permission, from D. Francis, 1987, What is communication? In *Unblocking organizational communication* (United Kingdom: Gower House Publishing), 3-20.

- **Coordination** to integrate harmoniously the activities of everyone

- **Convenient geographic location** of the organization's personnel and departments, allowing direct contact among those concerned

- **Direction and control** to facilitate the so-called downward flow of information. This will be effective only when you give people clear job assignments, allow some freedom of action within the stated objectives, and make sure that everyone knows your behavioral expectations.

Sustaining a United, Healthy Community

You can sustain a united, healthy community by nurturing the following communication characteristics in your organization:

- **Trustworthy managers.** This requires honest, consistent, and realistic feedback; integrity; follow-through on decisions; fairness; and a respectful attitude.

- **Mutual respect.** Make sure no one in the organization is put to a disadvantage or belittled for any reason, whether he or she is alone or in the presence of others.

- **Supportive teamwork.** People need to feel safe sharing ideas with each other and working together on projects.

Making Intelligent Decisions

An organization needs to make decisions all the time, but particularly in the event of threats or to take advantage of opportunities. Top managers can make good decisions when they have access to information from all levels. This involves the following:

- **Channeling information** through the management levels by direct contact with the staff, practitioners, and all involved in the sport through surveys

- **Facilitating communication** through an efficient system that avoids "red tape"

- **Nurturing managerial skills** to express proper and clear messages and use methodical approaches to deal with difficult situations, make decisions, and solve problems

Channels of Communication

The channels of communication follow the hierarchy of the staff members and include those listed here:

- **Vertical channels** follow the chain of command and start at the top level with parallel communication to subordinates.

- **Horizontal communication** is the message discussed among peers (managers or employees at the same level).

- **Diagonal channels** are for communication from management to specific departments concerned with a given plan.

- **Contact with the base** is informal contact by managers with the members of the organization, players, referees, coaches, and local members in a family-type atmosphere.

Communication Elements and Barriers

Elements of the message and barriers can affect how a message communicates. The basic *elements of a message* are accurate content, clarity, credibility, appropriate context, continuous flow of ideas, consistency of thoughts and words, and the use of adequate channels.

There are many possible *barriers to communication* between the sender and recipient of a message, and they are often disregarded. The most common barriers are sexual, political, and racial differences; prejudices and biases; enmity; social, religious, and age differences; superstitions; circumstances; multiple meanings of words; words taken out of context; poor timing; poor choice of communication means; lack of clarity; distance; and pride (see figure 3.2).

Communication Styles

Communication styles can fall into one of the following types:

Open communication is the most recommended type. It is similar to an open forum of communication. There are no secrets. Ideas, problems, and solutions are openly and freely discussed.

Unknown is a style that creates problems. The recipient of the message is not properly identified.

Diverted communication is shallow or on the surface. There is no reception and no feedback.

Devious communication is when some people know and others don't. The communication is a best-kept secret scenario. The manager may be the one who is not informed.

Communication Dangers and Solutions

Communication dangers include the following:

• **Ignoring the feedback loop.** Recipients should confirm that messages were properly received and understood and not ignore feedback.

• **Generalizing or stereotyping the audience.** Do not generalize about others. Speak to individual situations.

• **Falsifying information.** Avoid false messages or small print hiding the real message.

The following skills can help in avoiding communication dangers:

• **Understanding audience capability.** Environmental and personal experiences cause differences in individual perceptions. Attempt to anticipate your audience's reactions and their level of comprehension as you prepare a message.

• **Sharing and listening.** Communication calls for the mutual sharing of information. Within the organization, everyone should have equal access to information. Listening to people helps to improve communication and mutual understanding.

- **Managing change well.** The only certainty with respect to the future is change; nothing will be the same in terms of people, economy, markets, press, technology, and so on. Anticipating, preparing for, and dealing with change are a manager's job. This involves a flexible strategy. People frequently resist change and cling to the "status quo." Communication is the best way to anticipate conflicts in changing situations.

External Communication

In addition to communication within an organization, there is the task of communicating with those on the outside. This takes place through mass communication, publicity, and press conferences.

Mass Communication

This type of communication is essential to the promotion of sport and the key to a successful sport program. *Mass communication* involves conveying messages with the purpose of informing or educating individuals, creating impressions, reinforcing or exchanging opinions held by others, influencing behavior, reinforcing habits, exchanging fashions or trends, developing allegiances, or establishing attitudes.

Mass communication implies the use of publicity and the media. Both are ideal tools to communicate messages or influence behavior but require careful planning. There are different methods to use in getting your message out. Keep in mind the following factors as you plan your communication.

Live presentations offer immediacy and can encourage group feelings while television films can be carefully prepared and used in various settings. Newspapers are a permanent record whose regularity opens a channel for constant communication. Local radio stations, which are more in the background, can also carry persuasive messages. Poster campaigns get across simple but powerful messages, as do billboards on a larger scale. Books, brochures, and manuals allow complex information to be permanently available not only for the media but for participants as well.

Certain other tools generate publicity, promote PR, and even raise funds. These can also serve as a communications link with important groups since they carry a message for the particular target group. Organizational manuals and handbooks carry useful information that is more permanent, whereas newsletters and printed bulletins report up-to-date facts. Other communication aids include public meetings with a public address system, logos and mascots, window displays in public outlets, and bulletin boards and billboards to announce forthcoming sport events.

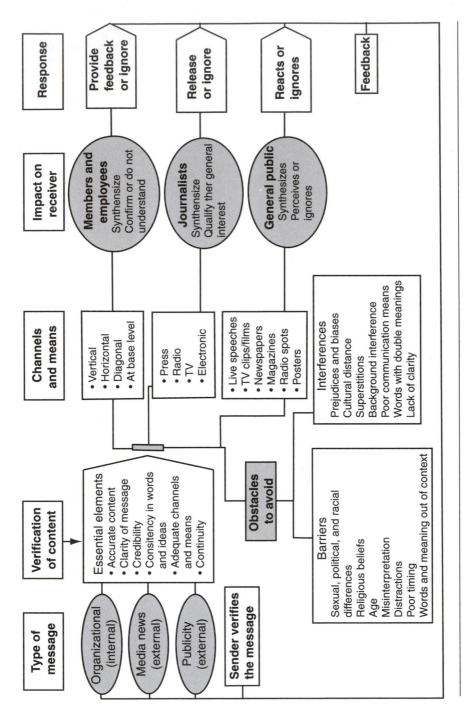

Figure 3.2 Flow of communication.

96

Publicity

Publicity is carefully planned and systematically distributed information with the aim of influencing others. The objective of publicity is to make the information frequently available in a variety of media so that the sport program remains in the public eye, unlike the news, which only remains in the public eye for a limited time.

Publicity can help to raise awareness; win the influence of supporters, individuals, and groups; and promote events. The publicity made by a NF in regard to its sport must be based on fact and reach the public through various types of media.

The print media include daily or weekly newspapers, journals, organizational and sport publications, and trade and business magazines. The daily, weekly, and biweekly publications of small cities give more weight to neighborhood happenings or events; use these vehicles for local competitions in preference to others. Daily papers in large cities may provide wider sport coverage of national leagues and professional or sponsored international events.

Columnists and feature writers give good publicity; international and national press agencies and wire services do as well. Use wire services for major, mainly professional, sport events. They pay attention primarily to professional sport athletes and teams and provide nationwide coverage.

Other types of print publicity include newsletters, direct mail, bulletins, press releases, posters, leaflets or displays, fliers, graphic and pictorial material, annual reports, banners, and stickers. Whatever the publication, it needs to be planned well in advance, created with imagination by professionals, and always evaluated in light of its results.

Printed Materials

Top quality design and printing must be fundamental to any advertisement, publication, or printed brochure. During the planning stage, carefully consider the following important points:

- **Paper size (A4/A5)**
- **Total cost** and cost per copy
- **Structure** (common cover, changeable paper inside, or fully printed brochure)
- **Printing schedules and frequency** of publication
- **Number of copies** to be printed
- **Creative artwork** (layout and design)

(continued)

(continued)

• **Rate per page of advertisement,** preferably color (at least the two sides of the back cover of a brochure to have publicity)

• **Advertising sales force**, who will be selling, and what strategy they should use (phone, door-to-door, person-to-person, business contacts)

• **Sale**, pricing and marketing, selling or giving away, determination of sales force, promotions to increase sales, and determination of additional benefits through advertisers (such as gadgets or tickets)

Audio-visual media encompass television stations (regular and cable), television advertisements, video clips and videotapes, and films and film clips. Television needs brief, dramatic, and visually and acoustically appealing stories.

Finally, the radio is an audio medium, as are public address announcements at events and meetings and organized word-of-mouth campaigns.

Press Conferences

Press conferences represent the most important contact with the media and for this reason should be very carefully planned. An appealing invitation will help motivate media representatives to attend (although a disaster is always possible, for example when only one or two journalists turn up). In all cases, circulate reminders and make telephone calls to the invited journalists the day before in an attempt to put the situation in the best possible light.

NF directors should not call a press conference unless there is no other way of disseminating the information with the same explosive impact. Be sure not to schedule it in conflict with other newsworthy events.

Before a press conference, a NF director should

- have newsworthy information;
- choose the best date, time, and site for the media representatives;
- provide adequate advance notice of the conference;
- secure necessary facilities (phones, electrical outlets, and lighting);
- prepare enough fact sheets plus photos (press clippings);
- personally confirm attendance by phone the previous day;
- begin on time;
- arrange for someone to introduce the speaker, who should talk briefly and mention by name others of importance who are present; and
- provide time and opportunity for questions and answers.

Press conference: The press is a permanent link between sport and its fans.
Courtesy of Nuova Immagine.

CONCLUSION

Communication is the oral, written, or visual transmission of ideas. A sport organization must maximize its use of organizational communication as well as communication to the public. Both are necessary for success, as the former improves the level of understanding inside an organization and the latter improves relationships with the external environment.

In its traditional meaning, communication conveys messages through any possible means in a two-way process that links a sender and a recipient, either directly or indirectly. Any type of communication, whether written, oral, or mimed, will only be able to fulfill its purpose when it contains the basic elements of a message. The wording must be accurate, clear, credible, and fit into the intended context; its ideas must flow easily with consistency from one to the other and be transmitted through the adequate channels.

Modern concepts of communication provide managers with tools to achieve organizational objectives through a good communication system. Organizational communication at its best enables the manager to keep the members informed, motivated, and confident in the organization. This calls for mutual sharing of information and mutual understanding, for which listening to people is essential. In addition, everyone must have equal access to information. The benefits include a shared vision; integrated efforts; a united, healthy community; and better decision making.

It is a manager's duty to anticipate, prepare for, and deal with change. Communication is the best way to anticipate conflicts in changing situations. Managers must have a flexible strategy, since people usually tend to gravitate toward the "status quo" and are resistant to change.

While organizational communication is within the institution, external communication is directed to those outside and includes publicity and mass communication. With careful planning, it distributes information with a lasting presence and influences others, helping to raise awareness; win the influence of new supporters, individuals, and groups; and promote events. To do this, you must frequently make the information available to the public in a variety of media.

News, in general, has a limited time span. Carefully plan press conferences since they represent the most important contact with the media to release your news. Before scheduling press conferences, make sure there is no other way to disseminate the information that will be as effective, and always avoid scheduling it in conflict with other similar events.

four

SELLING SPORT TO THE COMMUNITY

> **So much of selling a product, a service, or activity is selling yourself, putting your own ego on the line.**
>
> *Mark H. McCormack,*
> **What They Don't Teach You at Harvard Business School**

Sport marketing should not be mistaken for sport commercialization, given their totally different meanings. Commercialization is managing or exploiting sport for profit; sport marketing is buying or selling the image of an event to finance the event and other sport activities, while promoting the image of a product.

Although NFs are nonprofit organizations, they should be organized in a businesslike manner. They should be cost-efficient, highly productive, and socially viable and furthermore maintain an optimal relationship with the media. PR are essential to positively influence the perception that all members of the community (including the media) have of any given sport, its organization, activities, and objectives.

Relating With the Media

When an organization enjoys an optimal professional relationship with members of the media, it can be said that the organization has already achieved half its objectives.

Rubén Acosta Hernández, Report to the FIVB Congress

Major sport organizations that have national competitions, grassroots programs, and national team training programs and host international friendly matches or multilateral competitions will only gain credibility as professional organizations if they hire a full-time media officer to be in charge of PR.

Previous chapters have provided a thorough study of the world of sport organizations, sport identity and image, and the social setting of sport today. They also demonstrated how to establish a suitable organizational structure in sport activities and described the most common types of organization. Chapter 3 showed that the power of a sport organization's performance lies in specific keys to success, namely communication, working with the media, and marketing. This chapter will describe and explain the importance of having excellent relations with the media.

Keeping Excellent Media Relations

The managers of an organization must understand the mission of the various media. Nurturing a professional relationship with each organ of the media and, if possible, with each of the media types—press, television, and radio—is your most important duty as a sport manager. You must develop skills and a special sense to deal appropriately not only with journalists and television or radio commentators, but editors and directors as well.

The mission of the media is to communicate to the public. There is no way or method of obtaining full coverage of all sport events in the press or electronic media. However, their needs can be satisfied through the reporting of news that the public finds interesting and informative. Olympic Games and Football World Cup media success is precisely due to the public interest they arouse worldwide. Such success would never have been possible without full press coverage, not only during the events but also in every activity leading to the final stage; by portraying top athletes and describing their real or fictitious rivalries; and most of all motivating public imagination, while satisfying the need for information.

When Negative News Is Good Press

Volleyball had never received such extraordinary media coverage as it did in Barcelona (1992 Olympic Games) when the Control Committee decided to reverse the results of the Japan-USA match. Television, radio, and the press waited all night and several hours into the morning to be informed of the Control Committee's decision by the FIVB.

There was absolutely no doubt in the minds of Control Committee members that the referee had made a mistake against Japan when, at 14-13 with Japan leading in the fourth set, and two sets to one against the USA, he gave Samuelson of the USA team a second personal warning for another misconduct during that set. The rules state that a point must be granted to the opponent. However, the referee forgot to cancel the warning and ignored the call of the scorer that the point was the end of the match. Instead, he chose to let the match continue and the USA recovered the advantage, won the set, and later also won the tiebreaker and ultimately the match.

After a thorough 12-hour analysis of the situation, with repeated interventions of every jury member, the referees and scorers, the USOC president Dr. Leroy Walker, and USA volleyball representatives, the FIVB jury decided to revert the outcome and give the match 3-1 to Japan. The FIVB was accused of favoring Japan, and its influential members were criticized for making a biased decision. This episode made the headlines of newspapers and television news reports, thus drawing public interest to volleyball.

(continued)

(continued)

Subsequently, the American players shaved their heads and won all the following matches until they eventually lost to Brazil in a semifinal cliffhanger, and then went on to win the bronze medal against Cuba. Even if the American team had won against the Brazilians, volleyball would not have obtained as much media attention in the United States as it did thanks to the Samuelson case.

This is an illustration of the fact that negative news can sell better than positive news. Volleyball obtained worldwide coverage because it was the first time an IF had repealed the decision of a referee at the Olympic Games. The United States press did its job; the FIVB never questioned whether the reactions were normal, unfair, or even biased, but the press did a good job for volleyball.

Competitive sport cannot survive and will not develop without the media. For this reason, relationships with the press, radio, and television news departments should be

- **effective**, producing desired results;
- **continuous**, to keep information available nonstop in case there is space;
- **personal**, so the media representative knows who it is that is providing the information; and
- **open**, reporting only top quality, truthful information based on fact.

Send information to media representatives in a timely manner with pertinent facts arranged, if possible, in such a way that they can be used as is. Avoid giving out verbal information unless there are written statements to be distributed later. Always check and double check the accuracy of information, using terms that carry only one meaning in order to avoid misinterpretation. Once a competition has started, NFs should inform media representatives of the developments, situations, and results in a timely manner.

Different Types of Media

Each type of media has specific needs, objectives, and peculiarities. Therefore, it is important to offer and report only what is within each one's area.

Print

Print publications offer information that is long lasting, can be kept and reread at a later stage, relates facts, and comments on competitions in full detail. It can report a great amount of names, plans, comparisons, and statistics.

Radio

Radio offers emotional narrative, in either live or delayed form, with short but repeated news. Do not neglect radio and television sport news or even general news programs. These are broadcast at peak audience hours, and while only a few seconds of comments of an event may be broadcast, thousands of people will hear about it and it will generate public interest. Radio may have more time available for stories if they involve local teams and well-known personalities. Keep this in mind if you manage a local organization.

NFs should try to offer space beside the competition area for radio station logos in exchange for periodic short spots announcing the event. They can also grant exclusive radio broadcasting rights to a major radio station, if deemed appropriate.

Television

Television has the greatest impact of all media because of the powerful action of pictures. It is also informative through the sport news it broadcasts, which may contain excerpts of competitions reported, either in live or delayed form. Television can help popularize a sport. Its visual effects, using slow motion, replays, visual background, and visual aids, can also generate discussion on situations that arise in live competition.

Television requires short comments or short stories of the event, visually dramatic and appealing slides, and video clips. Television news stations can be invited to send cameramen to report on press conferences or events. A good relationship may help to convince them to send a crew.

Television will be interested in events with organizational quality, beautiful images, large crowds, extensive press coverage, and corporate sponsorship able to pay for broadcasting or commercial time.

The television rights value of an event will depend primarily on sponsorship availability, extension of the coverage (local, regional, national, or worldwide), public awareness of the event, and competitiveness of local athletes. In many countries national sport organizations trade television coverage (signal production) for national broadcasting rights without any charge.

Major sport events rate high in the eyes of most television networks. In the United States, the NBA, NFL, and MLB rate very high. Worldwide, the Olympic Games, Soccer World Cup, Formula One, athletics, and volleyball obtain their highest income from the sale of television rights.

This television cameraman captures the drama during a break in the action. Television is a perfect medium for sports because of the power of moving pictures.
Courtesy of Nuova Immagine.

Photography

Photography is also an effective means of communication. The written press should have access to photos taken by professional photographers who can utilize the photogenic values of sport actions in a very effective manner. Photography is a complement to written information. As a consequence organizers should, wherever possible, make photos available for use by the written press, either on the Internet or by distributing copies.

Running Media Operations

Media administration does not only mean providing services or polite attention to the members of the press, television, and radio. It also involves arranging for adequate facilities and working conditions for the media and preparing and distributing accurate and timely information. Major sport organizations running national competitions, grassroots programs, and national team training programs and hosting international events will only gain credibility as a professional organization by maintaining a constant dialogue with as many personal contacts in the media as possible through a full-time media officer.

The Role of a Press or Communications Officer

This person's duties will be to take personal care of the journalists and other reporters attending events, coordinate the organization of press conferences, follow up the press accreditation process, and supervise the press information flow before the event and the smooth running of the media center during the event.

Every international and national sport organization should have an officer responsible for contacts and personal relations with the media. Small sport organizations should try to obtain the voluntary involvement of a press writer or television or radio commentator who may be willing to help develop their sport. Or, they could ask an amateur of the sport to take on this assignment as a volunteer. Not only major sport organizations, clubs, and leagues but also major stars of the sport should have PR managers or communications officers to handle their image, information, match preparation and results, meetings, and special events.

Give all media contacts the name, address, and telephone number of the officer whom they may contact for data, statistics, or details regarding competitions, clubs, and outstanding competitors. This person will facilitate the work of the press and other media and, above all, will keep the flame of the sport alight in the public eye.

The press or communications officer should organize, implement, and monitor every project concerning journalists, photographers, news agencies, and in general all activities relating to the media. This includes providing action photos of the competitions and awards for the best press organization of a competition and the most outstanding international or national coverage of the sport.

This officer should accomplish the following duties in a professional manner:

• **Create a media guide**, as well as coordinate the design, planning, and implementation of the press arrangements for major championships and important competitions. This includes the preparation of question-naires and forms as indicated in the media guide, the constant supply of team and athlete information and competition results, and the drawing of lots.

- **Oversee press registration** to accredit the journalists planning to attend important events.

- **Supervise press services** for all important events, including the planning and implementation services (equipment and work material, and information to distribute), rooms for press conferences, working areas (telecommunications room and press stands), and rest facilities.

- **Prepare press clips** for all participants at the press conferences of the president of the organization, club, circuit, or league, including infor-mation sheets on controversial matters, souvenirs, a directory of partici-pants on the occasion of national competitions, reports and feature stories on sport competitions and the athletes involved, and other newsworthy items for the press, such as newsletters.

- **Create a communication plan**, establishing a detailed press master plan and operational monthly programs in order to ensure and expand the presence of the sport before the media. Keep updated media lists.

- **Organize a computerized filing system** for photographic archives, books, and publications.

- **Oversee the different projects** of the main operations plan for each national competition and the follow-up of each project.

- **Coordinate and collaborate closely with each department** of the organization, especially the technical, competition, and marketing depart-ments. Keep close contact with the organizers of circuit events in individual sports and with national league events in team sports.

- **Report activities and programs** of the different events held by na-tional leagues and local associations, keeping the media informed on ev-ery issue within its sphere.

- **Improve media relations** and establish contacts with leading news-papers and news agencies, international news agencies, and the heads of sport sections of major television channels to find ways of getting informa-tion on the sport reported. Contact media representatives at NOC meet-ings, press meetings, national competitions, and other events.

Contact Persons

The press or communication department of the sport organization needs to draw up a clear and accurate list of names and addresses of persons to contact in the various media organizations. It is advisable to prepare for each person an individual ID card with personal and family data, even hobbies. Contact people are listed by media type:

- **Written press/sport newspapers:** the sport writers and chief sport editors. The NF president should also become acquainted with the general manager or director of the newspaper.

- **Sport magazines:** the heads of the editorial staff or staff of the specific sport.

- **Other magazines and general newspapers:** the sport writers and chief sport editors. The NF president should become acquainted with the general manager or director of the newspaper.

- **Radio:** sport commentators, programming directors, and acquisition managers, the latter to be contacted by the NF president.

- **Television:** sport commentators, news commentators, news editors, programming directors, and acquisition managers, the latter to be contacted by the NF president.

- **News agencies:** on the occasion of national and international events, periodically brief the national news agency and foreign correspondents of international news agencies on the preparation of the event and especially invite them to attend. The NF president should become acquainted with the persons heading the national news agency and the local branch of each international news agency.

Operational Strategy

The organization's media officer should prepare and follow a communication master plan and a calendar of activities that includes the following:

- **Keep updated lists** with addresses, telephone numbers, e-mails, and faxes of all the international and national news agencies in the city of the NF's headquarters and the main media organizations of major cities in the country.

- **Send news releases** or newsletters to them on a regular basis concerning events of the sport, activities of the organization, national teams and athletes, and major clubs.

- **Keep at hand the names, addresses, and, if possible, hobbies of every press contact** so that news releases can be addressed to them. Add the following remark: "In case of absence, please hand to the person in charge of the specific sport or sport in general."

- **Inform sport editors and media contacts** in general of the names, addresses, telephone numbers, e-mails, faxes, and the different places where the NF's media officer may be contacted, or the media officer responsible for the event, the club, or the activity.

Preparing and Releasing Information

Every sport organization normally has communication staff to prepare statistics, reports, decisions, and other information of interest for all levels of the internal organization, the constituency, and the outside world. This information must be clearly worded to avoid misunderstandings, short and easy to read, marked with the date of distribution and the date for release of the information to the public, and released in time to meet news and publication deadlines.

Assigning the Task

Determine which level of an organization should prepare and release the information according to the type of event and media interest. This decision can be made based on the criteria listed in table 4.1.

World events are most likely to attract international attention, but special campaigns and PR programs can create worldwide awareness of other international competitions, such as continental championships and world championships qualifiers. Olympic qualifying events are important today because of the worldwide media coverage of the Olympic Games. Use such images from the press and television to your best local advan-

Table 4.1   Who Should Prepare and Release Information for Different Events

Level of event	Interested media	Who should prepare and release
Local	Only local press	Club/local association
Regional	Local, regional press	Club/organizer
National	National press, TV	NF/organizer
Continental	National press, TV	Confederation/organizer
International	Radio, press agencies (national and international)	NF/organizer
World	National, world press; TV; radio; press agencies (national and international)	IF/organizer
Olympic	National, world press; TV; radio; press agencies (national and international)	IOC/IF/organizer

tage even if your country is not taking part in that sport at the Olympic level.

Each international sport organization taking part in the Olympic Games should make video images and press clippings available to its members. This can help them make subsequent presentations as they seek sponsorship for the national team and athletes. The media coverage creates the mythical heroes that are indispensable to enhance the image of the sport as well as the individual athletes' chances of economic success.

Using News Releases

A news release is a brief, concise report containing facts of general interest to be made public. Carefully prepare the text in short, appealing, and interesting phrases without a headline, and type it double or triple spaced using normal fonts. Keep sentences short and sequential. Use correct grammar and spelling together with good sentence structure and, above all, accurate content. Include the organization's name and address.

The main rule here is to mention all meaningful facts or news in the first paragraph. Leave the least important or secondary details to the end. The text should be appealing and interesting. Photos may help to increase the impact. It is essential to answer the following questions when preparing a news release: Who? What? Where? Why? When? How? Three types of news release are most common: the advance story, the follow-up story, and the feature article. It is important to eliminate from a news release any clichés or humorous comments, irrational or biased statements, profanity, excuses, highly technical language, distortions, and inaccuracies.

It is equally important to prevent a news release's rejection for publication because of information with little or no appeal to readers, old stories or stale news, poorly written stories, exaggerated information, obvious inaccuracies or omissions, duplication of previous releases, or superficial information of little value.

In addition, the press might not publish a report because more interesting stories may be available at the time, it may appear too close to free advertising, the space may be unavailable, or the story may conflict with newspaper policy.

You can also use news releases in other ways, such as by displaying copies of weekly and monthly news releases for members. Alternatively, you can keep them in a special binder easily available to visitors in your reception area and display them in other ways to inform other departments and extend such exposure to other individuals.

Distribute news releases according to the potential interest of the media, depending on the type of event. As you prepare the release, consider when to distribute it. Before a sport season, a NF should announce its yearly activities, giving dates, sites, and names of likely participants in events or meetings it will organize. When an important event of the sport is imminent, use a different guideline: Except for a world competition when longer periods are recommended (such as two years for world championships), other events may use the deadlines suggested in table 4.2 to release the information indicated.

Table 4.2   Suggested Deadlines for Releasing Information About a Sport Event

Time in relation to event	Type of information to release
Two months in advance	Date, place, invited teams/athletes, general information
One month in advance	Details of the competition, history of the event, organizer, previous winners, importance of the competition, ticket sales, general competition timetables
Two weeks in advance	Complete information on the competitors' names and confirmed teams (including competitions they have won), photos, history of the event and novelties to be introduced, competition schedule, sponsors
Three days before	The arrival of teams/athletes, training sites and times, official meetings to be held, sponsors, clinics, inspection of the competition area, individual background of the most outstanding competitors
One day before	Opening programs; VIPs attending the opening; interviews of coaches, team captains, athletes with opinions of their first appearance, and cheerleading groups for certain athletes
During the event	A daily bulletin with competition results, team or athlete rankings, inside news, and as much information as possible
After the event	Thank all journalists for their help in the successful distribution or publication of information, especially those who attended the matches; personally present special recognition to editors and directors of newspapers, television channels, or radio stations that provided exceptional coverage

Press Expectations

It is always important to anticipate what the press expects from sport managers or sport organizations as a whole. This does not mean that sport managers themselves will perform the duties of the media officer, but they should supervise and follow up the responsibilities of the latter by being aware of media expectations.

Concerning Local and National Events

Representatives of the media, as all other individuals, welcome personal attention, courtesy, and consideration. Everyone with responsibilities in any organization should be aware of media expectations, including

- **facts on the forthcoming events**, clubs, and competitors (advance stories);
- **reports on sponsors** and facilities for upcoming events;
- **factual reports** that do not withhold sensitive information;
- **invitations to cover** the national teams' or national representatives' activities leading up to the events;
- **first-hand information** and feature stories on the teams, athletes, and the most charismatic participants;
- **invitations to accompany the national team and athletes** to important competitions or events, if at all possible; and
- **feedback from the NF** on published stories and recognition of the importance of media work.

In addition, the media expects the organizers and NFs not to have favorites or show preference for a specific type of media to the detriment of others. Press, television, and radio must be placed on an equal footing.

There is no better means of communication with the target groups, selected sectors of the population, and even the constituents of a sport organization than the written press and television. Fifteen seconds of television comments or half a page in a major newspaper can make all the difference between a successful sport program and one that is not.

Concerning World Events

Organizers of top-class events should pay special attention to the needs of the press and create a constant flow of communication, starting by inviting them in due time (6 to 10 months ahead of the event) to accredit their representatives. For worldwide events, NFs should try to involve journalists of the written press from as many countries as possible.

Fully involve the media from every participating country via constant bulletins from the organizer as well as each local NF. The press expects the organizer to

- **especially invite them to be accredited** and provide them with programs of activities and adequate facilities for work and transportation;

- **send an advance story** on the competition, its previous editions, and details of participating teams, athletes, and local and foreign participants;

- **send follow-up stories** through periodic bulletins and photos on the organization, competition halls, and statistics of previous events;

- **provide adequately prepared and accurate material**, whenever possible illustrated with photos, especially on the occasion of a major national or international event or press conference; and

- **provide adequate telecommunications facilities, material, and equipment** in spacious and well-arranged locations. Mechanical typewriters are a must, as are laptops, photocopiers, fax machines, and local and international direct dial (IDD) telephones in the case of international events.

Media Coordination at World Events

It is essential to involve all departments of the organization in the preparation and implementation of a plan that involves those departments in activities with or for the press.

Preparing a Media and Communications Plan

Prepare a special plan for media, two years if possible, but no less than one year in advance of an event. Implement this plan according to schedule, starting with the advanced registration of journalists, feature stories on previous events, periodic news bulletins, organization of a media center, and set-up of an accreditation procedure. All these activities must be arranged in chronological order for their implementation, but each item may be ready at any time. Consider that not all previously registered journalists will arrive at the event and therefore will not require actual accreditation.

Event Press Chief and Press Officer

The organizer of a world event appoints a press chief and the international sport organization concerned has a press officer responsible for press relations. Both must carry out assigned tasks and supervise the set up and operation of the media center and its various sections (working, telecommunications, and interview areas and lounges).

The press chief

- is responsible for the preparation of the press report after each heat, round, or match as well as for its distribution;
- is responsible for the official press interview to be held immediately after the heat, round, or match and must ensure the presence of journalists, interpreters, coaches, and competitors; and
- must not leave the technical bureau (or secretariat) before he or she has received the last results from the other venues.

The press officer of the IF

- must receive full access to all press and television areas; and
- coordinates the photographers' positions around the competition area or playing court and in specific, restricted positions with the organizer and the officials responsible for the competition area.

Preparing and Distributing a Daily Bulletin

The organizing committee of major events is responsible for a daily bulletin to be distributed to the media and officials at the competition venues. However, the committee delegates its preparation, contents, and coordination to an official named by the IF.

The first daily bulletin must be prepared, printed, and distributed *in each venue* the day before the start of the competition with the team composition and list of competitors of each delegation that have been officially approved and with other relevant information and activity schedules not contained in the handbook or in the official program.

The subsequent daily bulletins must contain

- the results of each heat, round, or match of the day;
- the daily results with team or individual ranking per pool, round, or heat;
- the daily events and their timetable; and
- any change in the training program.

The staff in charge of preparing and publishing the daily bulletin must remain on stand-by after a heat, round, or match to receive and process results from other venues.

After each stage of the competition, the daily bulletin must also contain

- complete statistics of competitors involved,
- information on how and where each team and athlete will continue the competition, and
- the time and place for the drawing of lots whenever needed.

One person appointed by the local organizer will be responsible for distributing the daily bulletin in locations determined by the IF and the organizing committee. It must be distributed at the end of the last scheduled competition, during the night, or very early the next morning (before 7 A.M.) as determined by the IF and the organizing committee.

Relating With the Public

Actual relations between human beings are the constituents of a society, not the human beings themselves.

Arnold Toynbee, "Study of History"

Chapter 3 of this book presented several important keys that lead sport organizations to success, while chapter 4 began with an overview of relations with the media. It continues with a study of what is potentially the organization's most needed and essential tool: excellent relations with people, other organizations, sponsors, and the media. This will result in respect and confidence toward the sport, the organization itself, and its programs. *Public relations (PR)* refers to communication outside the organization and *human relations* to communication within.

Internal Human Relations

Individuals only ever become full-fledged constituents of the organization through adequate human relations. Because it matters so much how you treat people, the measure of such relations may become the measure of the organization itself. The ultimate goal of human relations is to create allegiance and a feeling of loyalty to the organization. This involves instilling the feelings of belonging in its members as soon as possible.

Groups Within the Organization

Each group as a whole has a purpose shared by all its members. Subgroups may form part of the group where there is a mutual attraction, and some members find this smaller association meaningful. However, subgroups may become weak if they fail to offer desirable personal objectives.

Members' allegiance and loyalty to the main organization should not be seen as a threat to the internal identity of subgroups. However, in reverse, although conflicts may originate from the specific interests of subgroups, this does not imply the absence of a subgroup's loyalty to the organization as a whole.

While an individual is attracted to a group for various reasons and decides to become a part, the group is also the result of a collective decision on the part of the rest of the group. The individual must adapt his or her decisions or attitudes to those of the group in order not to be rejected or isolated from it. In order to attract people, however, groups need to offer something appealing and have structures for relating within the organization that respect those who are taking part.

Communication and Relations by Level

Human relations between members of an organization are a process of adequate communication between members and need attention at every level of the organization. If this process fails, the outcome will be relational conflict. Communication includes any way of giving and receiving data, ideas, suggestions, impressions, and concepts—those that are deliberate and formal as well as those that are subtle. The latter includes body language involving your eyes, eyebrows, hand gestures, and posture. Indeed, even silence can become a means of communication under certain conditions.

The exchange of messages called communication can never be completed in one step. It requires feedback as well. Interpretation is a stage of communication that follows the sending of the message. It will vary depending on how the message was expressed and other complexities of the process of communication, including competing communications and predominant attitudes.

Before communicating, sport managers must therefore learn to listen and catch the attention of those with whom they communicate. This communication process happens at different levels within the organization.

First Level   This is the top relationship between the number one person in the organization and its top leadership. For sport organizations, this means the president and the heads of each administrative unit (such as executive committee members, coordinators, directors, managers, and commission presidents) and eventually certain managers at lower levels.

Second Level   Relations of the second level occur between the coordinators, directors, commission presidents, and regional or continental representatives. They can make the difference between failure and success of the organization as a whole because they may easily become politicized and lead to the emergence of subgroup interests and even power struggles.

Operational Level   The most significant and closest human relations occur at this level. However, they do not preclude other levels of management from having a supervisory role in the organization's day-to-day activities.

Organizational Pride

Group feelings and loyalty might not be apparent within the organization, but they are very much present in the pride that comes from belonging to it.

Organizations can develop this pride by sharing information, using consensus to achieve agreement on objectives, and also stimulating participation.

Sharing information enables employees and members to better understand their duties and their roles within the organization. This requires informing them about things they may need or desire to know. When employees and members help make decisions about organizational objectives, their job satisfaction increases. Avoid any pressures to adopt unattainable objectives as this just creates frustration. Willing participation stems from positive feelings about the organizational environment and acceptance of common goals. Involvement in crucial tasks and satisfaction from achievement bring with them loyalty and a degree of pride in an organization.

A Positive Work Environment

Nurturing human relations within an organization involves a commitment of personnel and financial resources of the organization. Individuals thrive when they receive recognition for their efforts, and they welcome opportunities to earn it. For this same reason, assigning tasks that are difficult or impossible to achieve results in extreme frustration on the part of employees and low employee morale. Organizations can recognize members verbally through their supervisors, in organizational newsletters, or through other avenues.

Bad working conditions have a negative impact on employees' morale because of the impression that management is disregarding their needs. A workplace's emotional environment influences productivity just as much as temperature, humidity, lighting, and noise do. These conditions should all be adjusted to meet the needs of employees.

Whenever members or employees of the organization are convinced of the incompetence of their president or managers, they will not be sufficiently motivated to produce quality work. They will quickly lose interest in cooperating, together with any sense of pride they may have felt in belonging to the group. Top-level managers, commission presidents, and regional leaders must have the professional experience and authority to deal efficiently with problems raised by employees, members, and other organizations. Misuse of power by top-level management, even by accident or mistake, will seriously damage working relations within the organization. This will result not only in a loss of credibility and motivation but also in increased mistrust and suspicion within the organization itself. The first management level embodies the trend and spirit of the organization. Whatever those managers do and say is seen as representing the organization's leadership. If they are incompetent, the president and the organization as a whole will also be viewed as incompetent.

When you dismiss an employee, a member, or a commission president, you send a message to other members and employees: "Beware, this organization does not provide any guarantees and will discard you when you are no longer needed!" Employees expecting to be dismissed at any moment will naturally show less loyalty toward the organization. It is important to assure members and employees that they are really part of the group, to affirm their abilities and to build on their strengths. To avoid incompetent or power-hungry managers and painful dismissal procedures, hire people with proven records and never as favors for any individual, no matter how influential.

External PR

Organizations direct PR toward public opinion in much the same way as they direct marketing relations toward sponsors, be they individuals or companies. PR influences the perception of members of the community at all levels in connection with a sport, its organization, activities, and objectives. The end result of a good PR plan will be a more positive image that can create in turn true, long-lasting, and effective support from important segments of the community.

Through Member Behavior

It is well known that the conduct of the members of any sport organization influences the perception of the media and the general public about that sport and its programs. PR activities can in this way influence both the image of a sport and its reputation. For this reason, organizations should communicate to members and participants the significance of their conduct.

Through the Perception of Programs

If the sport program is seen as excellent, practical, and beneficial to youth, it will be able to successfully promote a variety of products and communicate its value to society at large. National sport organizations should strive to communicate the values of their sport positively through PR activities. Mason and Paul recognized back in 1988 that "PR is the process of getting the right facts to the right people at the right time and in the right way." Influencing people's perceptions is a large part of PR work.

Through PR Flexibility

PR flexibly promotes positive thinking about the sport and organizational programming in many different ways. The PR process should emphasize positive feelings and a good image, creating harmony and understanding between sport programs and the public through a well-designed plan. You can easily influence human behavior by affecting individual and group perception in a way that reinforces positive feelings while eradicating negative attitudes.

Need for a PR Plan

Every sport organization should have its own PR program to improve the image of, and create public confidence in, its sport and the organization itself (figure 4.1). Organizational activities, personal contacts between the members of the organization and the general public, professional working relationships with members of the news media, and formal public speeches are all part of PR.

Good PR flourishes with good communication between the sport organization and various sectors of the public, including media and sponsors. The basis of good communication is true, accurate information coming from people who can be trusted. This also explains why misconduct and scandals concerning members may destroy the credibility of the sport and the confidence in the organization.

The organization should have someone who speaks on its behalf. The best speakers are the athletes themselves, who experience the benefits of the sport they practice. Alongside athletes, NF paid staff and volunteers play an important role in promotion and PR activities.

Image-Enhancing Tactics

The use of excellent facilities and premises, which are properly maintained and well operated, creates a positive image of the NF and of its programs. Furthermore, its involvement in national activities, charitable projects, service clubs, and professional sport and nonsport organizations will also enhance its image. This is especially true when it enjoys a good profile and high visibility, as these result in greater esteem and respectability both for itself and its programs.

Participation and active involvement in community programs are important to create a better image and increased public awareness of the NF and of its programs. Every occasion in which a NF participates may serve to promote its image, if it is adequately intertwined with community activities and well publicized.

Class and Style

Every activity, participation, or contribution should be marked with class and professionalism for the best possible reflection of the organization and its programs. The professional organization of sport events, coupled with the responsible behavior of participants, officials, and spectators, adds class to the image of a sport. Adequate housing of media members, sponsors,

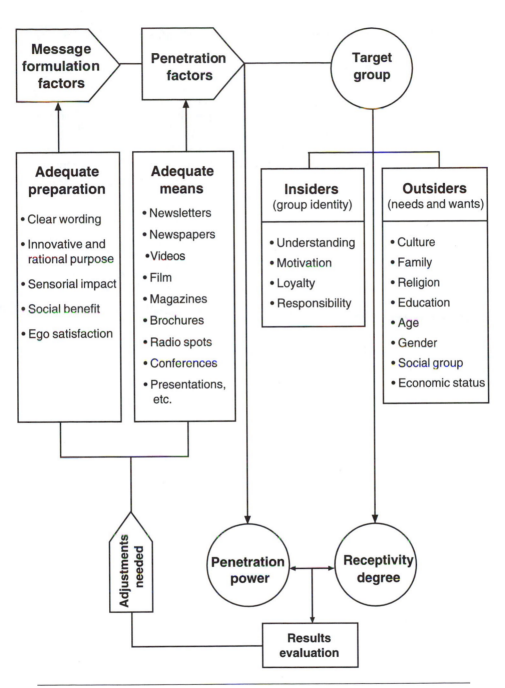

Figure 4.1 Decisive factors in a PR plan.

authorities, and guests at an event, together with intermission shows, adequate seating, and a cheerful attitude of organized groups, all contribute to a positive image and enhanced reputation of the NF and its activities.

Conducting the program of activities as scheduled will always generate a positive image and a good reputation. Changing the date and place of events destroys credibility and tarnishes the image of a NF.

Good organizational structure and smooth working routines based on procedures and policies bring high visibility to the activities and create public respect. The publication of a printed, full-color leaflet containing the profile of the NF, its objectives, grassroots programs, sponsorship opportunities, and important national or international events will help to make a good impression on sponsors.

PR From Different Perspectives

Before choosing and preparing the best communication means, it is necessary to take into account important group factors that must enter into people's minds before communication can have any influence on their attitude. Sport managers should also remember the fact that PR activities can take different shapes and be the subject of particular considerations in accordance with the perspective of the individual concerned or the organization's framework, as shown in table 4.3.

Objectives of a PR Plan

A sport organization's PR plan may have many different objectives, depending on the organization's situation or the problems it needs to solve. The following are possible organizational goals:

- To integrate the sport organization into the sport community of the country, or in the case of international organizations, into the world sport community
- To create favorable attitudes on the part of the population, governmental authorities, media, companies, and other public and private sport organizations toward the sport
- To promote a positive social, political, and ethical image of the organization
- To establish links with every person or organization involved in sport who could help achieve its objectives
- To foster interest, respect, and support on the part of the media for the organization and its programs and objectives
- To promote grassroots sport activities in its own sport

Table 4.3   Media Officers Responsible for PR for Organizations and Individuals

Organizations or individuals	PR agents or speakers
Governmental agency	Public affairs bureau
Educational institutions (schools, colleges, universities)	Promotion and fund-raising departments
Political or interorganizational	Lobbying agents
Entertainers or artists	Press agents
Athletes	Sport agents
Sport organizations (according to subject) a. Press affairs b. Marketing and sponsoring c. Political affairs d. Fund-raising and development e. Recruiting, promotions, etc.	Marketing agency or internal marketing unit a. Communications/press relations office b. Marketing officer/agency c. Political contacts d. Development office e. Public relations office

- To earn support and recognition from public and private organizations
- To periodically evaluate the attitudes of the media, authorities, and other sport organizations before readjusting its PR program
- To communicate to employees, members, and executives the influence that their individual attitudes and behavior may have on the public image of the organization, its programs, and objectives

As mentioned earlier, PR objectives should be flexible, acceptable, and adaptable. The PR plan should emphasize positive thinking and creating a good image as well as harmony and understanding between sport programs and public opinion. Human behavior is easily influenced, affecting individual and group perception. The goal of PR is to create a positive image that will in turn create long-lasting support on the part of important segments of the community.

Getting Started in PR

Before implementing PR activities, it is necessary to undertake PR research to pinpoint the problems to be tackled, judge the facts, and make decisions.

PR Research

To understand the problems properly and determine the need for a PR plan, sport organizations should start a PR research program and periodically repeat the process. The purpose of the research is to

- find out what the public at large, the government, sport practitioners, sport institutions, and the media think of the organization, its programs, and its activities;
- ascertain the logical, illogical, or emotional basis of the opinions they have formed; and
- determine how to judge those facts and make decisions.

Putting PR Research to Use

During the preparation of a PR plan, follow these steps in the decision-making process:

- Make an analysis of the situation without relying on feelings, pre-judgments, preferences, and fears.
- Analyze the facts without prejudice, avoiding biased opinions.
- Combine the facts to form proposals.
- Combine these proposals to come up with pros and cons.
- Draw conclusions based on arguments (combination of proposals and principles) that should lead to the definition of a course of action.

PR Planning

Once the organization has concluded the PR research, made the decision to proceed with a PR plan, assessed the public image of its sport, and carefully studied all the information collected, it should pay special attention to internal and external characteristics. You can complete such a three-step process as follows.

Step 1: Assess the Public Image of the Sport

Use scientific polling methods, such as mail surveys, telephone calls, and personal interviews or focus groups throughout the area where the sport is present (from local to worldwide), with total or scattered coverage in critical target points. The research and polling should determine

- how the general public perceives the sport;
- where, geographically, the sport is recognized;

- who practices or watches the sport;
- which sports are practiced by the majority of the people surveyed;
- what kind of information about the sport, its leaders, or the organization itself circulates among those people; and
- which information retains their attention.

Step 2: Study the Data Collected and Draft the Plan

The following activities and decisions are necessary as you study the data and draft the plan:

- List the objectives and goals established in the mission statement of the organization.
- Determine whether such goals and objectives suggest the need to build a positive image or to modify a negative one.
- Choose the target groups of people for the PR plan.
- Determine the kind of message to send and the channels of communication.
- Decide how you will evaluate the results and who will do it.
- Assign specific responsibilities with deadlines.
- Prepare a budget, with necessary expenses and sources of income.
- Prepare a master plan, with a timetable for all PR activities.

Step 3: Deliver the Plan

This consists of the internal and external development of the plan, which take place within and outside of the organization.

Internal Steps These steps have to do with affecting the attitude or behavior of the constituency, members, and employees. It is common knowledge that, whatever the activity, the conduct of the members of any sport organization will influence the perception that the media and general public have of their sport program as a whole and of the sport itself. Therefore, the PR-based image and reputation of the organization should be made clear to those inside the organization right away.

The organization should then establish principles pertaining to the behavior of its members, employees, and leaders who must face the outside world; receive visitors to the organization; answer telephone calls; and attend sport, cultural, or social events. Such principles should be established after considering the following questions:

- Are all members, executives, and employees of the organization equally aware of expectations for behavior?

- Has confidence and trust between the constituency, employees, leaders, and units of the organization developed through common information channels?
- Do members and employees feel that the organization's units or leaders will listen to them and consider their needs?

External Steps These steps affect the public at large, spectators, media, sponsors, and authorities. A sport organization or NF must effectively and efficiently communicate the values of its sport in a positive manner through PR efforts. As we said earlier, Mason and Paul stated in 1988 that "PR is the process of getting the right facts to the right people at the right time and in the right way."

People must see the organization, its objectives, and its sport program as excellent, practical, and beneficial to youth in order to promote the image of the sport and to communicate its value to others. The organization should therefore establish policies and procedures on

- attitudes and behavior for receptions, assemblies, conferences, congresses, and press conferences;
- negotiations of cooperation with other sport, cultural, and social service organizations to establish joint projects; and
- recruitment of personnel and volunteers for sport events (sponsors and media, clubs, coaches, judges or referees, and journalists).

It is also important to identify the target group of the PR plan and choose the most adequate means and persons to carry out the plan. This involves

- outlining the profile of the public involved in the sport, their values, attitudes, social and economic status, age, and sex;
- outlining the profile of sponsors whose marketing objectives, mission, product, or image could see a marketing opportunity in the sport;
- finding the vehicle (person, means, or group) who has the greatest influence on public opinion, sponsor decisions, and media attitude; and
- choosing the most effective communication means with the largest acceptance and best public image (magazine, television channel, radio station, newspaper, or newsletter).

The plan is now ready to be implemented according to the organization's policies. It just remains to be decided who will be responsible for carrying out, following up, and periodically evaluating the PR plan.

Managing the PR Plan

The PR plan could be entrusted either to a manager of the organization or to an outsider (PR agency), but the huge cost of the latter option makes it unrealistic for most sport organizations. A basic knowledge of PR should therefore be provided to a responsible person within the organization whose duties will include the following:

- Be aware of all internal and external situations that could affect the relationship of the sport or its organization with its constituency or public, and make sure the president and general manager know.
- Detect or anticipate the attitudes of the sport's target groups toward the organization or its activities, and report them to the president and general manager.
- Maintain close contact between the leadership of the organization, its constituency, and the public in general.
- Draw up a realistic PR plan on the basis of the organization's own situation, historical setting, and moral and ethical atmosphere.
- Prepare adjustments or elaborate a new PR plan and attend public ceremonies requiring the presence of the organization.

PR and communication both reflect the quality or efficiency of their respective development. In addition, better communication usually means better PR. The organization needs good communication systems with its own public, but also a specific PR plan prepared with regard to its unique nature.

Influencing Results

Sport managers are advised to consider several factors that influence the result of any PR activity and make the difference between success and failure.

External Factors

External factors include the formulation of messages, the selection of the most adequate market penetration factors, and the resistance or support of group factors for the effective reception of the message.

Promotions

Good promotion campaigns will be very effective at stimulating market penetration and public awareness. The manager could try distributing some free tickets, coupons, autographed photos of outstanding athletes, gifts, samples of souvenirs, event logos, and other items that do not exceed budget limitations.

Positioning

Positioning is also important, ever since Al Reis and Jack Trout added this dimension to marketing in the mid-1980s. They stressed the importance of positioning a product (sport or event) in the minds of consumers (potential practitioners, sponsors, media, or spectators). Successful positioning will help to influence consumers beyond traditional marketing and advertising strategies by

- emphasizing that the event is the first of its kind;
- searching for the gap left by other events and emphasizing the edge this event has over others (if the event is not the first of its kind on the market);
- using a simple, easy-to-remember name; and
- mentioning previous successful events.

PR is the vehicle for positioning, and marketing purposes are its end. It refers to the perception of the service, product, or individual by the customers or supporters in connection with their needs and wants.

Evaluating Results

Once the PR plan is implemented, the organization must proceed to evaluate its results. You want to be able to measure that

- the organization is making progress toward achieving the established goals and objectives (and how much progress has been made),
- targeted groups experienced some impact through the PR message,
- positive or negative effects on the image are noticeable,
- the budget is cost-effective (properly serving its purpose), and
- human and material resources are being used efficiently.

Promotion and Fund-Raising

Public Relations can serve as both a supportive and corrective function to marketing" (including promotions and fund raising).

John White, How to Understand and Manage Public Relations

Good promotional activities should inform, remind, and persuade. There is little doubt that an organization needs to adequately plan such activities around themes or slogans, implement them well, and periodically evaluate them. NFs and leagues should only promote success, not failure.

Fund-raising strategies or plans may only be implemented via promotional activities and PR efforts. This being said, not every promotional activity or PR program is implemented to seek money. Most, in fact, are aimed at improving the image of the organization and its perception by the public at large.

Successful promotion requires a quality in the communication process known as "persuasive communication." It requires communication based on similar understandings between the sender and recipient and must avoid communication obstacles and distortions. Promotional tools are only effective when they have been carefully planned, abide strictly by PR principles, and respect the organization's principles. Promotional tools include personal sales, publicity, and advertising.

Personal sales happen through lectures, seminars, and clinics—which offer a great opportunity to sell the sport or event to prospective media agents, sponsors, and institutions—as well as individual contacts. Individual contacts are made by service personnel whose friendly manner and warm attitude serve to create customer satisfaction and loyalty to the sport, event, or program. Instruct personnel involved in organizing a sport event to smile constantly at spectators and be especially courteous, polite, and friendly with media and sponsor representatives, making them feel at home.

Publicity is a free means of conveying information about a sport. It is commonly made in the shape of news releases, interviews, television or radio presentations, television coverage of ceremonies, and public service announcements. Sport organizations need to publicize their activities through carefully planned press relations and communication.

Advertising is a paid form of announcement via radio, television, magazines, newspapers, billboards, newsletters, mail, posters, signs, and other promotional products. To be truly effective, an advertisement must contain a message that satisfies four customer needs:

- A rational reason to practice or watch the sport or buy the product (to become stronger, jump higher, run faster)
- Sensual satisfaction (something pleasant to see, hear, feel, or smell)
- Social satisfaction (the chance to meet pleasant, important, beautiful, powerful people)
- Ego satisfaction (a suntan to look attractive, exercise to look younger, or sport ability to be more fun to be around)

You will need innovative approaches to show how the sport satisfies these needs and procures style, a way of life, and enjoyment. Then, intensive distribution becomes an important issue.

Promotion As a PR Activity

Promotion is essentially a PR activity enabling a sport organization to make contact with people within the chosen target groups, provide them with a tangible proof or taste of the sport or event, and positively influence their perception of it. The aim is to foster the want, develop a need, and ultimately create the demand, all with the understanding that the product (sport or event) is within their economic, cultural, and social reach.

Promotional Planning

Promotional activities could be defined as the actions undertaken by a sport organization to position itself, its sport, or events (championships, cups, tournaments) in the minds of the public, both members and customers (practitioners, spectators, media, sponsors), through free distribution of the organization's symbols, logos, sport event programs, star competitor photographs, coupons, free tickets, and gifts, among other things. Paid advertising, publicity, and direct sales of gadgets during events can also be powerful promotional tools.

Means of Communication

Event organizers should be familiar with the best available communication means prior to drawing up any advertising or promotional strategies so they can effectively reach the targeted groups.

Organizers should pay most attention to the formulation of the message. As mentioned before, effective messages must be ego-indulgent and contain an expected sensorial satisfaction, an expected social satisfaction, and a rational reason for why spectators should attend the event.

Special attention must be given to the media *impact* on target groups and to the *frequency* of the message, including advertisement scheduling one month prior to the event and follow-up advertising one week before. This frequency should apply to each phase of the organizational process including the beginning and end of qualification rounds, the list of teams or athletes attending, the drawing of lots, and the competitors' arrival in the city hosting the event.

Specific Promotional Activities

As previously mentioned, good promotional activities should inform, remind, and persuade. The following are more specific aspects of promotional activities.

National Leagues and Other Competitions

National leagues or circuits of individual sport events should promote the competitive dimension of the sport, the excitement of that competition, the achievement of competitors, and the accomplishments of the league or circuit itself. Consider the following questions to prepare selling points for potential sponsors:

- Do you promote quality and class in the competition?
- Is there sufficient public interest in the sport to draw spectators to the events?
- Which television channels are interested in broadcasting the competitions?
- Do the planned competition areas have adequate facilities for spectators to ensure that they will enjoy the show?
- What are the sport achievements?

Tactics in Promoting Sport

NF administrators should use their own imaginations, those of their staff, and all manner of tactics deemed suitable to inform the general public and the media of their sport and of its activities. This includes

- publicizing natural rivalries existing between competitors and coaches;
- involving public figures such as politicians, artists, and company CEOs as VIPs, inviting them to make or receive the first pitch or serve, trigger the starter's gun, deliver an opening speech, or confer an award;
- staging presentations or appearances of special guests during competition intervals;
- bringing in special organizations such as the Red Cross or UNICEF;
- delivering certificates or congratulatory letters to journalists, authorities, sport heroes, etc.;
- using every occasion to thank others publicly;
- organizing annual gala dinners or special luncheons (such as press lunches);
- displaying banners and signs in every possible visible place; and
- opening a national Hall of Fame, a Pioneer's Hall, or a national All-Stars Gallery containing photos, trophies, and other items.

Use of Merchandise and Cross-Marketing

Only high quality, first-class merchandise may be used to promote events or programs. Clearly identify the purpose in using it and the benefits you anticipate. Then it is important to decide whether to give merchandise away or sell it and whether you will print sponsor logos or other advertisements.

Cross-marketing is a very powerful tool to motivate public involvement and attract them through the offering of premiums as a result of their participation in games or contests.

The objective of merchandise and cross-marketing is to promote and publicize the sport events and programs on the basis of the initial interest they raise. They must have a certain intrinsic value to the recipients; otherwise the effect will be counterproductive.

Strategic Planning

Strategic planning is the blueprint of an organization. Through such a plan, the organization decides what type of action will be undertaken, which internal operations are needed to deliver the desired results to the constituents of the organization, and how to achieve the organization's objectives and mission statement.

Planning has two faces, strategic and operational. The *strategic planning* process links the sport organization with its institutional mission and objectives relating to sport participation, public image, and generating revenue. It consists of establishing guidelines and setting long-range goals and includes

- planning which constituent groups (community groups, development groups) to target,
- communicating with the targeted groups,
- marketing services to these groups, and
- identifying services for resource development.

The *operating plan* determines the day-to-day activities and responsibilities of the different units of the organization, which are adequate enough to ensure that the NF serves the expectations of the sport practitioners and club members as well as those of sport fans and spectators.

Constituency Development

Constituency development is achieved through the planned programs and activities to be implemented in a community in order to identify, retain, and serve those already taking part in the sport (or those who are favorable to it) and reach other groups in the community who are not yet involved in the sport organization.

Fund-Raising Activities

These are typically North-American activities successfully developed by the sport directors, administrators, or managers in a region where people are always ready and willing to support junior high, high school, collegiate, and national sport activities.

The activities to be performed in this context require a minimum level of competence, technical skills, and decision-making ability. Fund-raising tactics, promotional activities, and PR efforts are intimately connected. Any successful sport program depends on the precision of the coordination within the administrative structure of the organization, national league, or professional club (including colleges, universities, and local sport associations), as the case may be.

Elements of Successful Activities

Specific elements are required to carry out fund-raising activities or to promote an organization's specific sport program:

- The media (radio, television, press)
- Publications, photos, and printed material for advertising such as programs, schedule cards, posters, pens, calendars, and billboards
- Buildings, equipment, and supplies
- Image-enhancing activities (joining organizations or projects that lend respectability)
- Operational activities such as policies, procedures, routines, and priorities
- Merchandise for distribution, sale, donation, and exchange
- Committed athletes, volunteers, and coaching and administrative staff
- Coherent sport programs as the basis for the fund-raising activity
- Adequate PR and promotional activities

Type of Activities to Consider

Promotional activities are always necessary to obtain good results in fund-raising programs. Such promotions must be cost effective without sacrificing quality in the gadgets offered in exchange.

- **Approaching individuals** for money, services, or products, going person-to-person, door-to-door, or via telephone but always exchanging logos, pins, or small mementos
- **Approaching businesses** to request sponsorship or corporate partnership
- **Profitable units** such as parking, shop sales, tickets, clinics, camps, and merchandise sales (pins, caps, T-shirts, banners, mascots, and logos)
- **Promotional activities and special events** aimed at improving the image; increasing attendance at matches; or providing recognition for team members, coaches, sport supporters, and sponsors

Recommended Personal Attitudes

Conducting promotional and fund-raising activities requires fixing important projects as the beneficiaries of the campaign results. Volunteers must be properly educated and trained in the following principles.

- **Keep efforts in the proper perspective** and remember that fund-raising is a means to ensure the progress of a sport rather than a personal vehicle to public recognition.
- **Bear in mind primary responsibilities** and do not neglect day-to-day functions or duties. Overdoing it in fund-raising activities could be detrimental to other duties.
- **Adapt previously known fund-raising programs** instead of simply repeating them. Look for successful programs and adapt them to your environment.
- **Keep things in perspective.** Look around at the sport environment and assess the organization's position; it should be no more and no less than what it is. The fund-raising strategies, promotional activities, and PR efforts should be compatible with the particular situation of the sport organization and with the circumstances prevailing in the country.
- **Above all, be optimistic.** Do not let poor public response or initial failures destroy enthusiasm.

Planning and Development

The success of PR, promotional, or fund-raising activities depends on the solidity of the ground where such activities are performed. This ground will be as solid as the quality of the organization, management, and administration of the sport organization performing the leading role. See figure 4.2 for a chart showing the process for an organization's promotion, fund-raising, and PR.

Organizations must be able to rely on an organizational structure with a minimum level of management and adequate administration to accomplish the following basic tasks:

- **Planning:** establishing goals and objectives as well as selecting resources and determining what should be done, how, when, and under what conditions
- **Organizing:** allocating resources and tasks in units or departments with clearly determined responsibilities, functions, authority, and power
- **Staffing:** allocating sufficient and competent individuals and groups to perform each task, matching their capabilities and skills with the appropriate area of responsibility

- **Directing:** providing guidance and leadership to personnel inside and outside the organization
- **Coordinating:** matching the tools and resources available, placing each in the right perspectives of time, place, hierarchy, and line of authority
- **Reporting:** ensuring that members follow the chain of command and that the accountability of each individual and unit is clear
- **Recording:** keeping records to avoid confusion, document activities performed, and maintain accountability
- **Facilitating:** supporting each member of the organization and providing assistance as required
- **Evaluating:** controlling or assessing periodically the effectiveness of individual and collective efforts
- **Budgeting:** allocating funds per area of responsibility in order to provide financial support. To make money available is to put the organization to work. This financial allocation should be made after an appropriate budgeting process.

Essential Factors for Success

Certain operational conditions have a positive or negative effect upon the desired results. Aiming at a final success, it is important while drafting a plan to keep in mind the following essential factors for success: time, personnel, equipment and supplies, facilities, reputation, image, past accomplishments and achievements, status, and money.

Time

To successfully run sport programs, each administrative unit must have enough time to carry out its assigned duties properly.

Personnel

Not only quantity but also quality, capability, and competence are the essential ingredients for successful sport organization personnel, both internally (full- and part-time staff) and externally (volunteers). In other words, just like in any business, you will need enough qualified staff to maintain smooth operations.

Equipment and Supplies

Modern and appropriate office material is important for good personnel productivity: computer software and hardware, plus typewriters, copiers,

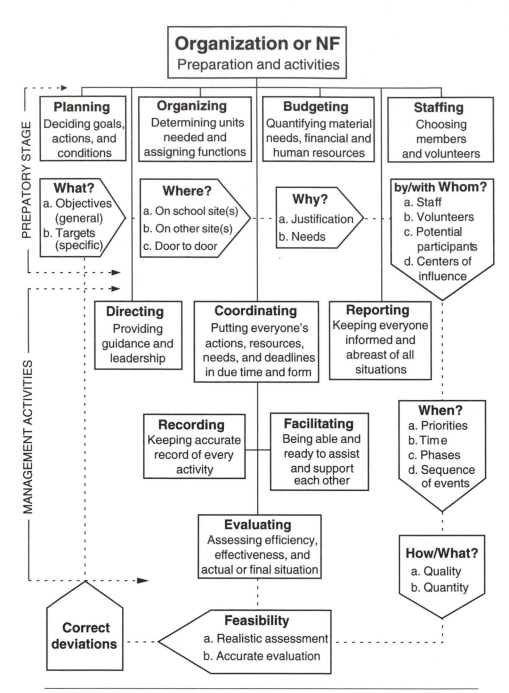

Figure 4.2 Organizational process of sport promotion, fund-raising, and PR activities.

fax machines, telephones, paper, and so forth. These are essential ingredients for an office to run in an efficient and organized fashion.

Facilities

Office space, sport facilities, meeting rooms, and dining halls may be used extensively in the development of programs. When newly born groups or associations do not have access to such facilities, it will always be possible to find a church priest, factory owner, schoolmaster, or even a city council member who could gladly support the association by providing some of the space or facilities required.

Reputation

What others think or feel about the NF and its principles and values is important. Having a positive reputation can open doors and facilitate support for operations and programs. Although reputations are gained over a period of time and after a series of achievements, they can be easily lost following one mistake or miscalculation.

Image

Closely linked to reputation, the image is the impression that a sport activity or organization creates when other people watch its activities closely. While the reputation has the effect of influencing individuals who have had no personal contact with the organization, the image is usually the result of personal experiences obtained through PR activities, contacts, or dealings with the organization.

An image may be created deliberately or accidentally and may be real or only perceived. It can have a positive or negative effect on individuals or groups targeted as potential supporters of a sport organization. The way staff dress for events, the behavior of athletes, and the manner of arranging competition areas and setting up press and VIP facilities may all have an adverse effect on companies, the media, or even individuals.

Past Accomplishments and Achievements

Past achievements can be a tool used to hire the services of a sponsor or to obtain support for a given program. Winners attract supporters. The opposite may also happen, and spreading rumors of previous failures will scare potential sponsors and even terminate actual sponsorship relations.

Status

The good status gained in the sport community is a result of ethical or legal behavior of the NF or its involvement in sport events, activities, and social gatherings. This status is often self-perpetuating and makes potential sponsors receptive or ready to cooperate.

Money

Money is important, but not indispensable. Different strategies such as "trade-outs" may secure products and services from other sources; even professional personnel from a given sponsor may be "traded-out" for billboards, publicity, or partnership. The internal or external atmosphere or properly equipped premises and expensive equipment may constitute the adequate environment in which to influence the attitude of a potential sponsor. It could even prove decisive to engage the sponsor's participation in much better financial conditions.

The financial climate is as much a part of an organization's environment as the political climate and should influence the launching or termination of a sport program based on this support.

William F. Stier, in his book *Successful Sport Fund-Raising*, has made a graphic representation of the excessive quantity of contacts needed in every stage of the process in order to arrive at the end and have no more than 10 percent successful contacts (figure 4.3).

Marketing Sport Events

The consumer demand for a sporting event is ultimately generated by the potential spectators.

Peter J. Graham, Sport Business,
Operational and Theoretical Aspects

Even though the market is the actual buying and selling of a product and not only the place where this physically occurs, sport in itself is not for sale and, as such, is not on the market. What people, sponsors, and the media buy as products are the events, the names of athletes and their popularity, or the image of a sport organization. As such, these are commodities that can be used to increase public interest in another product or service.

This chapter has already demonstrated that a successful campaign to sell sport programs, activities, or events to the community requires excellent PR. This is how the sport organization positively influences the perception and opinion of the general public, media, sponsors, and spectators by enhancing the image of its athletes, clubs, leagues, and leaders.

This chapter will now explain some marketing concepts and the reasons for sport organizations to define a marketing strategy and outline a marketing plan for their activities. Do this methodically, after extensive research to identify public and sponsor preferences, and then determine the type of

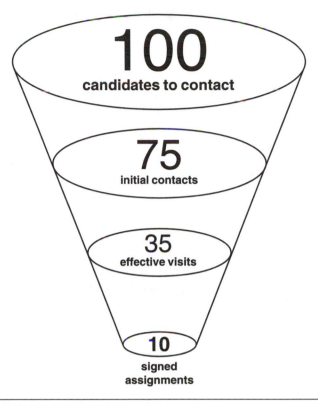

Figure 4.3   The funnel concept in fund-raising.

From William F. Stier, Jr., 1994, chapters 4-5. In Successful Sport Fund-Raising, edited by Chris Rogers (Dubuque, Iowa: Brown & Benchmark), 60-88. Reprinted by permission from William F. Stier, Jr.

events you wish to stage and market, the image you wish to portray, the marketing mix most suited to your objectives, and the specific situation of each sport event.

Sport Marketing Definitions

Sport marketing may be considered from three different points of view, depending on the focus of the marketing activity. First, when the focus of the activity is on sport units like athletes, sport events, and sport programs, which a company considers as potentially satisfying its marketing needs or as representing adequate tools to reach its marketing goals, the term is *corporate sponsorship*. Second, the buying and selling of an image, name, or logo to obtain cash for athletes, teams, leagues, circuits, or event organizers is called *endorsement*. Third, the marketing plan of a sport organization on the occasion of an event, for the primary benefit of that sport, is called *event marketing*.

Marketing Terms

Marketing relations have to do with sponsors, be they individuals or companies, as PR relates to public opinion. Sport organizations often confuse terms such as publicity, advertising, marketing, or positioning because of the small range of their activities to which such concepts apply. Nonetheless, it is important to understand their exact meaning. Study and remember the following terms.

PR

PR, as an externally oriented communication process, includes the activities, attitudes, and behavior that an organization or individual uses to influence, modify, or improve public opinion (potential sponsors or supporters). The aim is to create or change the public's perception of the message or image of the organization (service), the sport itself, a sport event (product), or an individual.

Advertising

This a paid message using any communication means or media vehicle, whether newspapers, magazines, television commercials, billboards, or brochures. A more general definition is to announce, through presentation to the public, the actual or future existence of services, goods, or things (including a person, a group as a whole, or a fact).

Publicity

Publicity is the methodical and systematic notice to the public of services, goods, or things (including a person or group as a whole or a fact).

Marketing

Marketing is the offer and acquisition of products or services to satisfy specific needs of people in exchange for cash or value-in-kind. Products can include use of the organization's image, logo, and space; services include sport events, billboards, and titles.

Trends and Fads

Sport organizations promoting sport events or new products (such as discipline or practice within their sport) should be aware of the difference existing between trends and fads to shield their members from possible disappointments. Trends find their source in consumers and generally last many years, whether on a continuous basis or periodically. They affect events, sport meetings, and cups that may become traditional and boost the culture of the sport. Fads should not be granted the image of the organization because they are normally short-lived, even though they sometimes become traditional events.

In a certain respect, the sport of beach volleyball could be considered as being trendy. However, in view of the long tradition of beach events in many countries and the ongoing TV, media, and economic success of the sport, it received Olympic sport recognition. It has become a hot product in its own right and is in the process of building a culture of its own.

Marketing Concepts and Definitions

To properly draft your marketing strategy and marketing plan, everyone taking part in these drafts should share the same understanding of key concepts and definitions. What follows are definitions of some of the terms you should know.

• **Sport marketing:** The sale by a sport organization of the image of its sport and of its events to satisfy public demand. Organizations can do this on their own behalf or by professional managers or marketing agencies who understand the process of sport marketing and have the necessary selling power.

• **Marketing mix:** The management of certain elements (price, promotion, product, place, public—the 5Ps) to influence and increase demand on the part of the public, consumers, or followers for a given sport, sport events, sport news, sporting goods, and sport organizations.

• **Market research:** The study of people's attitudes toward a product or service and of the elements that influence their behavior as consumers (practitioners, spectators, television viewers, or sporting goods buyers) of that product (sport) or service (organization).

Need for a Marketing Plan

As with any other business, sport organizations and sport events need to emphasize customer satisfaction and pay attention to the spectators, media, and sponsors of their events. They should also keep in mind the need to satisfy their constituency and their own sport practitioners. The way to do this is through a PR or promotional plan.

New organizations or sport events do not require the same tools to satisfy their new customers. But mature and professional organizations need a marketing plan to achieve superior goals or ensure that their sport makes its way into the group of major sports. Marketing opportunities are never there for long and do not wait to catch the eye of sport organizations. They come and go and must be seized ahead of competing organizations. Use some marketing concepts and information during the strategic planning stage, when you are selecting actions, to ensure that the organization is ready and fit to take action.

Defining a Marketing Strategy

Before successfully carrying through any marketing activities, a sport organization must prepare its own marketing strategy for the given event or for the whole sport as a competitive sport activity. In preparing such a strategy, the organization should follow a step-by-step approach as follows:

1. Assess the identity and image of the national or international sport organization and the sport disciplines under its authority.

2. Develop a strategic plan to modify and enhance the image of the organization and of each of its sport disciplines.

3. Communicate with the organizational units involved and implement the plan at the various levels (world, continental, or national).

4. Evaluate the marketing effectiveness and make necessary adjustments at all levels.

5. Prepare marketing plans to satisfy needs, wants, and demands for the sport by different types of sponsors.

6. Define both the process of negotiation and the text of the agreement with potential sponsors to make clear the exchange of product (event or presence at an event) and value (financial or in-kind payments to the sport organization).

7. Identify the needs of youth, spectators, press, and potential sponsors as you formulate your strategy. The marketing plan should include specific proposals to obtain their involvement in the sport events.

8. Analyze marketing opportunities by assessing
   - whether people have the time needed to practice or watch the sport;
   - who pays the money for it,
   - who are potential sponsors, those having a strong financial situation and being willing to link their image to the sport to satisfy their marketing objectives;

142

- the strength of other sport organizations; and
- whether the sport mission statement fits the needs and wants of people selected as potential practitioners, spectators, or sponsors.

9. Define target groups (customers) for the sport: men, women, boys, girls, young, and old and the potential growth of these groups in the community.

10. Estimate income: Define the range of income of people included in the target market.

11. Define marketing mix: Determine what people must give in exchange for practicing or watching the sport (prices); how to put those people in contact with the sport and its events (promotion strategy); and who will deliver the sport organization's or event's image and where (distribution strategy).

Planning Marketing Relations

Marketing relations are activities or means used by the organization to obtain cash or value-in-kind in exchange for services rendered (use of sport image) or products sold (event benefits). Before being able to serve or sell products, sport organizations must find their own specific market place and their own customers, identify those customers' needs and wants, recognize which strategic actions are being used by other sports, and have a clear understanding of the most important marketing concepts.

Positioning the Sport

Positioning the sport means to place the image of the sport organization, its sport, or event in the minds of its customers and to influence the perception they have of the organization and its products (disciplines and events). Positioning the sport requires the prior identification of the needs and wants of its potential customers at a given moment and an awareness of the position of other sports and their strategic actions in the customers' minds.

Sport organizations should understand that they are satisfying human needs rather than their own. The needs will actually grow in direct proportion to the number and intensity of activities undertaken to meet the human needs.

Sport As a Need

How strong an individual's need for a given sport is will determine the type of strategic actions that sport organizations should undertake to satisfy effectively that need and all the subsequent side-needs associated with practicing or watching the sport.

Whatever the priority of their needs, individuals do not actually wish to satisfy such needs and, least of all, to satisfy them with a particular satisfying agent, which will be chosen according to their culture, biological constitution, and impulses. Such individuals might feel compelled to satisfy one need rather than another and to use one satisfying agent rather than another according to their economic, social, ethical, or religious condition.

Demand

In this context, *demand* means a willingness and capacity to purchase goods and services. Along with the feeling of need, people have the impulse of relieving that need or the desire to fill that state of insufficiency (want). Individuals will only be able to do so as allowed by their material, mental, moral, or legal constraints, which may force them to hold back the wish for satisfaction. Those constraints find their origin in economic limitations, cultural shortcomings, religious obligations, and age limits.

Such limitations oblige sport organizations to offer a product (sport) that equals the need for that sport in a measure that practitioners or spectators can afford and that represents their demand. Customers will choose the satisfying agent or sport that best corresponds to the wants stemming from their demand. The actual market for sport organizations is construed by potential competitors, spectators, sponsors, and the media interacting within their own community at the local, regional, continental, and world level.

Marketing Process

Three phases make up the marketing process: the analysis of marketing opportunities, the selection of target groups, and the marketing mix. These phases must be implemented in that order. You could not determine a marketing mix without knowing which event is being organized, who is taking part, and where.

Phase 1: Analyzing Marketing Opportunities

This first phase consists of collecting accurate information that the sport organization will use to assess the chances of success of a given event, program, or activity. The information must include the following:

- The possibilities of organizing an important event, its cost, and the best location
- The difficulty of competing with other sport events, the drawbacks, if any, or the advantages
- The quality or importance of other sport competitions or events already scheduled within its territorial limits

- Whether or not the event or competition falls in line with the organization's mission and corresponds to its objectives, material possibilities, human resources, and financial means

Phase 2: Selecting Target Groups

This second phase consists of measuring market demand, identifying market segmentation, and determining market targeting. You must also develop tactics for influencing consumers to choose your sport over competing ones. Figure 4.4 portrays market targeting and market segmentation for volleyball, swimming, tennis, and athletics.

Market demand is measured with the help of public response to other previously staged similar events, taking into account television audiences, tickets sold, licensing and merchandising results, and so forth. Actual and future growth are also considered, together with the possibility for the public to be ready for another event in the light of possible shifts or changes in the mood or perception of sport events.

Market segmentation means to identify people who could be involved in the event as spectators, practitioners, supporters, sponsors, and media attendants.

Market targeting will answer the questions of who and where are the best potential spectators (members of the organization, regular attendants of public events having the necessary time and financial means), practitioners (team selection), sponsors, and media representatives.

Phase 3: Marketing Mix

The third phase consists of determining the product, place, price, public, and promotion and requires answers to the following questions:

- Which type of spectator regularly attends the sport and which type prefers to attend other sport events?
- With what frequency do the targeted groups normally attend the events staged by the organization?
- What kind of action or promotions could attract new types of spectators?
- What kind of needs or wants of the potential spectators could be satisfied with the event or with promotions based on tickets sold, especially for low-interest competitions?
- Which price will the targeted spectators deem to be affordable?
- What is the best type of media to encourage the attendance of spectators at an event or to motivate them to approach ticket sales offices?

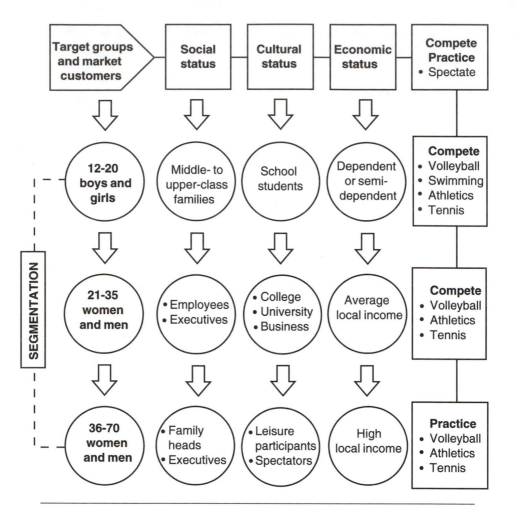

Figure 4.4 Market targeting and market segmentation of sport practiced by students (volleyball, swimming, tennis, and athletics).

The actual design of an effective marketing mix represents the most important decision to be made in placing a sport or event within the reach of spectators or consumers. Product, price, public, promotion, and place (the 5Ps) are the keys to a successful marketing mix and to a better outcome of the plan.

• **Product** means the organization, sport event, or program at its best or highest expression, and each one under top professional conditions.

- **Price** is the contribution to the sport in exchange for the participation of individuals or companies. Decisions on price must take into consideration the adequate balance between the size of the sport or event and the needs and wants of the customers (spectators).

- **Public** means the spectators or participants identified in groups whose needs and wants create the demand. In this sense, the public represents the potential individuals, companies or institutions, constituents, and customers.

- **Place** means the distribution points or outlets where customers (spectators, practitioners, media, and sponsors) can access the sport, the location of the sport organization staging the event, and the location where tickets are distributed.

- **Promotion** means the activities undertaken by the organization to put the sport and its symbols in direct contact with the customers (spectators), or the way in which the sport and the public make contact. It is also called strategy.

Marketing Sport Events

Before choosing any specific marketing approach or tools, sport organizations should assess their present life stage and the current state of the sport in their environment. This is illustrated in table 4.4.

Avoid designing your strategic plan in a rigid manner based on the present stage or situation. Rather, continue to update the plan according to the new conditions arising from current marketing results. One of the first steps is to identify target markets. For a NF, these targets include people involved in the practice of the sport, people involved as spectators, media representatives, and companies or products suiting the needs of people involved in the sport.

Table 4.4 Life Stages As They Correspond to the Current State of a Sport

Life cycle	State of the sport
1. Introductory stage	1. Actual public awareness of the sport
2. Growth stage	2. Increased number of sport events
3. Maturity	3. Multiplication of top-level competitors
4. Decline	4. Lack of public awareness of national athletes

The second stage is to identify other sports attractive to these targeted groups and develop tactics to compete with them from the most advantageous standpoint (choosing the battlefield). A third stage is to design an effective marketing strategy to reach the people and companies targeted and provide the best possible services to meet their highest marketing expectations.

Clients Served

A sport organization is forced to provide, on an ongoing basis, a wide range of services to different groups of people, including participants, spectators, and so on.

Participants

The best services that a sport organization can provide to participants include

- clear-cut sets of rules for sport practice and participation in competitions;
- well-organized units for the daily or weekly practice of the sport (clubs and leagues operating at the local, city, provincial, and national level);
- a regular calendar of competitions or events at all levels (including international if possible); and
- information for referees, officials, and coaches on new rules or trends, as well as continuing education courses in a permanently established recycling process.

Spectators

Spectators must be identified in order to determine their needs. They include those not attending in person (but listening or viewing electronically), those attending (regularly or occasionally), and the media. Spectators and participants should be identified by various criteria in each country:

- Geography: region, size of community, climatic condition, and population density
- Demography: race, family size, sex, occupation, education, national origin, annual income, religion, family life cycle, and age
- Behavior: stage of readiness to practice the sport; attitude toward a given sport; benefits sought through the practice of that sport; loyalty, frequency, and amount of practice; and frequency of attendance as a spectator
- Sociology: social class, lifestyle, and personality

Market Research

To develop a sport marketing program properly, some data are essential. The following are important topics to keep in mind for your market research.

Ticket Purchase

Think about who decides to buy tickets for events. Buying tickets is natural for the traditional fan but can be motivated in others by carefully planned promotion and timely information in the right place.

People have a need for free-time entertainment with family members or friends. They must be aware that a sport event will provide them entertainment and self-satisfaction; they must have the information within reach in entertainment leaflets or newspapers, on television, or on a person-to-person basis.

Promotion

You must provide potential spectators with enough persuasive information to attend a particular sporting event: time, price, and benefits. This information will influence a decision either to buy or reserve a ticket or not to go (if the price is too high or the tickets sold out).

Spectators' Importance to Sponsors

A company will be motivated to sponsor an event or sport on the condition that its own target market (population) is either attending, viewing on TV, or reading about it in newspapers. Potential spectators for a sporting event generate the consumer demand for that event; therefore it is important to know the characteristics of these spectators in order to develop properly the essential elements (the 5Ps) for a successful sport marketing plan.

Customer Satisfaction

Keep in mind that a satisfied customer will usually come back for more. After attending a sport event, an individual will assess the performance, having either been satisfied (and be back next time) or not satisfied (and most likely not return).

Corporate and Event Sponsorship

Corporate and event sponsorship are two different aspects of sport marketing. Both presuppose the realization of the objectives of the companies on the one hand, and of the event organizer on the other.

From the point of view of a company, *corporate sponsorship* is the identification of the company's product, name, or logo with the image of a sport-related unit, such as athletes, officials, national or international sport bodies, and championships or cups, to achieve corporate objectives or marketing goals. This is one of the most productive sources of income for an organization having a marketing strategy and a plan.

Through corporate sponsorship, companies enjoy promotional flexibility. They can achieve different promotional objectives through different levels of participation as either title sponsor, main sponsor, cosponsor, presenting sponsor, official sponsor, official supplier, participating sponsor, or licensee.

Companies may search for marketing combinations to obtain maximum benefits, depending on the objectives they wish to achieve. The elements of promotion found in corporate sponsorship are PR, advertising, publicity, personal sales, and sales promotion. In accordance with their objectives, companies can consider corporate sponsorship as one of those in this list or as a hybrid form of communication. Corporate sponsorship offers cost, market, and geographic flexibility through different types of events and free media coverage to increase credibility, improve image, and generate higher levels of awareness.

Event sponsorship, also called marketing of sport events, brings income in exchange for the use of a sport event's image in publicity campaigns; the use of its facilities during the event for sampling products or the sale of beverages, food, or gadgets; or the use of available space for advertising. These opportunities may be offered to several different companies that consider the sport event appropriate for their corporate marketing objectives. Event sponsorship can meet corporate objectives to create, maintain, or reposition the corporate image; generate sales revenue; provide community support; and fulfill corporate social responsibility.

CONCLUSION

Nurturing a professional relationship with the media is one of the most important duties of sport managers. They should develop special sensitivity and obtain as much information as possible to perfect contacts not only with journalists and television or radio commentators but with editors and directors as well.

Competitive sport can only survive and develop with adequate media coverage, providing the necessary input to a major sport event and bringing it to the forefront of current news. A relationship with the press, radio, and television news departments should include an effective, continuous flow of information ready for use in the case of available space.

A full-time media officer manages the distribution of information. This person will take personal care of the journalists attending events, coordinate organization of press conferences, follow up the press accreditation process, and supervise the press releases before the event and the smooth running of the media center during the event.

An organization must also be aware that PR activities influence the image and reputation of the sport and its organization. Capitalize on PR at every available opportunity. This starts with the conduct of the members of the organization, which should be positive to reflect well on the group.

Creating allegiance and a feeling of loyalty is the ultimate goal of human relations within the organization. In this regard, every organization should produce in its members the certainty that they belong to it. However, their allegiance and loyalty should not be used to avoid dealing with conflicts inside the organization. Although internal conflicts originate in the specific interests of a subgroup, their existence does not imply the absence of that subgroup's loyalty to the organization as a whole.

Group feelings and loyalty result in the sense of pride that comes from belonging to the organization. Pride can be developed by sharing information, reaching common agreement on objectives by consensus, and increasing participation of members. Employees' or members' feelings of involvement, satisfaction, and pride are by-products of having a way to gain recognition, getting recognition for achievements, an agreeable atmosphere, employment security, justice, equity, and competent management within the organization.

The other major aspect of PR has to do with relations outside the organization. The first management level embodies the trend and spirit of the organization. Whatever they say speaks for the organization's leadership. If they are incompetent, the president and the organization as a whole will also be viewed as incompetent.

The organization should have someone who speaks on its behalf. The best speakers are the athletes themselves, who experience the benefits of the sport they practice. Alongside athletes, NF paid staff and volunteers play an important role in PR as well as in promotion and fund-raising activities.

Promotion is any way in which the sport or its symbols and the public make contact. Good promotional activities should inform, remind, and persuade. Plan such activities around themes or slogans that are well implemented and periodically evaluated. NFs and leagues should only promote their own success, not failure, and avoid mentioning others' failures.

National and local organizations must be aware that promotional and PR efforts are essential to fund-raising. At certain times they specifically seek money; most of the time they work to improve the image of the sport or the organization and a better perception by the public at large.

People Leading the Way

Worldwide organizations are not the only ones with people leading the way in sport; national and local organizations originate proposals that are eventually approved at the world level. In the next chapters we will see that every person responsible for a sport organization, association, or national federation is leading the way for many people involved in sport practice, promotions, and even business.

Sport managers are important, but every city and region involved in sport also plays a key part in sport leadership, from the point of view that they are at the terminal end of the chain. Communicators, marketing agents in sports, sporting goods manufacturers, journalists, television commentators, and many more are part of the sport world, and in many respects they are also part of the people leading the way.

five

BEING THE SPORT MANAGER

Courtesy of Nuova Immagine.

> **And when we think we lead, we are most led.**
>
> *Lord Byron,* The Two Foscari

This chapter is dedicated to sport managers, the people supposedly leading sport organizations, but who, unfortunately, find themselves very often led against their will by political, economic, and a host of other factors. Sooner or later they find themselves feeling the same as Lord Byron in this chapter's opening quotation.

This chapter will deal with one of the most sensitive aspects of this work. Everybody knows that human relations more often than not depend on the character and temperament of the individuals rather than their intelligence. The chapter will explain some management concepts regarding the organization's internal and external environment, which sport managers have to understand and learn to manage. It will also examine some important principles that facilitate the management of an organization, its members, and employees and include a description of the world of sport managers.

Chapter 4 has already considered the internal and external factors of a NF or sport organization and how you could analyze and manage such factors to create a marketing plan for the benefit of the organization. This chapter will examine the role of managers and what your attitude as a manager should be when handling specific situations.

Basics of Sport Management

The value of a state [organization in general] is in the long run the value of the individuals who constitute it. A state [or organization] that belittles men in order to have them in its hands as docile instruments, even for beneficial purposes, will find that with little men nothing great can be accomplished.

E. Burke, Thoughts on the French Revolution

To be an effective sport manager, you should know the general fundamentals about management, understand how they can fit into the sport arena, and then apply them to your own type of organization. You will come back to these fundamentals again and again throughout your career.

Management Concepts

Management duties are fundamentally oriented toward planning, organizing, coordinating, and controlling. A good manager needs these skills as well as personal work performance and decision-making abilities.

Traditional concepts of management have been classified by approach, such as classical, behavioral, management science, systems, and contingency. Each approach helps us understand how and why managers function as they do. This being said, each manager's personality and behavior will influence his or her own personal management style.

Classical Management

Classical management is basically founded on the belief that each manager must master a high level of skills as well as abilities for planning, organizing, coordinating, and controlling. This relates to work with employees and collaborators, as well as local and regional units of the entire organization, affiliated members, clubs, leagues, and other affiliated organizations. This concept is closely linked to the following definitions:

- **Planning:** the establishment of goals, objectives, and strategies
- **Organizing:** the selection and grouping of appropriate actions to accomplish the organization's strategies and the design of suitable structures to assist in attaining the organization's goals and objectives
- **Coordinating:** interrelating people and departments to assure that each unit functions as a whole and maintains its activities in line with organizational goals and objectives
- **Controlling:** overseeing the maintenance of a course of action, the completion of plans, and the correction of mistakes

Behavioral Management

Behavioral management is based on the principle of people's motivation, which goes beyond planning, organizing, coordinating, and controlling. Individual productivity improves when people are motivated by their own needs, wishes, and desires. They will more readily achieve goals they willingly undertake. Treating people with dignity and individual consideration helps them identify with the organization.

Management Science

This style uses the precision of statistics, mathematics, and high technology to assist management more effectively. Operations like manufacturing have been boosted significantly by the introduction of computers and robots.

This concept is also valid for NFs as there is increasing need to give demographic information to sponsors, technical statistics to the media, and even more sophisticated online statistics to television broadcasters. To satisfy this need, the FIVB has, for instance, prepared its own Volleyball Information System (VIS) and is currently working on the development of its "Volleyball Demographics." This will instantly provide valuable information to sponsors, showing volleyball and beach volleyball participation at all levels and outlining the economic and social conditions of participants. Football, ice hockey, and other IFs have also made similar studies.

This style of management works well with operational tasks, such as planning sport events, controlling goods and services, monitoring employee satisfaction, and stock-taking. The latter is not only related to sport material and equipment but also to the calendar of traditional events in which national teams and athletes participate at home and abroad, considering that the top quality of such events makes them marketable products.

Systems Management

This concept is based on the coordination of all aspects—planning, organizing, and controlling employee behavior and operations—so that together they function as an integrated system. The better such general functions are coordinated, the more successful management will be.

Every organization is a system consisting of duly integrated parts. Managers must therefore ensure that all parts function as a whole in order to meet successfully the goals and objectives of each part and the organization as a whole.

Contingency Concept

This concept asserts that there is no "best way" to manage a given organization. Management depends on the context of each particular situation. Managers will find adequate solutions on a case-by-case basis.

Managing in the Sport Environment

The environment of national sport organizations is made up of internal and external factors. External factors, those found in the outside world, include economic, political, cultural, or social conditions faced by individuals involved in sport activities. Internal factors include the sport organization's internal working conditions and administrative activities.

The success of operations depends on the awareness by managers of internal factors such as job levels, skills, employee capabilities, roles, and motivation in regard to the objectives of the organization. Of equal importance are the external factors, such as the global economy, local economy, technology, politics, competitor penetration of the same market, youth needs and trends, and the social and cultural environment of youth. In a perma-

managers, forcing them to be selective and discouraging them from taking undue risks by recruiting unqualified personnel.

Choosing Your Staff

Before fulfilling the primary responsibility of choosing staff and employing a person for the organization, you as a manager should take the following steps:

• Describe the job profile exactly, defining the demands, particularities, experience, and abilities needed for the position.

• Rely on the advice of competent external organizations and people.

• Compare the candidates during the interviews, and ask yourself the following questions in the process:

• Does each person have the qualities required to fill the position?

• Are one person's shortcomings a decisive factor in determining competence for the position?

• Has each person given sufficient reasons to be identifiable with the organization or the position?

The best candidate will be the one whose efforts will best contribute to the goals of the organization and who is capable of working efficiently and in harmony with other colleagues.

Management Function in Sport

All levels of management are present in any organization and each level calls for individual technical, human, and conceptual skills. At the same time, every manager must perform a range of basic functions: organizational, interpersonal, decision-making, and informational.

The most important quality for a successful sport manager is to know how to motivate, coordinate, and improve employee productivity, interpersonal relationships, and strategic actions within the organization. Employees are an organization's bottom line of success or failure.

Previous sections depicted managers within the context of their organization and briefly considered the internal and external environments that affect the outcome of management decisions. This section will define the manager's function, executive powers, authority, qualities, decision-making abilities, and the need to delegate. Closer consideration will also be given to ways of motivating people, coordinating efforts, and communicating the compelling vision of the organization. It is vital to learn how to exercise leadership and to understand what exactly is expected from a leader. To this end, an explanation is given of some important rules for managers, which have been grouped under what are known as the "Lundborg Laws."

Defining the Manager

The definition of "manager" found in dictionaries gives us a few clues as to how to identify the managers of organizations. *Collins English Dictionary, Millenium Edition* defines a manager as "a person who directs or manages an organization, industry, shop, etc.; a person who controls the business affairs of an actor or the training of a sportsman or a team." Peter Drücker (1954) defines managers as follows: "Managers are the highest ranked employees or persons in charge of an organization who, because of their responsible position and the knowledge they possess, have to take decisions in the parameters of their work, decisions which have an important effect on the progress and results of the organization in general." To this should be added that managers are also those persons in charge of units of the organization whose decisions have an important effect on the achievement of the objectives assigned to their units and of those of the organization as a whole.

Executive Powers of Managers

The executive powers come with a manager's job description, even if sometimes managers do not know how to exert such power. Managers, coordinators, and directors can be found at different levels of the organization, where they deal with duties similar to those of the general secretaries or president. The duties of the former also include planning, organizing, controlling, integrating, motivating, and evaluating, even if their field of action is more limited than the latter's. See figure 5.2 for a graphic image of a manager's responsibilities.

Executives Versus Administrators

Authority is vested in the managers of the organization to a greater or lesser degree. Theoretically, authority increases in high-level managers and decreases in low-level managers, because of the responsibilities assigned to them. Naturally, the responsibility to do a job implies the authority to accomplish it.

It is sometimes said that administrators are not managers and vice-versa. This observation refers to the supervisory role of managers through which

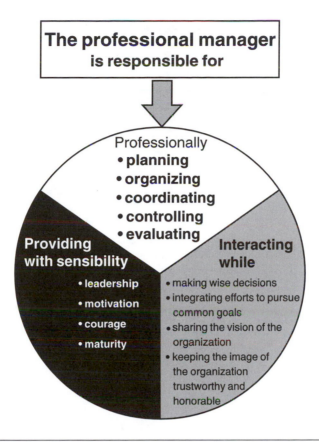

Figure 5.2 The three facets of the professional manager.

they can influence the attitude and behavior of others. When power and authority are in good balance, subordinates unhesitatingly follow the requests formulated by their managers. Some administrators are not managers because all they do is supervise the work of other employees, without giving any orders pertaining to the character of the work to be performed. It also happens that administrators are not managers because they do not actually supervise a specific group of employees, even though they do make decisions that have an important bearing on the results of the organization.

Exercising Authority

The president and general secretary, as chief executive officer (CEO), chief organizational officer (COO), or executive director of a sport organization, together with their various directors, must give their employees necessary guidance. It is equally important to ensure that employees do not lose interest in fulfilling their responsibilities. In addition, they should also ensure that their managers do not entrust their own tasks to those they are responsible for supervising and unfairly take advantage of a given situation. Appropriate delegation of tasks is the subject of a future section of this chapter.

After a trial period, employees must know how to perform the tasks allotted to them. In instances where they are required to apply criteria, make decisions, or correct reports or memoranda, the president, general secretary, or their directors should avoid taking over the duties assigned to such employees. A manager must be able to teach an employee how to improve performance without imposing the manager's own work methods. The idea is to inspire confidence in such a way that employees find their own work methods.

Delegating Authority

Effective managers should understand that they can delegate to their subordinates only specific tasks and responsibilities and not overall responsibility. A manager who delegates always remains responsible for the task that has been entrusted. However, delegation is only effective when it goes hand in hand with the authority to accomplish the task properly. If this is not the case, the result can be a power vacuum and ultimately anarchy.

Power and Authority

Power and authority should be vested in the same person in order to legitimize the instructions issued to that person's subordinates. Do not circumvent the supervisor or director of a section by issuing orders from a higher level of authority. Avoid conflicts of authority between an employee's supervisor and a manager occupying a higher position. To maintain peace in the workplace, do not break the chain of command.

Giving and Receiving Work Instructions

Employees should generally implement instructions they receive. However, it is advisable for managers to accept certain initiatives on the part of subordinates and occasional—but not regular—resistance from them when they are given irrational or improper instructions by a superior. They may be courageous enough to say "no" or they may just remain silent. To a certain extent, that "no" can protect superiors from their own blunders and should not be viewed necessarily as a sign of rebellion.

Subordinates must be able to negotiate with their supervisors in the case of unreasonable demands. Some delays, for instance, are impossible to

When delegating to subordinates, managers must be certain to delegate *specific* tasks and responsibilities and never the *overall* responsibility.

avoid; some tasks are beyond human reach. However, it is not suggested that a superior renounce a decision; rather, be prepared to discuss it openly with the employee and be receptive to questions raised by the latter, in particular with regard to deadlines.

Decision-Making Power

Decision-making power is a characteristic of managers, although it is often a means to achieve more important goals such as efficiency, productivity, or coordination. Those managers who are responsible for obtaining maximum returns for their organization and achieving the most favorable balance in its overall activities are genuine manager-administrators. As such, they have the responsibility and the authority to make decisions that will decisively influence the results of the organization.

To obtain superior and lasting results, a manager-administrator needs time to consider what the impact of his decisions will be on the attitude of his or her employees and on the output of their final work. When studying a given situation in order to make an important decision, it is necessary to keep in mind not only the immediate effects but also the long-lasting results of that decision. Reaching an objective or failing to do so is a temporary issue, whereas permanent consolidation takes considerably longer.

The Decision-Making Process

The main challenge in a decision-making process is how to choose the best available option rather than just any one of them; the biggest risk is choosing the option that leads nowhere.

There are six steps in the decision-making process:

1. Determine the need to make a decision.
2. Establish criteria (or key points) to be applied.
3. Assign priorities for each of the criteria.
4. List alternative choices.
5. Select the best alternative.
6. Implement the choice and evaluate its effectiveness.

These are all simple, straightforward steps. However, there is more to making a decision than these steps. Before making a decision, you must do some research. Always know exactly what you're getting into by making sure all the facts are available. Take advantage of history by finding out precedents in similar situations. You might be surprised at the consequences others had to face for similar or opposite decisions. Finally, time the decision well; complex decisions need time for plenty of consideration. The decision-making process will be made easier by the establishment of realistic criteria, after a careful analysis of options.

As a manager, it is important that you become an excellent decision maker and surround yourself with a staff that possess good decision-making qualities, such as the following:

• **Experience.** Fewer mistakes will come from those having made similar decisions under similar circumstances.

• **Creativity.** A valuable skill in decision making is being able to find other options or angles for approaching problems.

• **Good judgment.** A good decision maker must have common sense and strong business sense.

• **Quantitative skills.** Being able to analyze market and economic trends, event reports on television or in the press, and related research helps people make sound decisions.

Different Types of Decisions

In your career, you will encounter different types of decisions. Understanding these can help you become a good decision maker. Decisions fall into either the programmed or nonprogrammed categories.

Programmed decisions are guidelines prepared for certain situations, such as employee regulations, equipment standards, competition regulations, and safety requirements. These decisions are based on policies, regulations, guidelines, or standards; for example, the mattress for the high jump and the mattress for the pole vault are described by IAAF. When applying for approval, the decision will be made by the IAAF after comparing the specified standard with the sample provided. *Nonprogrammed decisions* are different because of their singularity. They could relate to establishing a new competition, event, or category, or drawing up a new program. These decisions are made by middle- and upper-level management. However, group consultation of the people involved is important. The selection of 5 officials out of 50 candidates for an event is an example of a nonprogrammed decision.

Motivating People

The most important quality for a successful sport manager is to know how to motivate staff to improve employee productivity, interpersonal relationships, and strategic actions of the organization.

Pinpointing the true nature of motivation implies discovering the essence of human behavior. Herzberg (1959) defines motivation as "a personality trait that directs intensity and initiates behavior. It cannot be observed, only inferred." This definition applies more specifically to individual perception. However, from the organizational point of view, motivation is the force moving employees and managers in a sustained effort toward prompt achievement of the goals and objectives of the organization. Motivated employees increase productivity, raise work levels, and identify their individual interests with those of the organization.

The motivational process is closely linked to goal-directed behavior. It starts with an unsatisfied need (or goal) that an individual wants to satisfy or achieve. Motivation can be easily transmitted to others, which is why highly motivated members, collaborators, and employees can easily obtain enthusiastic responses from other people, are easy to convince, and are willing to take part in the sport or become involved in the organization itself. The result is goal-directed action or behavior.

A highly motivated person who achieves a goal is never entirely satisfied with the achievement and will consequently turn to another objective. In this case, there is the risk of job burnout if the unsatisfied state continues to repeat itself. When such a case is detected, that person should be reassured of the manager's confidence and recognition of his or her achievements by the organization. It would be convenient to grant that person a leave of absence but not to reduce his or her responsibilities.

Motivation Theories

Some people often miss goals because of their failure to adopt a goal-oriented behavior pattern. Combining planning and goal-setting skills from the management-by-objective process is the key to motivation. A priority goal system for management may avoid job burnout and facilitate employee motivation in the work assignment. Several theories try to analyze and explain motivation.

Maslow's Theory This theory on hierarchy evaluates motivation in the priority that an individual assigns to his or her needs and establishes five levels of human needs outlined in order of lower-level to higher-level needs:

5. Self-actualization (total fulfillment in all areas of human growth and potential)
4. Self-esteem (recognition by others)
3. Social needs (love and affection)
2. Safety needs (shelter and protection from physical harm)
1. Physiological needs (primary biological needs)

Maslow's (1954) theory states that each stage must be fulfilled before the next one can be reached. Some critics agree that individuals vacillate from stage to stage at various times during their careers. Furthermore, not everyone is willing to, or capable of, being driven toward the self-esteem or self-actualization stages as a result of their job experience. They fulfill these stages outside their job environment.

Another stage was added by Sergeoroni and that is self-autonomy, between self-esteem and self-actualization, representing the employee's need for greater control. Lower needs are satisfied more through external rewards whereas higher needs (esteem/actualization) are fulfilled through internal satisfaction.

Maclelland's Theory This theory states that the primary motivations for an employee in the workplace are achievement, affiliation, and power. Some people need to succeed only for the success itself. They wish to do things better, so they do well with moderately challenging goals and rapid feedback on their performance. They are very competitive by nature and dislike improvisation or situations left to chance, as well as tasks that are either too difficult or too easy. The need for affiliation and power is a greater motivation for success today than is the need for achievement. Among managers, the need for power is greater than the need for affiliation.

Herzberg's Motivation Theory   This theory, from 1966, states that two kinds of factors are involved in employee motivation:

1. **Maintenance factors.** If these factors are absent, employees are not satisfied; if they are present, employees are not sufficiently motivated. Employee satisfaction is strengthened by the presence of factors such as salary; job security; status; working conditions; satisfactory interpersonal relationships with peers, subordinates, and supervisors; company policy; and administration. But these are not enough to provide motivation.

2. **Motivational factors.** The absence of these factors does not bring dissatisfaction to employees, but when present they help to motivate employees. They include achievement, recognition, advancement, responsibility, possibility of personal growth, and the challenge of the work itself.

Maintenance factors are external to the job, while motivational factors are directly linked to the job. Organizational principles such as delegating authority and decentralization, as well as greater autonomy, self-esteem, and self-control, can be effective motivational weapons within the organization.

Theory of Expectations   This theory is based on expectations linked to certain job elements, such as job description, personal ability, and requirements of a job situation. When the job description and the requirements to do a job are clearly explained and identified with the employee's personal ability, you can drive motivational behavior.

The degree of motivation is linked to the degree of certainty that an expected outcome will follow and how attractive that outcome is to the individual. The will to produce something at a certain time or in a given situation depends on the individual's goals and expectation that they are achievable. The strength of the effort is directly related to the strength of the belief that the goal will be achieved through that effort. A manager can influence the individual's degree of response by acknowledging his or her special needs and strengths and providing support and advice.

Factors in Employee Motivation

In sport management of personnel, equity and money are important factors that may affect employee motivation. There are some differences in these factors between the public and private sectors. It is believed that public sector employee motivation is low, although this is not always true. Research has found that the public sector does already offer employees job security. For this reason, self-actualization is a better motivating factor for them. They are also more satisfied with direct economic benefits than are private employees.

Equity   Individuals are concerned about equity not only in terms of the absolute reward provided to them by the organization, but also in terms of how their economic gain for work performed relates to that of others. When ratios are equal or similar, equity exists, positively affecting the work environment and motivation of employees. When there is not equity, problems arise. Rewards that are proportional to effort are critical in satisfying employees and motivating job performance. If an individual's productivity is higher than others while earning a similar salary, there will be tension at work.

Money   Money is a high motivation for some people; for others it is not. Whenever money is the motivating factor, there must be a link between performance and reward. People looking for money are really motivated to better performance only if they perceive the link between their increased performance and their reward in the form of more money. Money seekers will be motivated only when they see a monetary reward as able to satisfy their personal goals and when it is clearly perceived as conditional on performance criteria.

Understanding Leadership

A sport organization needs leadership, just as a community, society, or enterprise needs someone in charge of the day-to-day affairs, solving differences of opinion, and choosing from available options. This person will have the overall responsibility and thus must be given the authority and powers required to fulfill the function in accordance with the expectations of the group and maintain their efforts in line with the objectives of the organization.

Leadership requires the ability to influence others and the capacity to assume a position of responsibility. It is intertwined with all managerial functions. To implement programs, to ensure that departments are organized efficiently and operate effectively, to motivate employees, to make decisions, and to manage by objectives, managers have to lead other people.

Leadership Theories

There are three theories explaining leadership: *trait, behavior,* and *contingency.*

Trait   The *trait* theory claims that leaders are born with specific traits, such as charisma, intelligence, assertiveness, enthusiasm, empathy, courage, and loyalty. This theory neglects the fact that many people with all these traits are *not* leaders.

Behavior   The behavior theory concludes that leadership as a behavior can be taught. Some authors, such as Professor Lekert of Michigan University, say that successful leaders are considerate toward employees and skilled at defending and organizing jobs and departments. Lekert speaks of two kinds of leadership: employee-oriented and production-oriented. Employee-oriented leaders are more effective. Production-oriented leaders show low productivity and greater job dissatisfaction among employees. Being considerate toward employees is paramount to effective leadership behavior.

Other authors find that most successful leaders use the "Management Grid," which consists of a series of links interconnecting people to develop mutual goals and respect between managers and employees by creating a shared vision of the organization.

Contingency   The *contingency* theory explains how leaders can adapt their interventions and decisions to be made in the domain of their responsibilities to different situations. This model is focused on the autocratic-democratic continuous model. Employees are more satisfied under democratic leaders who elicit feedback from them and involve them in decision making. Yet, while some groups under democratic leadership are very productive, others are even more productive in an autocratic mode.

Your Leadership Style

Overly routine and structured jobs create a desire in employees for greater control and less leadership. Complicated or ambiguous jobs make employees more likely to require leadership. Pay attention to the strengths of employees as you assign tasks. A successful leader has mastered two important management areas: assessing the needs in a given situation and understanding employee needs and wishes.

Less educated employees, as well as those who are inexperienced or not internally motivated, require a more *autocratic* style of leadership. Autocratic leadership is required in situations involving new employees executing simple tasks. Highly educated, self-motivated employees want to take part in the decision-making process and require a more democratic leadership style. The *participatory* leadership style is recommended when dealing with complicated tasks that are entrusted to experienced employees. A good leader results in good followers by hiring the right person for the right job, establishing a shared vision of how to accomplish job goals, and understanding that every work situation and specific employee will need a different leadership style.

Characteristics of Good Leaders

Sport managers need to administer, facilitate, guide, and coordinate the activities of employees, volunteers, and affiliated members toward achieving the goals and objectives of the organization. To do this well, they must model leadership with courage and maturity to the employees of the sport organization. These characteristics will help maintain the services and loyalty of skilled and motivated workers, which is essential to the organization. Good leaders are also loyal, supportive, and unbiased when overseeing others, motivating them, and evaluating their actions. They give employees due credit for their work. Effective leadership then provides confidence, receptiveness, and meaningful work for employees and volunteers as they work to attain goals and objectives.

Along with the charisma required to rally everyone behind them, leaders must also have credibility, determination, knowledge, self-confidence, and empathy. Additional qualities essential to leadership include articulating and communicating ideas in a simple, precise, and coherent manner. You need to be able to attract voluntary cooperation, as well as present yourself appropriately.

Attracting Voluntary Cooperation

A sport manager should also lead by attracting the enthusiastic and voluntary cooperation and participation of people to whom the accomplishment of a common task will bring personal or collective benefits.

Good leaders are not tyrants or despots who exercise power in an aggressive manner to impose their will on others. They have personal inborn or acquired qualities that make people want to follow them with faith and enthusiasm. There are born leaders in history, but most of them become leaders through a series of social influences and personal learning experiences. Among other qualities, a good leader

- knows where to go and how to get there;
- has determination, courage, and a tenacious character;
- acts in line with principles, never trading them for personal gain or profit, and has people's trust;
- articulately and enthusiastically communicates the importance of tasks and a feeling of confidence in the accomplishment of objectives and goals; and
- communicates self-confidence to employees that they can accomplish the tasks they are assigned.

Presenting Yourself

A leader projects a charismatic profile and appears to always stand alone, be self-assured, and unfailingly face up to responsibilities. Physical qualities that can help in the early stages of a career include charm, appeal, and good looks. However, these qualities are not essential to a leader.

It is important to note that leaders are not mere conductors of the masses or groups, but individuals who speak with clarity and precision. They are able to instill faith in the followers themselves and in the mission they want to accomplish. They are winners whose spirits, without anticipating results, provide a winning morale to their followers.

The Lundborg Laws

The following principles are known as the "Lundborg Laws," and it may be useful to keep them in mind to improve managerial performance:

1. Do not make unnecessary efforts (law of the least effort). Managers should not take all the workload on themselves.

2. Select only the best and most worthy. Worthy collaborators are difficult to find, difficult to manage, and difficult to control, but in the end their merits produce higher productivity and less expenditure.

3. Do not settle for mediocrity. Mediocrity is the organization's worst enemy.

4. Allow freedom of movement. First-class employees will not improve results if they are not allowed a little latitude.

5. Do not seek excuses. If something goes wrong, do not make up excuses nor look around for a scapegoat.

6. Work while keeping an eye on the clock. Keep track of schedules and deadlines. First deliberations must be completely planned.

7. Look and communicate with eyes and ears. Make contact.

8. Keep the motor running and well oiled. Try always to be first and in good shape.

Enhancing Your Management Abilities

Every position in a hierarchical organization is eventually taken by an incompetent person, because generally the managers or directors have risen step by step until they exceed the limit of their competence. This is called "Peter's Principle."

Peter Drücker, The Practice of Management

Having studied essential items relating to the management of the organization and the functioning of the sport manager, it is necessary to provide the manager with some clues as to how to improve fundamental skills in making decisions, assigning functions, selecting assistants, appointing managers to the different divisions of the organization, and managing time effectively. At the same time, it is essential to safeguard one's own health, that of one's family, and, last but not least, the organization's.

This section will also address several other important tasks, such as handling documents, using a secretary's capabilities to the full, organizing archives, knowing how to manage sport conflicts, and applying disciplinary measures in the office and among the members of the organization.

The Fundamentals

If sport organizations are to be led properly, leaders must pay special attention to the management skills required in any kind of organization:

- Know how to get organized.
- Learn how to control time and schedule activities.
- Avoid useless paperwork.
- Organize archives and files in process.
- Understand leadership and know how to be a leader.
- Understand the function of command.
- Know how to select collaborators.
- Consolidate a working team.
- Establish a good system of organizational communication.
- Coordinate public relations properly.
- Maintain high morale at work and an atmosphere of identity within the organization.
- Control any disturbances in the work environment and avoid conflicts between power and authority.

The first two major decisions of managers should be 1) to identify their personal objectives and those of the organization, since together they constitute the standard values that will form other priorities and 2) to wisely distribute working hours and establish an order of priorities for their work.

Managers of national sport organizations receive different titles due to the different administrative or even cultural or political approaches of sport practice in each country. This is usually why their management responsibilities do not correspond to their titles, whether they be president, general secretary, secretary of commission X, Y, or Z, treasurer, event coordinator, technical coordinator, and so on.

Recently established national sport organizations often lack professional staff, which does not imply that they lack a manager. Usually, this position is fulfilled by a person carrying the title of president or general secretary, who is responsible for managing the affairs of the new organization and for this reason must be familiar with what a management function entails.

Selecting Managers

The selection of managers of major professional sport organizations can be done by recruiting in-house persons already serving in the organization or by hiring professionals with academic backgrounds and prior sport knowledge. When considering prospects, it is important to know the development potential of the candidate and his or her personal ambitions. Keep in mind the quotation of "Peter's Principle" at the beginning of this section.

It is not necessary to give too much importance to the actual positions of managers, but rather to obtain the necessary information concerning their potential development in order to focus on planning their futures in the organization. In general, managers or coordinators concentrate on the development of what they know they are capable of doing well. This knowledge gives them the peace of mind and sense of security that they are looking for.

Self-Management

Managers must put their own activities in order before trying to establish order in the activities of their colleagues. This order will be established through global and personal planning.

Global Planning

Self-management is a method by which each director or manager prepares a general schedule or global plan as part of a working agenda. Within this plan, managers must allocate the time necessary to inform, guide, control, and supervise people reporting to them as well as keep open the channels of personal communication with all other employees.

A manager prepares a general schedule for her or his own guidance, which contains an overview that includes an introductory stage, the time required for completion, and the key dates or deadlines for the completion of each essential operation.

Personal Planning

A good president, general secretary, or coordinator has to get organized. This involves clearly sorting out ideas and defining priorities. The following checklists may be helpful in this task:

Example 1: Determining Priorities

- At the end of the day write down by order of priority the six most important tasks to be done the following day.
- Early the next morning start off with priority task number one and proceed to number two as soon as the first is completed.
- At the end of the day, tear up that day's priority list and work out another in the course of the evening.

Example 2: The Edwin Bliss 80-20 Rule

- Every evening, make out a list of the 10 most important things to do.
- Take time off each morning to work on the first two activities on the list.
- Complete the first two tasks chosen in the time allotted, and start on the next one as soon as this is done.

Analysis of the Job (by Joseph Tricket)

This method was adopted by General Electric during the 1970s with the aim of improving management planning and employee efficiency by saving time in the performance of the duties listed in their job descriptions or profiles. In a series of seminars, employees were instructed in the use of this method, which seems complicated and time-consuming, but which once properly understood is useful for weekly work planning. Managers and supervisors were instructed to proceed as follows:

From their job profiles:

Do the following:

1. **Make out a list of all the activities** that the job entails. Include all the routine and foreseeable tasks. Take 15 minutes to draw up this list.
2. **Analyze the activities** on the list and determine the importance of each task. Move the tasks from the first list onto a second list that has four columns:

Column A: Very important (must be done)

Column B: Important (should be done)

Column C: Less important (not necessary but useful)

Column D: Not important (can be disposed of)

3. **Analyze the tasks in column A by order of importance.** The activities on the first list should now be put onto a third list with four columns:

Column A: Very urgent (must be done urgently)

Column B: Urgent (should be done)

Column C: Not urgent but necessary in the long term

Column D: Time is not the prime factor

4. Study all the tasks to help **decide whether any of them can be delegated.**

5. In order to make a fourth list, **compare the second and third lists and then give priority** to the tasks on the basis of importance and urgency.

6. The fourth list will have as many columns as there are collaborators, including the president of the sport organization or its director.

Column A for the manager: **"I have to do."** List here only the most urgent and the important tasks, even if not urgent.

Column B and following: **"Others can do."** Make a list of the urgent but less important tasks and delegate to a less competent or less expert (in that matter) subordinate. Delegate to the most competent subordinate the most important but less urgent tasks.

7. **Prepare a fifth list** of four columns based on the first list as follows:

Column A: People to speak to directly

Column B: People to see often

Column C: People to see fairly regularly

Column D: People to see less frequently

(The list in column A should have notes on the people with whom contacts should be maintained during the accomplishment of a job.)

Delegating Functions

When delegating functions or tasks, a manager should apply the following basic principles:

- The president or general secretary of the sport organization must handle special problems only and delegate all that is routine. Subordinates should be able to handle the foreseeable problems while superiors must concentrate on the more difficult ones.

- Presidents, general secretaries, or directors must personally carry out the activities for which they have the most expertise and delegate those jobs in which they have the least.

- It is important to delegate work to subordinates who are capable of fulfilling the job as well as, if not better than, the managers, who should retain the work they can do much better than a subordinate.

Handling Documents

Remember this saying: "Have one place for everything and everything in its place." It is important to foresee a place for every document or file in process and to always maintain other documents and files in their initial places.

When papers and documents are badly arranged or spread all over the desk of a president, director, or coordinator, it suggests they lack control in fulfilling their tasks. Such disorganization entails a loss of time and disorderly follow up. The desk should always be tidy and clean and should not be used as a wastebasket by piling up documents or papers. A file, folder, or document should only be on the desk when it is being consulted or processed. When work on that particular document is completed or suspended, the document should immediately be returned to its initial place before work is started on another document.

In instances where documents are to be consulted or worked on periodically, the use of a "pending" tray is recommended. Each time a document is used, it should be taken out and placed on the desk's working surface. If the work is suspended and the document is still likely to be used, it should be placed in the "pending" tray. However, if the document was entirely processed and its file is no longer needed, then the document should be placed in its file and replaced in the file drawers. File documents correctly so as to avoid confusion or loss. Be sure to take all necessary actions on all points in a document before considering it processed.

Whenever a response cannot be prepared immediately, the manager should note, in the margin beside each different point, "agree," "in order," "to be rejected," "finished," or "decision to be made"; if a reply is necessary, write "to be dictated" or a few basic ideas so that the secretary can reply. If a reply on all items is not possible because of the complexity or lack of information, the document should be put in a "pending" tray while the manager asks for the information or particulars needed. It could also be added to the agenda for the next meeting with the collaborators concerned or responsible for such items.

Documents usually lie around on the desk because of the indecisiveness of the person dealing with them. You can effectively handle the indecisiveness by simply addressing the different points in a document that is before you.

When choosing a technique to handle correspondence, you can take into consideration the following methods:

- **Write on the original received.** It is possible to reply to many letters simply by writing on the original, or on a blank piece of paper attached to the original, of which a copy is filed.

- **Use preprinted forms.** These are useful when replying to routine requests for information. Upon receiving a request or letter, the manager marks the correct information on the preprinted form and then sends it.

- **Reduce the contents of a letter to a strict minimum** by noting the points essential for the reply on the original or an attached sheet of paper.

- **Make a draft** rather than scribbling a reply or a few words in a margin, or even tape-record some words or the entire response. It is recommended that the manager and the secretary agree to the method that suits them best, which could be to write out a whole draft or just the points to include in the reply.

Working With Your Secretary

Even if not everyone is able to have a secretary, keeping in mind some of the following points might be useful for you to take proper action by yourself or be prepared for that moment when you will be able to get secretarial support. You will then know what to do!

A secretary assists a manager, director, or coordinator to administer the clerical work of the office. This includes handling correspondence, files, and important documents; keeping records; and following up on specific matters. However, this definition is far too formal and restrictive.

A secretary is not a tool or instrument at the disposal of the manager, but instead a most valuable assistant in fulfilling responsibilities. The secretary is an efficient collaborator whose work entails arranging documents in an orderly manner by classifying, processing, and filing them. Manager and secretary are on the same team, playing for the organization under the same rules and on the same side of the court. They have to know and understand each other, establish a common working and filing system to maintain order, and share the same criteria for the treatment of problems they handle.

Some managers do not understand the need to maintain an ongoing dialogue with their secretaries, though the secretary is supposed to know all the secrets of the department and as much as possible about the organization. Managers must regard their secretaries as true professionals and appreciate them as a confidants, consultants, and colleagues. Secretaries should keep the agenda up-to-date and remind the director of deadlines and important appointments.

Managing Paperwork Together

The manager and secretary must coordinate the management of their papers, documents, and work in general in a way that does not hamper either one's initiative nor submit them to purely administrative working routines. The purpose of being orderly and methodical is to eliminate the tension that comes with disorderliness. Work with your secretary to establish procedures to determine which papers to keep and for how long; file documents by department, project, or another method; and label files to make their contents clear and to avoid searching in more than one place.

Whether you are fortunate enough to have a secretary or are managing your system alone, it is important to keep it organized. The next sections will make recommendations for the areas listed previously.

Creating the Filing System   The alphabetical system is recommended when there is only one type of document to be filed. The pitfall is when there are multiple subjects. A manager's category system has to reflect exactly all activities and functions: each area of responsibility, reports received for review, reports that are "in process," and the coordination of activities between departments and outside groups. A personal filing system is necessary for questions concerning personal activities related to the function of the manager or coordinator. When the director is a member of other organizations or commissions with different activities, a reference file must exist with relative documents included for the next meeting. However, when the meeting is over only file the official reports; the rest can be thrown in the wastebasket.

Computerized processing avoids a certain amount of disorder but does not eliminate the paper element, often coined "paperwork." So as to leave nothing to guesswork, your document handling must be organized and systematic. Lack of order when handling documents or a faulty filing system can prove to be expensive and time consuming. It can result in great delays in the transmission of documents or, worse still, in their loss. Consequently, the manager will not have them when they are needed. It is important to institute a double control of all documents you handle. If, for any reason, you cannot find a document in its file, you will feel relieved that your secretary has a chronological filing of documents she has typed, thus enabling you to find the much needed copy.

When devising a filing system, create the following elements to ensure a properly working double control:

- An organizational scheme or diagram that takes into account all the activities of the sport and clearly indicates the intended location for each document or file
- A list specifying which documents you will keep and for how long
- Instructions on the control of incoming and outgoing files and documents. This control could consist of an index card with the name of the actual file and the date, time, name, and signature of the person taking out the file. Be sure to also record the date when the file was returned.

Filing subject categories required in a sport organization include the following:

- Affiliated clubs, recognized promoters, organizers, leagues, and regions
- Suppliers of equipment and services
- Marketing and promotional activities
- Media outlets with contact information
- Scheduled competitions and their results
- Courses, seminars, and symposia
- Fund-raising activities
- Sponsors for grassroots programs
- Individual sport events
- Players' transfers
- National circuits and tours
- Meetings and congresses
- National athletes
- Federation employees
- Demographics on coaches, referees, judges, officials, and athletes
- Technical commissions and councils

Filing System Upkeep Once the manager and secretary have decided which papers need to be filed and for how long, the secretary should establish a plan for keeping and destroying documents. This plan should be based on a schedule that tells at a glance how long to keep each file: one, two, three months, or more. Establish clearly how long to keep each file and note it on the file. Using a computer avoids a certain amount of disorder but does not eliminate the need for marking details on each file. Whoever is responsible for the files should devote part of each week or month, depending on the amount of documents, to keeping the files up to date. It is advisable to devote a small amount of time every day to this task, so as to facilitate the management and location of documents.

If your organization is large, the central system should satisfy the needs of all the working departments and sections. As the size of the system expands, it may be necessary to employ one or two people to manage and supervise it. The size and diversity of a large filing system requires well-defined control.

Showing Appreciation

The manager's appreciation toward support staff for quality work is essential in communicating the importance of their role. Secretaries who are useful and supportive to their bosses and the organization as a whole must have a reasonable knowledge of all affairs, programs, and projects concerning the department, office, or section. When they understand the importance of their job and the reasons for the goals or tasks they are given and can fully identify with the manager's working methods, they will take pride in their department or section.

Working With a New Secretary

When a new secretary is hired, the manager assumes the responsibility for training. Several decisions must be made right from the beginning between the manager and the new secretary in order to lay down the personal rules of their cooperation and the working methods they will follow.

This initial meeting is not a lecture by the manager or the coordinator to the secretary, but a sincere and honest exchange of views on personal working preferences. Both should agree on how to implement the basic "house" routines and share their own working methods before starting a long-lasting partnership.

Managing Conflicts

Appropriate and effective management of minor differences of opinion can prevent major conflicts in sport. Managers should be sure that organizational policies include proactive policies for dealing with conflict. It is important to be clear about the different kinds of conflicts that may stem from the following situations: interpersonal, institutional, working, and sport-related conduct in competitions. Effective managers should distinguish the kind of conflict situation they are confronting and make sure that all parties involved are fully aware of the regulations with which they are expected to comply. Working relations must be handled in accordance with contractual terms, and managers are expected to follow local customs and legal working conditions.

Enforcement Methods

Regardless of its size, an organization is a community (small or large) in which law and order must govern internal relations that are normally based on common benefit. Managers must enforce law and order, and top-level management must also respect it according to the principles of justice and equity. The problem will always be to decide which enforcement methods the organization should use.

Disciplinary Power It is common practice in some sport organizations that top leaders or first-level managers become defendants, judges, and jury, often performing these functions without the required legal principles or procedures which should exist. In such organizations, managers are able to take disciplinary measures on an arbitrary basis and by unilateral decision. When this occurs, people will see the result as unjust even if the sanction imposed is eventually changed on appeal.

The least a manager should do before imposing a sanction is to implement the following three steps:

1. Collect information and verify it.
2. Request evidence and verify it.
3. Whenever possible, hold a hearing and listen to the parties involved.

The Sport Tribunal Sport organizations should foresee the need for an independent body for appeal in extreme cases to solve complex or legal controversies that may arise. As a manager, you may need to enlist the help of someone else to set this up. Do not perceive this as a failure on your part, but rather a method of taking appropriate action.

CONCLUSION

The executive performance of managers is measured by their personal work; decision-making ability; and their manner of planning, organizing, coordinating, and controlling. Internal and external factors constitute the environment of sport organizations and create their working conditions.

Some of these conditions (economic, political, cultural, or social) originate in the outside world; other factors are part of the organization's own administrative activities and internal working conditions.

A manager's awareness of internal factors, such as job levels and skills and employee capabilities, roles, and motivation, is important to a successful organization. Equal importance, however, must be given to external factors, such as the global economy, local economy, technology, politics, competing organizations' share in the same market, youth needs and trends, and the social and cultural environment of youth.

An organization is as good as its managers and as valuable as the people working for them. Motivated employees perform better and are more productive. Managers must bear in mind the fact that openness in communication eliminates conflicts and that the proper handling of employee interpersonal relations helps to obtain better performance levels.

The belief that administrators are not managers and vice-versa refers to the supervisory ability of managers to use their power (that is the ability to influence the attitude or behavior of others, particularly those they are expected to supervise). When power and authority are in good balance, subordinates unhesitatingly follow the requests formulated by their managers.

Specific tasks and responsibilities can be delegated to a manager's subordinates, but not overall responsibility. The manager who delegates still retains responsibility for the task that has been entrusted. However, delegation is only effective when it goes hand in hand with the authority to accomplish the task properly. If this is not the case, the result can be a power vacuum and ultimately result in anarchy.

Vest power and authority in the same person to legitimize the instructions issued by that person to subordinates. Do not break the chain of command by issuing orders from a higher level of authority. To be effective, a manager must also provide courage and maturity to the people working for the sport. This kind of leadership will provide confidence and meaningful work for employees and volunteers toward the attainment of goals and objectives.

Tyrannical or despotic managers who exercise power in an aggressive manner to impose their will on others will never be able to provide true leadership. They will not make people want to follow them with faith and enthusiasm. Among other qualities, good leaders know where to go and how to get there with determination, courage, and tenacity. In addition, they have credibility and people's trust that their deeds will line up with stated principles; they will never trade such principles for personal gain or profit; and they articulately communicate self-confidence to followers.

Before accepting positions, managers are expected to 1) identify personal objectives with those of the organization and 2) make a wise distribution of working hours, establishing an order of priorities to help organize the work. Once established in the organization, directors and managers must manage themselves through a global plan. Within this plan, managers have to allocate the time necessary to inform, guide, control, and supervise people reporting to them and approach all other employees to keep open the channels of personal communication. Delegate work to subordinates capable of fulfilling the job as well as, if not better than, you but keep for yourself the work you can do much better than a subordinate.

Appropriate and effective conflict management is the best way to prevent major conflicts in sport. Managers should pay attention to the manner in which rules and regulations are approved and ensure the inclusion of provisions for handling conflict. It is important to identify the different conflicts that may stem from the following situations: interpersonal, institutional, working, and sport-related conduct in competitions.

Hearing the parties concerned is the least a manager should do. Before imposing a sanction be sure to collect information and verify it, request evidence and verify it, and whenever possible, hold a hearing and listen to the parties involved.

six

PLANNING YOUR ORGANIZATION'S WORK

Courtesy of Herzog Photography.

> **There is no better comfort against the failure of a plan than to have another in reserve or immediately to prepare a new one.**
>
> **_J.-P. Sartre, French writer_**

Planning in any organization is not the task of one individual, even if it is a primary responsibility of the manager. Every level of the organization should be involved in planning activities. In particular, every manager and employee should take part in operational planning as a part of their duties. This is known as modern _collective planning_, which is sometimes also referred to as _participatory planning_. Lack of coordination and the absence of information in the planning process result in poor participation or the absence of participation by employees. No planning at all implies no targets, no goals, and no programs and means task duplication, plus a general waste of time, energy, and other resources.

All sport organizations and their managers should possess a meaningful knowledge of planning techniques that will be studied in this chapter—in particular, the need for participatory techniques, the process of SWOT analysis, how to implement the plan, and how to divide it into action programs. Finally it must be clear who is to assign responsibilities for each program and it is essential to foresee a contingency plan.

Planning Process

You can never plan the future by the past.

E. Burke, "Letters"

Planning is the act of establishing objectives and goals, followed by selecting actions required to achieve them, assigning tasks (labor division) in compatible administrative units, and arranging administrative units in an organizational structure able to operate as a system. (A _system_ is a series of interrelated, interdependent, and interacting elements, each one reacting as part of a collective entity to a given stimulus.)

Before studying problems and solutions in planning for your sport organization, it is important for you to know the steps in the planning process. Here are some steps you should keep in mind as the manager of your organization:

1. **Selecting objectives** is the most important part of the plan. To successfully achieve a plan, the objectives must be clearly defined and unequivocally understood. All members of the group should be aware of the

plan's preparation, their options for possible involvement, and the means available to enable them to participate.

2. It is essential to have **flexible objectives and actions** to achieve them. The objectives take the form of dynamic human activities that may be modified and for which you should foresee optional courses of action.

3. **Administrative provisions are the backbone** of a plan. They provide the financial, material, and human resources required to complete the activities. Expenses and income should be part of a balanced budget that includes costs for the participation of volunteers, employees, and members, as well as material and operational costs. (See chapter 7 for more information on the budgeting process.)

4. **Follow-up and evaluation** are essential. Each phase, goal, or target of the plan must be measured and its finances compared with the budget. The follow-up of the plan is essential to detect deviations and correct them in a timely fashion.

5. **Planning and control complement** each other. Planning should follow technical requirements and respect methodological principles. Managers can then control the process, supervising the costs and keeping an eye on starting dates and deadlines.

Before entering into significant program planning, managers of a NF should

- understand their organization's operating environment (internal strengths and weaknesses, as well as external opportunities and threats);
- determine its identity (mission statement or compelling vision); and
- understand the importance of the three primary resources (human, material, and financial) and their interactivity.

Planning starts by describing *what* the organization wants to accomplish and which tasks will make this possible, *how* the tasks will be accomplished, *which means* are appropriate to measure whether the organization is moving toward its objectives and when the goals and objectives have actually been reached, and *how* the organization could easily adapt itself to changes in the external environment or those required for the work to be done. If all participants recognize their role in the operation of the plan, it will dispel doubt or confusion regarding what the organization expects from them and reduce job duplication and useless activities. In addition, clear deadlines and priorities in the plan will facilitate a productive environment.

Preparing the Organization for Planning

The process for preparing a plan should follow a certain pattern:

1. **Identify the sport organization's operating conditions** through environmental research and an evaluation of its internal and external factors.
2. **Determine the mission** statement (or "compelling vision").
3. **Set goals** and select objectives.
4. **Allocate necessary resources**—human, material, and financial—to implement the plan.
5. **Implement the actions** under professional management.
6. **Determine a schedule to review and evaluate** the effectiveness of actions and the plan as a whole.

Participatory Strategic Planning*

Preparing a plan is the most difficult and important stage for a sport organization seeking to establish its current identity and determine its own future. The underlying problem is how to put ideas and problems in the right perspective when trying to achieve the goals of the plan. One solution is not to plan at the top of the organization but rather through the participation of individuals representing the whole spectrum of the organization, working in small group sessions that include the most knowledgeable and experienced members. This process is also known as *team planning*.

Group Approach to Problem Solving

Based on a structure similar to the well-known "think tank" sessions, the success of this type of planning depends on the structure, motivation, and involvement of the members, as well as the group-handling skills of the facilitator.

The group will generate plenty of ideas, filtering each one of them through lengthy discussions, adopting or rejecting them by consensus, and leaving only the most acceptable ones for the purposes of planning. The process first requires freewheeling brainstorming of ideas without discussing their validity or quality. Only at a later stage are the ideas analyzed, criticized, and put in order as actual suggestions for planning.

---

*This text is adapted, by permission, from D. Stevens, 1993, *Participatory Business Planning* (Australia: Wrightbooks), 41-66.

Forming a Planning Group

When you are forming a planning group, invite members from various important areas and levels of the NF. Some of them should be able to contribute technical know-how, others administrative skills, decision-making ability, or problem-solving talents. No single person should dominate the others because this could lead to group conflict and professional intimidation.

The planning group should include no more than 10 members and no less than 8 and could comprise the following:

- One top-level coach and another for low-level athletes
- One top-level judge or referee
- A representative of the most active and competitive club or sport institution
- A representative of a regularly participating university
- A representative of the educational sport system
- A press representative
- The president or head executive of the organization concerned
- The national league executive or the most important organizer of a top sport event
- A representative of one marketing agency or interested TV network

The tasks of the small planning group will be to identify existing problems, find specific solutions to each problem, and determine the internal and external resources that those solutions require.

Role of Facilitator

An external facilitator is essential to the success of think tanks for ensuring everyone's active participation during the planning sessions. Psychologists are the best choice since they can provide motivation and supportive technical information, provoke discussion of controversial issues, and even mediate corporate or interpersonal conflicts.

The role of an external facilitator is to

- focus the group's efforts on positive interactions and general participation;
- ensure that ideas retained include technical expertise, problem-solving approaches, and a clear understanding of the decision-making process;
- avoid individual or group dominance over the majority;

- maintain a creative agenda for long sessions and ensure an adequate physical environment;
- reject professional intimidation by specialists in one area over others; and
- avoid or minimize interpersonal or group conflicts, providing a satisfactory process for dealing with conflict whenever it is needed.

The facilitator can argue, plead, or guide the sharing of opinions, with the aim of ensuring general participation and a sharing of values and information. Facilitation might involve well-placed provocative comments to raise controversial issues or deal with interpersonal conflicts among members. Once the facilitator has explained his or her role, the group will be asked to nominate candidates for the following positions:

- **Holder of the bell,** in charge of sounding the bell if a member breaks a rule

- **Recorder,** to write the policy recommendations in brief or in full when the group is able to articulate the proposal after a lengthy discussion. All such recommendations are written on one sheet of paper for review at the end of the session.

- **The person in charge of the butcher paper,** who will pin the working papers of the brainstorming session to a wall or board and will also write notes on the papers

- **The supplier of additional information,** to keep a record of any important statements that may contain valuable data unrelated to the issues under discussion but which are potentially critical to the organization

Once the group is organized, they may determine by consensus the timetable for the period needed to implement the plan and proceed. All should share their ideas of what a major achievement of the plan would look like by the end of the chosen time period.

When this preparatory session is completed (40-45 minutes), the whole group is ready to tackle the next phase of participatory strategic planning, which consists of preparing a list of ideas through a brainstorming session (another 40-45 minutes). This brainstorming session will subsequently be filtered and analyzed via the strategic diagnosis, also called the SWOT analysis (8-10 hours).

Creating a Strategic Diagnosis

The next step is the process called *strategic diagnosis,* or *SWOT analysis,* which consists of the study of the **S**trengths and **W**eaknesses of the sport governed by the organization, followed by the **O**pportunities and **T**hreats it faces.

The brainstorming session consists of preparing a list of ideas as qualities, flows, and conditions that favor—or situations that prevent—the practice of the sport in question and will go through the following steps:

1. The first individual lists what each of the group members considers to be the **strengths** of the specific sport throughout the country. This list is written on the blackboard without discussion or evaluation. Every other member does the same, adding new or similar strengths, sometimes repeating previous ideas.

2. When the last member writes the last strength, he or she will become the first to write a list of **weaknesses** of that sport in the country. He or she will be followed by the previous member and then by the others in reverse order until reaching the first member, all of them listing what they see as the weaknesses of the sport.

3. This same person is now the first member to list what he or she considers **opportunities** or actions that will lead that sport to success in the country. The next member will add other opportunities and so on until the last member.

4. The same will be done backwards for listing **threats** hampering that sport's development or success in the country. Each member will list situations, attitudes, organizations, individuals, or whatever they consider to be obstacles to the success of the sport that the organization should remove or fight against.

5. Once this is finished, ask all members individually one last time if they have something to add to any of the four lists of strengths, weaknesses, opportunities, and threats. It is important to ensure that nobody has left an idea out of the lists and that such lists are in view of all members, either on the wall or blackboard.

After the brainstorming session, the real strategic diagnosis or SWOT analysis of the four lists of ideas shall be conducted to determine by consensus which of them are recognized as strengths, weaknesses, opportunities, and threats for the sport in question. The examination of each list starts with a clear general definition of the meaning of "strength," taking into consideration each example on the respective list as something that represents an advantage for that sport over other sports in the country. Once the definition is agreed upon by consensus, then the group discusses each idea on the list in light of the definition. Anything that is shared by all other sports must be eliminated because it does not represent a strategic advantage, one that is exclusive to the sport under discussion.

The diagnosis continues with weaknesses, as you clearly determine the meaning—factors that represent a strategic disadvantage for the sport under discussion. Each definition must be prepared on the basis of the corresponding list, which was decided by everyone in the group. There will be a list of weaknesses, a list of strengths, a list of opportunities, and a list of threats. I cannot invent a hypothetical definition without having the above mentioned lists. In this case, you may list weaknesses that are common to other sports. Explain that if the sport finds a way to overcome or solve a weakness listed that is common to each and every other sport, then that weakness will become a strategic advantage for it. Accurately define "opportunities" and "threats" in relation to the sport and its environment, both internal and external.

The so-called diagnosis or *filter debate* takes place when you analyze each idea in relation to the definitions and either put it on a new list or drop it if it does not fit the definitions determined by consensus (never by vote). It is necessary to ensure that the group discusses and evaluates *all* ideas before either discarding them or considering them for the final list of critical elements.

Sometimes it appears during the discussion that a specific issue leads to another and subsequently to yet another (the latter known as the "presenting problem" in opposition to the first issue called "causal problem"). In this case, the group must pay attention to solving only the first (causal problem) and the last issue (presenting problem) and ignore the others. Each final list will have its own heading, such as "Advantages of the sport," "Intrinsic problems to be solved," "Situations to capitalize on," and "Obstacles to overcome."

Once the group has gone through the long list of ideas generated during the brainstorming session, all that will be left are those that match perfectly the respective definitions. Keep these four lists under the general title of "Critical elements of the organization," meaning its actual strengths, weaknesses, opportunities, and threats.

After the final debate of ideas, destroy all the sheets or working papers so that the elements remaining in each of the four final lists will reflect the sport's real situation in the country. Thus, through a process of discussion you will have reduced each list to the critical elements that will constitute the basis of the plan.

Example of a SWOT Analysis
Performed by a Local Athletic Association

Once the brainstorm session had produced four lists of ideas headed by the titles of **strengths, weaknesses, opportunities,** and **threats,** the group

proceeded to determine by consensus which of the ideas in each list satisfied the meaning of each title, discarding those that would not fit.

The members of the group, appointed by the local athletic association, agreed to the following definitions by consensus.

1. **Strength should be any quality, trait, or attribute that advantages only the practice of athletics over other sports in their community.** They discussed each one of the ideas on the list, qualified them, and by consensus decided which ones constituted a real advantage (strength) for the practice of athletics.
2. **Weakness should be a fault, defect, or shortcoming that constitutes a disadvantage or situation against the practice of only athletic activities.** All the weaknesses on the list were then discussed, and by consensus, the group decided which ones were real disadvantages (weaknesses) against athletics.
3. **Opportunities should be situations, favorable circumstances, or chances that can favor the practice of athletics.** All ideas were qualified and agreed on by consensus. The group decided which ones were real opportunities for athletics.
4. **Threats should be situations particularly harmful to the practice of athletics.** All ideas in this column were also filtered through this definition and each approved by consensus or eliminated.

Once all the ideas were discussed and approved or discarded, the ideas remaining in each of the four lists became the *critical elements,* which the group then considered as the basis for the final plan.

With these critical elements, the group may proceed to determine the mission statement or compelling vision of the sport organization or NF and establish the objectives, with mention of each of the critical elements. Immediately afterward, the group discusses the accountability matrix and assigns responsibilities for implementing each of the selected actions, once again by consensus. Those people who are assigned a responsibility propose the time and deadlines for accomplishing their tasks and the kind of resources (human, material, and financial) needed. This constitutes the *resource allocation.*

Making an Action Plan

There are many ways of creating and implementing a strategic plan for the sport organization or NF. Some guidelines are provided here for doing this through a standardized and efficient process that uses the following steps:

1. Research and evaluate the internal and external environment.
2. Draft a mission statement or compelling vision.
3. Establish goals and objectives.
4. Develop a strategy.
5. Allocate resources (human, material, and financial).
6. Implement programs of the plan.
7. Evaluate periodically.

Strategic planning consists of the implementation of each of these steps.

Environmental Research and Evaluation

The research consists of asking questions about the conditions the NF faces in the external world: political and economic conditions, public perception of the sport, and the social and cultural backgrounds of the people for whom the activities are planned. It also involves asking questions about the operational situation of the NF, in terms of available personnel and technological, technical, and economic means available to make the plan possible.

If you already have a plan for managing the organization's image, then this initial stage has been completed. If not, you could use the simple and advisable SWOT method already explained in this chapter, which involves identifying and listing the organization's **Strengths**, **Weaknesses**, **Opportunities**, and **Threats**.

As previously mentioned, this method is designed to analyze both internal factors (strengths and weaknesses) and external factors (opportunities and threats). The analysis will show the "gaps and gains" of the organization and provide a planning platform of critical elements for overcoming gaps and taking advantage of gains. There are many methods to carry out the environmental research and evaluation of a sport organization, including SWOT analysis, surveys, work-planning groups, think tanks, and brainstorming sessions. The most effective process to use with any of these methods, *participatory strategic planning,* was described on pages 192-194.

Mission Statement or Compelling Vision

This statement or vision corresponds to the definition of what is to be accomplished and should usually contain the critical elements of the four environmental conditions identified during the SWOT process. This statement needs to be revised periodically (at least every five years) to keep the operations in line with new environmental conditions (both internal and external). It should be realistic and achievable.

A worldwide organization working at continental and national levels may determine its mission statement and offer it as a guide for its continental and national branches. However, each continent or country may need to introduce some variations into its own statement to take account of particular regional conditions.

For example, the International Volleyball Federation has incorporated its compelling vision in the following mission statement:

> **The Fédération Internationale de Volleyball (FIVB) has the mission to govern and manage all forms of volleyball and beach volleyball world-wide through world-class planning, organising, marketing and promotional activities aimed at developing volleyball as a major world media and entertainment sport.**

The members completed that vision by establishing its organizational goals and objectives, stating that

> **In co-operation with its more than 200 affiliated Federations, the FIVB will achieve this mission through:**
> - **the staging of world-class international events;**
> - **the development of quality programs and resources;**
> - **the application of modern management principles.**
>
> **In all its activities, the FIVB will endeavour:**
> - **to provide equal opportunities to men and women, and maximum enjoyment for participants and spectators;**
> - **to maintain the values of FAIR PLAY and PEACEFUL PARTICIPATION.**

Choosing Organizational Goals and Objectives

Organizational goals and objectives are a more detailed explanation of the mission statement or compelling vision. Each objective should eventually become the subject of a specific program of the plan with details of operational steps by department or section. The mission statement is the source of the organization's objectives, and each objective has specific goals that become partial achievements of that objective, thus making them consequent with the mission statement. The goals and objectives may be based on the critical elements obtained after the discussion of the organization's environmental conditions during the SWOT analysis.

Objectives must be precise, clear, achievable, measurable, realistic, and interesting. People responsible for the actions necessary to achieve the goals must measure their efforts by the accomplishment of such objectives.

The theory called *management by objectives* (MBO), conceived by Peter Drücker in 1954, says, "If objectives are established concurrently by management and employees, they will be realistic, achievable and motivating." People strive for what they perceive as being within their reach. Mutual discussion and joint decisions between management and employees can establish individual and common goals that further the organization's overall mission. Again, the best method for implementing this stage is the SWOT analysis, most effectively carried out through the participatory strategic planning process.

Developing Strategic Actions

Strategies come from combining means and efforts to find the best possible way to reach established goals. The strategy must show the path to follow from the present position to the desired position. *Strategic planning* is making systematic decisions about the human, material, and financial resources required for activities and programs necessary to achieve predetermined goals.

The words "strategy" and "strategic" are often used. Just like the word "businesslike," these words indicate order, discipline, and a professional approach. The word *strategy* has been defined by Franklin Language Master as follows: "Strategy is the science and art of command aimed at meeting the enemy under conditions advantageous to one's own force" (*Franklin Language Master Dictionary*, London), in other words the method chosen to achieve an end. There is no need to stand in awe of these words. Everybody follows a certain strategy for the many things done in private life. To plan in a strategic way actually means to systematize actions in pursuit of personal goals.

Opposite of strategic planning is *operational planning*. It is important to realize that operational planning is needed as well, but you must be aware of the difference between strategic and operational planning. To simplify, the difference between strategic and operational planning is that a strategic approach is needed when deciding or planning *what* to do, but deciding or planning *how* to do it requires an operational approach.

After setting objectives, you must draft an action plan to give direction to the operations. This stage consists of matching the actions to the objectives and arranging their implementation at the operational level. *Strategic actions* could be events, promotional activities, or specific competitions that lead to the achievement of organizational objectives in certain areas. You can focus on one or more areas and be more or less intensive. You can use a marketing approach, such as in the following types of actions:

- **Market penetration** involves action(s) directed toward the groups of people (children, students, or workers) already involved in a given sport.

- **Sport market development** is when you address your action to specific new groups of people you want to incorporate into sport activities, services, or events, thereby developing your market.

- **Sport diversification** is when you diversify by offering a new activity, service, or event to the new group of people being targeted. This requires more personnel and more money and time for publicity, public relations, and services, as well as new strategies for advertising, promoting, and organizing events.

The FIVB took one of the most successful actions in sport diversification and development with the meteoric incorporation of beach volleyball at all levels—national, continental, world, and Olympic. Diversification is costly so you will need to generate sufficient financial resources to cover the inherent cost or leave only a minimal budget deficit.

Allocating Resources

Both the preparation of a plan and the implementation of each program require human resources, together with financial and material means. These resources interrelate and operate in a coordinated manner under the guidelines issued by the management of the organization. They must operate harmoniously with effective intercommunication and work toward achieving the same objectives with clearly defined targets, common tactics, and strict programming. More detail on these different types of resources follows:

- **Material or physical resources** are operational, marketing, and other manipulatable resources such as office space, data processing or duplicating equipment, transportation, and communications equipment.

- **Financial resources** are the funds required for the plan. If human and material resources are not available in the NF or organization concerned, their foreseeable cost must be indicated per year for the whole period to be covered by the plan.

- **Human resources** are the personnel. You must foresee the quantity of people needed to carry out a specific part of the plan; the period for which they will be needed, including starting time; and their salary or compensation.

The NF or organization must prepare an estimated budget and a list of materials with cash-flow dates when each piece of material needs to be available. It is recommended to estimate the resources in a three-part table, indicating in each section the type of resource and specifics in columns as needed. You can obtain resources through fund-raising campaigns, governmental allocations, event sponsorship, and other means. Cash and value-in-kind should not be the only resources you use to cover costs; consider other means of substantial support, like discounts, lotteries, wholesale purchase, and used material.

Implementing the Action Plan

Once the task of packaging actions is completed, the entire plan of the NF for the following years can be considered as ready. However, if everything stops here, nothing will happen. The plan needs to be implemented. The implementation is not the most complicated part of the process, but somehow many plans in various organizations have failed because of problems during this phase.

The main reason for this might be that it is difficult to switch from the very strategic approach to a more operational or practical approach. Therefore, consider changing those in leadership during the planning process, exchanging some of the very creative people for others with a more practical sense with an executive mentality.

The implementation stage must convert plans into concrete actions connected with the resources at hand (finances and personnel). This will involve specifying *how* the actions will be carried out, *who* is going to do them, and *how much* of the available personnel and financial resources will be required.

Private enterprises call the set of activities pursuing a given target or objective *business portfolios* or *units of the plan;* in a sport organization, these correspond to the different programs. Each program should contain the actions required to achieve a certain objective or goal in relation to growth, development, social penetration, or diversification of activities.

Phasing and Scheduling

Phasing is timing the different blocks (phases) of action needed to complete a whole project, and this timing can never be arbitrary. Scheduling is establishing the sequence of phases according to the requirements of the strategy. A schedule is necessary so the project moves through intermediate targets before rushing toward final goals. Base your phasing and scheduling on logical justifications, with a maximum of flexibility and stability at the same time.

Project Management

Successful implementation of any plan depends on adequate management. All those involved must be fully aware of their duties, responsibilities, and authority, as well as be properly informed on the relevant procedures. The project manager (or leader) of a NF or another organization must attend to four aspects of management: adequate organization, clear descriptions of positions, accurate policy statements, and clear system definitions. Refer to chapter 5 for more specific discussions of management issues.

Adequate Organization   You must be able to describe an organization in a structural diagram of boxes placed at different levels and interconnected by lines. The lines represent the relationships between the tasks assigned to a group in one box with those tasks assigned to other boxes. Downward lines represent channels of authority and upward lines represent accountability channels. In general, all lines represent communication channels, but in any case each box represents a set of duties and a scope of authority. The duties are actions to be done by direct order or by an established procedure, while the authority is the decision-making power to carry out those actions. *Immediate command* is the power to override the authority of lower-level people even if that power is not used. *Extended command* is the power that spans to two or three levels below. See figures 2.4 and 2.5 on pages 74 and 76 for sample organizational charts.

Clear Job Description   Specify the following in regard to all positions. (The first three points are typically a part of a *job description* for a position.)

1. List the specific duties and responsibilities of the position. The employee is directly responsible for each one of the tasks and cannot delegate that responsibility. Remember: Even if you can delegate the task itself, you will always be responsible for an adequate execution.
2. List each person who reports to that position and the person to whom that position reports.
3. Describe experiential or educational qualifications for the position, if appropriate.
4. Clarify the scope of authority to make decisions without submitting them for approval.
5. Go over the limits of authority in relation to a higher authority and organizational policy.

Accurate Policy Statement   Policies are compulsory rules for all employees and members of the organization. They protect the general interest of the organization and ensure smooth operations, swift coordination, and higher efficiency. It is important to update and circulate each new or modified policy in a timely manner.

Clear Description of the Organization's Systems   Organizational systems are mechanisms of control to facilitate a fluent operation and reinforce accountability. They constitute a way of detecting breaches in the operations and therefore facilitate the tracing of responsibility.

Creating an Overall Accountability Matrix

You can now make a general description of all programs and activities. Include the links between different activities, the schedule with different phases, and the management of the various projects. At this stage, the action plan is ready and must tell us *who* is going to do *what, how, when,* and through the use of *which resources.*

It is important not to enter into too many details. However, you must list the essentials, such as the nature of the project; final and intermediate objectives; the schedule and phases of the activities; and the personnel, materials, and facilities needed for its implementation. The cost of the plan must mention the amount of money needed to pay for each part of the plan, where the funds will come from, and any specific financial arrangements.

Assigning Responsibilities

Most human activities are part of a plan. But in an organization, as in personal life, if no one accepts responsibility for the implementation of each phase or sets deadlines, that plan will eventually be forgotten. Such will not be the case when the plan includes official assignment of responsibilities and a process for periodic review, evaluation, and adjustment. Assigning who is accountable for what is the most important part of the planning process and the last stage of participatory strategic planning.

The Matrix

The matrix is a record of responsibilities, time frames, costs, goals, actions, and resources needed to achieve an objective. Through this matrix, prepared immediately after the strategic diagnosis, the mission statement, and the objectives are established, the distribution of the critical elements or actions to be undertaken is made among the competent members of the NF that volunteered to undertake each responsibility and who are supposed to be the best for the job. Each issue has one or more goals. Each action will be the responsibility of one person within the organization— and only one. This person is 100% accountable for the accomplishment of that particular action. All people involved indicate the time needed to accomplish the action(s) they chose for themselves and will also set their deadline(s). Encourage people to set realistic timetables and cost estimates. A first-level manager is assigned the responsibility to oversee the implementation and follow-up of the plan as a whole, as well as the responsibility of coordinating the managers responsible for each critical action included.

Periodic Review, Evaluation, and Adjustment

You must develop a process for continual supervision of the progress toward achievement of the goals. Assess progress weekly, monthly, quarterly, annually, or biennially. When a plan specifies goals, strategy, and concrete actions over a long period of time, you also need a system of evaluation and adjustment.

Evaluate the progress on intermediate goals as established for each phase of the plan at least once a year, circulating and celebrating each successful period. Outstanding success in the long run is only possible through several minor short-term successes. Encourage employees to be flexible in anticipation of possible adjustments along the way, since external changes may affect the planning at any point.

The Contingency Plan

If financial, material, or human resources are not available in the amounts required by the original strategic plan, you will need an alternative plan consisting of shorter, more realistic projects. At that point, the NF or organization will need to prepare a contingency plan that includes only those strategic actions for which it has already secured the necessary human, material, and financial resources.

Long-Term Planning

> *When society requires to be rebuilt, there is no use in attempting to rebuild it on the old plan.*
>
> John Stuart Mill, Essay on Coleridge

This chapter has already described the process of planning and its essential principles. Sport managers can now proceed to prepare the organization for long-term planning, which is fundamental to consolidating its operation and identifying its members with the chosen objectives.

Plans can be sorted into short term (one year), medium term (three to four years), or long term (five or more). This section now carries out an overview of the specific needs and problems of a long-term plan, explaining how to start such a plan, describing the advantages of strategic long-term planning, and presenting the questions you need to answer beforehand through environmental research.

Defining Long-Term Planning

Short- and medium-term planning are normally used to settle specific operational matters and PR activities that affect the organization's image, whereas long-term planning concerns the whole structure acting during a long period of time that is needed to reach a very important goal in line with its mission statement.

Collective Effort

A long-term plan should not be a series of good intentions for political purposes, but instead a united effort at all levels—local, regional, and national—involving concerted action. The plan not only helps unify the workplace, but, more importantly, is a genuine and permanent effort to identify the local, regional, and national sport context, along with institutional advantages and shortcomings, and make improvements. The plan should appeal to all individuals in the organization to fight weaknesses and take advantage of every opportunity at their respective levels.

The objectives outlined in a long-term plan require collective participation in their preparation and endless effort in their pursuit. People who genuinely believe in the cause of their sport won't remain passive, as spectators on the sidelines of the program, but take an active role. Everyone has a role to play, and employees of sport organizations should be concerned with the success of national sport activities and play their role well.

All individuals who are deeply involved in a sport, in whatever capacity, as athletes, team owners, promoters, coaches, associations, members, employees, or volunteers, should have similar concerns. For long-term plans to become reality, these individuals must also share the same goals, move as one muscle, and behave as one mind, since all together they will reflect the image of their sport.

Planning Steps

Each long-term plan requires specific goals; strategic actions; deadlines; and attention to material, human, and financial means. During the preparatory process, you must foresee how these will fit into the planning process. Review the first half of this chapter for recommendations concerning general strategic planning by a sport organization. Each long-term plan could be implemented in several stages, whether those stages are shorter or longer (ranging from one to more than five years). Those stages should resemble the pattern described on pages 197-205 and are summarized as follows:

- Undertake environmental research (internal and external factors).
- Select objectives and determine goals.
- Select strategic actions or conceive new ones to consolidate objectives in units or programs.
- Allocate material and financial means to implement the plan.

- Establish evaluation standards to assess the effectiveness of actions and the plan itself.
- Determine a periodic review and evaluation process of actions and effects.

In addition, separate shorter-term action plans could form part of a longer-term plan, as midcourse goals and targets.

Addressing Long-Term Planning Problems

Long-term planning by sport organizations begins with a serious analysis of their current situation from cultural, economic, and political standpoints and continues through action steps to evaluation. This section will look at some of the particular problems faced in longer-term planning and some ways to address them.

Problems

From a cultural point of view, sport organizations often lack the necessary technical knowledge for professional and methodical planning of their activities. This explains why many of them are satisfied with the preparation of a calendar of national events and international competitions that they refer to as their "annual activity plan," but which is not a plan in the full sense described here.

Single sport organizations are not the only ones to suffer from this cultural shortcoming. Indeed, a number of multisport organizations in many developing countries face similar problems, as they often ignore planning techniques and methods and cannot afford professional advice. Such organizations then hamper other national sport bodies by not providing them with necessary support in the form of clinics or seminars on the subject of planning, which would far improve the operation of sport activities.

From the economic point of view, no plan is feasible without sufficient resources, whether material, human, or financial. Frequently, sport organizations are unable to identify a source from which to obtain resources in sufficient quantity for the implementation of their plans. Quite obviously, a plan without resources is like a car without fuel, wheels, and a driver.

Additionally, multisport organizations may not require overall action plans from single sport organizations because they wish to avoid embarrassing situations, such as having to turn down a request for material support destined for the plans that they had asked to be presented. For these reasons, even if a calendar of competitions is not a full-fledged plan, multisport organizations are quite happy to go on using them, allowing each sport leader to work without an organizational scheme, without medium- or long-term goals, and very often without immediate goals as well.

Possible Solutions

Unfortunately, despite the problems inherent in long-term planning, without it national sport organizations are unable to fulfill their missions or effectively pursue any objectives—short-, medium-, or long-term. For this reason, it is important to address long-term planning problems with the best solutions at your disposal.

Sport organizations facing the challenges mentioned previously can still take some steps toward long-term planning. From the practical point of view, they can consider certain daily working habits and customs as the basis of a long-term operational plan. To do this, you must at least organize each activity and have a plan for each event, using whatever means you have secured. The purpose of such plans would be to put the different tasks or activities of the organization, whether individual or group responsibilities, in a logical order and place them under the respective department, section, club, or team.

Without going into a lengthy process, permanent long-term plans could also be built from the *administrative policies* and *operational procedures* already adopted as criteria. *Administrative policies* are general guidelines for deciding the course of action in routine situations that individuals or groups frequently encounter in the performance of their activities. *Operational procedures* are concrete and detailed instructions on how to perform a given activity on a step-by-step basis. Although their implementation is a concrete process, operational procedures are not permanent, nor are they for general use.

As already discussed, a sport organization will solve its practical problems better and faster if it has a plan for coordinating a series of orderly actions leading to the same objective. To this end, the organization could create a range of programs devoted to public relations, marketing, fundraising, sport promotion, and so on. Even if such plans are not part of a long-term plan, they can still be considered as the solution to certain problems and thus become a clear statement of the specific programs in the organization's yearly plan.

Benefits of Long-Term Plans

In spite of the difficulties inherent in long-term planning, to end up with a quality event sport organizations with major sport events, such as world or continental championships, should prepare a master plan and include long-term planning principles in the programming of their activities. The same goes for national teams and athletes preparing for the Olympic Games or world championships, formal pro league or pro circuits having professional teams and athletes, and marketing programs dealing with sponsors and national television broadcasting. In all these major events with essential marketing and communication activities, nothing can be left to chance. You need to plan long term; establish your strategy, policies, and controls; and periodically carry out program evaluations.

Advantages of long-term planning include the following:

- It prepares the organization to operate under real conditions and enables it to adapt easily to changes in the external environment created by actual working conditions.

- It reduces organizational conflict. If people in the organization recognize their role in the operation of the plan, there will be less doubt or confusion as to what the organization expects from each of its members over a given period of time.

- It helps to increase work efficiency by reducing job duplication and useless activities. Deadlines and priorities for activities that are established in the plan will facilitate a productive environment.

The 10 Golden Rules for a Successful NF

Now that you know what you need to make your organization successful and how to approach problems to secure the smooth running of the different administrative units, you are ready to understand your priorities. In addition, when making plans it is important to know the golden rules for a successful organization.

1. Have full-time, efficient, and dynamic staff ready to implement national programs and sell the image of teams, athletes, and sport events to television, sponsors, and the press.

2. Use governmental funds for grassroots and educational activities, while generating your own financial resources to ensure a sound administration of activities free from budgetary deficits.

3. Set up, together with national coaches, annual national team or athletes' programs to guarantee training, friendly events, and competitions over a five-month period, followed by no more than six months continuous activity in national leagues or circuits of sport events.

4. Organize fund-raising activities, PR, promotional events, and sport programs, and license the image of your top teams or athletes (sharing

(continued)

(continued)

revenue or allowing them to cash it entirely), engaging at least one main sponsor for them.

5. Develop and promote the identity of the sport with television by securing the broadcasting of national events, leagues, circuits, national championship finals, and all events and tournaments of the major national teams or athletes.

6. Guarantee a year-round system of friendly events or competitions for the local club teams or athletes and continuous sport events for the national league or circuit.

7. Encourage clubs and local sport associations to improve their own management, administration, and financial structures, granting them broad support for self-management and securing at least one major sponsor for each club taking part in the sport events of their leagues or circuits.

8. Work closely with the NOC and governmental sport authorities of the country to promote grassroots and educational sport, while ensuring respect for the independence, authority, and freedom of action of the NF.

9. Establish personal relations and maintain permanent contact with the media by regularly supplying information about national teams or athletes, the league or circuit, grassroots sport, and all activities of the organization in general.

10. Improve the flow of communication with the clubs and bodies affiliated to the NF, particularly with regard to decisions, rules, refereeing or judging, competitions, courses, and seminars, originating from the sport's international organization.

Creating a Medium-Term National Plan

Only yesterday, I walked on earth by chance and thousands of paths fled before my steps because they belonged to others. Today, there is only one way and only God knows where it leads. But it is my way.

J.-P. Sartre, French writer

After addressing the planning process and unique aspects of long-term planning, this chapter now moves to the specific situation of a sport organization that has decided to prepare a medium-term plan.

The explanation of this process will include how to study the organization's environment, select objectives, draw up a national strategy, and improve actual operational conditions, including specific information for organizations in developing countries. Some examples of specific programs are also presented in the rest of the chapter, such as how to operate national sport events circuits, prepare grassroots sport programs, restructure top-level national competitions, improve local conditions for competitive sport, and raise the performance level of national representatives.

The National Sport Environment

National sport organizations and particularly NFs should implement suitable strategic actions in their countries to bring the sport to the front of mass media reporting. To this end, national sport organizations should carefully study and understand the external environment and general conditions of sport in their country prior to examining their own internal working conditions. This study will enable the organization to understand the role of sport in the country, assess school attitude and public perception of the sport, and determine which goals are achievable under the given conditions.

To understand the role of a sport in a country, you must carry out sport marketing research not only in regard to the specific sport but also in regard to more general attitudes. This includes researching the attitude of the central government and local authorities toward sport as well as the attitude of other social forces, including national and transnational companies operating in the country, the press, television, radio, and marketing agencies. The aim is to detect reluctance or eagerness on their part to support or sponsor sport activities and events.

You will also want to find out about the educational system's approach to sport activities in elementary schools, high schools, colleges, and universities, as well as the public's perception or willingness to be involved in promotional actions with children or youngsters. This, too, will affect your planning.

Formulating a Mission Statement

Once the external social conditions are understood along with the internal operations of the particular national sport organization, you can proceed to formulate a mission statement that would fit the national setting and be feasible under the local sport conditions. Most established national sport organizations will already have some kind of mission statement, so the next step to focus on is selecting goals and objectives.

Selecting Goals and Objectives

National sport organizations may choose to pursue goals and objectives similar to the following:

- To turn the sport's disciplines into competitive sport activities in the country
- To transform the most important competitions into media events, fully televised and totally financed by major companies
- To professionalize the administration of the sport organization as much as possible in the short term and orient it toward becoming a financially self-sufficient organization
- To raise the competitive level of the national team or athletes and motivate local clubs to organize sport events that are appealing both to spectators and individual competitors

Goals and objectives should be accepted by the sport organization's board or executive members. Sport organizations will next choose programs for their medium-term plan that will implement these goals and objectives.

One of the most important evaluations to be made before you establish your long-term plan is to properly take a look at the internal structures of the organization and evaluate its basic components, for which you must ask yourself the following questions and find the response.

1. Does the organization have units adequate to the awareness of the mission statement and objectives?
2. Does the organization have the means and resources to support the operation of the organization units and individuals?
3. Are the managers the kind of leadership necessary to oversee the objectives and fulfill the mission statement?

For your better understanding of the basic components, see figure 6.1.

Designing a National Strategy

A national sport organization should have already set up a fact-finding panel to assess actual conditions, determine by consensus the organization's mission statement, and select goals and objectives. The next step is to determine suitable targets and actions based on the elements required for improving executive performance (see figure 6.1).

The organization should proceed to select the group of experts from different areas of the sport who will determine the strategic actions leading to the achievement of the goals and objectives. This strategic planning should include a detailed explanation of each objective already chosen, followed by the precise actions considered as appropriate to reach those selected objectives and goals.

Basic components		
Organization Establishing adequate units needed for the achievement of **objectives, goals, and targets**	**Administration** Supporting, facilitating, and following up the day-to-day operation of the office, units, and individuals for a better and prompt achievement of goals	**Management** Leading people to accomplish the **objectives, goals, and targets** through a resourceful use of materials, means, time, knowledge, and abilities

Their definition as parts of a system		
The process of arranging a coherent structure of interdependent and interactive units, sections, or divisions into a whole system	The process of running and supervising the operation of an office for the correct implementation of plans, decisions, and strategic actions undertaken by the organization	A set of coherent decision-making procedures to select activities suited to allocate resources and motivate the members, employees, and volunteers toward the achievement of sport objectives, goals, and targets

Actions and means to make them operative		
Organizational means	**Operational means**	**Management skills**
• Strategic planning • Coherent structure • Organizational communication • Unit interactivity • Choice of organizational objectives, goals, and targets • Compelling vision (mission statement)	• Competent staff • Adequate equipment and facilities • Material and financial resources • Comfortable working environment • Appropriate working policies and routines	• Planning, organizing, and controlling • Decision-making power • Leadership and coordination • Managing and motivating people • Supervising and evaluating • Selecting staff • Organizational communication and PR

Figure 6.1   Elements for improving executive performance.

There are a wide variety of clearly defined important actions or programs that NFs could choose as actions. Among many others to take into consideration are the following:

1. Improve the working conditions of the organization's administration and management.

2. Improve the structure and operation of national junior and youth programs.

3. Create national councils and operate a national circuit of events for each sport discipline.

4. Prepare grassroots sport programs for each sport discipline.

5. Improve local social, political, and economic conditions for sport activities.

6. Improve the competitive level of teams or athletes.

7. Promote the image of each discipline as a top national competitive sport.

Each of the previous actions could lead to the creation of particular programs. Different departments or sections of the national sport organization would then be given the responsibility for implementing these programs. In the case of small associations, such actions may be entrusted to specific persons or volunteers. The group or individual who will be carrying out actions must estimate, through the preparation of a budget, the resources required to launch the program and for its follow-up, periodic evaluation, and successful completion. It is essential that no action be started before having secured the financial and material means described in the estimated budget.

Improving Operational Conditions

Lack of administrative facilities and minimal managerial skills are two of the major obstacles to the advancement of sport in developing countries. Three basic elements must be available before progress can be made: office space, office equipment, and personnel. The following recommendations are intended more specifically for emerging or newly created NFs.

Office Space   The first duty of a president is to provide a place to work and the material needed to operate. A personal home or office is not suitable. NFs should lease and if possible buy premises in which to locate their office, with a minimum of two 24 square-meter (258 square-foot) rooms for administrative activities and meetings. If they are unable to do so on their own, they should seek to identify a sponsor willing to provide such space.

To meet the need for office space, sport organizations may use any one of the following strategies:

- Elect a president who loves the sport and is able to come up with a solution to obtain the required space and equipment, or even purchase suitable premises for the NF.

- Elect a president who loves the sport and whose contacts in the government will either lease premises or assign governmental facilities for the NF.
- Search for sponsors to donate the required premises in exchange for publicity in well-organized, top-class national or international events.
- Organize fund-raising campaigns through galas, dances, other social events, or lotteries to obtain the necessary financial means to lease or buy premises.

Office Equipment A minimum quantity of equipment is needed for any organization to operate successfully. Necessary office equipment includes a word processor, computer, or at least a typewriter; a photocopier or at least a stencil duplicator; a fax machine if possible; a telephone; and desks, tables, chairs, and filing cabinets. The same strategy used to obtain office space may be used to obtain this equipment. Businesses may be willing to donate some equipment.

Human Resources The problem of human resources is one of the most difficult to solve. It is recommended that a NF have at the very least, along with the president,

- one full-time executive officer (preferably bilingual with English as the second language) and a secretary/typist (paid staff);
- one technical organizer (volunteer);
- one press chief (volunteer);
- one managing director responsible for communications, public relations, and fund-raising (volunteer); and
- one person responsible for referees, coaches, and sport activities at school events (volunteer).

Everything possible should be done to recruit experts or volunteers, even though this may entail some risks. A NF may consider the following options:

- Invite the best available fans or NF members to accomplish specific tasks.
- Hire professional personnel where possible.
- Approach major companies to request the professionals needed (preferably full-time and for a fixed four-year period or indefinitely) in exchange for marketing opportunities.

Technical Personnel Technical personnel are essential for improving the administrative and management capabilities of sport organizations.

To ensure that such personnel are available, the organization should improve refereeing and coaching resources as follows.

For officiating and/or refereeing improvement, consider the following steps:

- Ask schools to select their sport events officials or referees from among the children practicing the sport.
- To facilitate the recruitment of referees and officials, encourage the systematic employment of school boys and girls as officials and referees at school competitions.
- Regularly hold one or two full-day officiating or refereeing clinics in conjunction with major sport events.

In addition, take advantage of the expertise available in the IF of your sport. Approach the international officiating or refereeing body of the IF and request detailed instructions on

- organizing national programs to prepare referees or judges, organizing clinics for children and young beginners, and engaging local international officials or referees to conduct them;
- setting up a national structure for judges or referees and drawing up a curriculum for the preparation of national judges or referees;
- organizing clinics for the training and upgrading of judges and referees; and
- evaluating the performance of national officials.

For coaches' improvement, a sport organization should choose the most suitable actions to increase the number of national coaches and develop their capabilities. Some possible actions include the following:

- Propose the creation of an official degree in sport coaching, or a coaching specialization as a part of another degree, to local educational institutions, especially universities and physical education schools.
- Organize seminars and sport events to initiate school teachers in the practice of the sport and to show them how to teach children basic sport techniques. At the same time, extracurricular sport clubs headed by teachers might be useful. Do this in cooperation with the ministry of education and the ministry of physical education and sport as a way to support the school sport programs.
- Organize specific sport activities to initiate school teachers in the basics of the sport and convince them to pass on their knowledge to their

pupils. Recommend the use of special equipment developed for school-age participants, if such is available.

In addition, contact the corresponding technical body of the IF for information on

- promoting the formation of competitive sport clubs, centers, units, or teams with newly trained coaches;
- preparing a national curriculum intended for school teachers and sport practitioners wishing to become coaches; and
- obtaining a suitable list of books and videos for coaches to improve their knowledge and skills.

Improvements in a Well-Established Organization

Regardless of its current managerial qualities and available resources, every sport organization can become even better prepared to meet the new

Organizing a seminar for coaches is a good way to improve your organization's administrative and management abilities.
Courtesy of Nuova Immagine.

217

demands of modern sport. The following are some actions that a well-established organization might take to improve its services.

- Focus on its organizational and administrative structures; the managerial abilities of its leaders; the competitive sport level of its affiliated clubs and national teams of athletes; or the organizational quality of its sport events.
- Learn how to better manage the actual sport environment by identifying possible risks and obtaining up-to-date information on sport management, sport marketing, and public relations. Apply the concepts included in this book or use it as a guide to improve the abilities and techniques of the organization's managers.
- Seek constantly to improve the professional knowledge of the organization's general secretary and technical director (if not the president) by encouraging them to attend as many management seminars as possible (preferably those related to the organization's own sport).
- Organize seminars and courses featuring world-renowned experts, carefully selecting the location to minimize travel and accommodation costs for the members, institutions, regional associations, and others wishing to participate.
- Join with a local marketing agency to organize competitions, events, and tournaments with high profile sponsors, television broadcasters, and prize money for individuals and teams.
- Raise the professional level of the organization and promote better preparation of its members.
- Recognize professional leagues, circuits, teams, or athletes as an essential part of the organization, granting them reasonable operating terms and conditions to maintain the unity and indispensable coordination of sport activities in the country.
- Emphasize that the successful participation of national teams and athletes in international events heightens the media value, potential sponsor interest, and professional image of the national sport, increasing the potential profitability of both the clubs themselves and the athletes concerned.
- Create new or incorporate existing professional leagues or circuits into the national sport organization by granting them adequate facilities and a certain autonomy under your umbrella.
- Encourage professional organizations in the sport to feel they are an essential part of the national sport organization and that it is in their own interest to contribute to the national team's program and cooperate with the national sport programs as much as possible.

- Open a register of individual athletes practicing the sport to establish the national ranking for men and women.

Junior and Youth Programs

National sport organizations must organize and promote junior and youth competitions in a carefully conceived grassroots program drafted according to the following principles:

- Find out from the IF's technical commission or from national education authorities the most suitable age at which children should begin competing in events at the national and international levels.
- Find out from the IF's technical commission up to what age special sport equipment for children should be used. In conjunction with the local education authorities, decide on appropriate use of such equipment.
- Apply the national sport organization's own special rules in national events for children up to the age of 12 in coordination with local educational bodies.
- Organize promotional activities and PR campaigns to find sponsors for junior and youth competitions, mainly for children up to 12 years of age.

Creating National Councils and Circuits of Sport Events

National sport organizations are advised to take the following steps to create national councils or a national circuit of events:

- Adapt the administrative structure to incorporate national councils for each sport discipline, with full powers for programming and conducting technical affairs and competitions.
- Seek advice from the IF of its sport on the structure best suited to a national council and on the best way to recruit competitors, promoters, marketing agents, and media professionals.
- Ask the IF of its sport to propose guidelines for the creation of national circuits for professional players, athletes, or teams.
- Counter independent professional circuits of the sport with as many activities and interesting competitions as possible, sponsored and publicized under the umbrella of the national sport organization.
- Seek private promoters and marketing agencies to enter into joint ventures to secure sponsorship, prize money, and organizational expenses for its events.
- Copy international forms used to register competitors in their sport to include them in a national ranking based on points earned after each event of the national league/circuit.

Preparing Grassroots Programs

The actions in this section have the objective of promoting educational and social activities within the community and obtaining the participation of school children, youth, families, and individuals from as many social layers of the community as possible. Grassroots competitive events should be supported according to guidelines for use of the funds granted by the government to the national sport organization. In any event use no more than one third of such grants for management and operation expenses. Program ideas for grassroots activities follow.

You can use resources received from the state or designated donations to promote and support competitions for teams or individuals of different social groups (such as competitions for families, companies, or universities). You could also organize competitions in the sport in three categories, the first two being recreational and educational, using only available public funds, and the third being the most competitive, including top-level national and international events, using your own funds or contributions received from sponsors. As much as possible, avoid timetable conflicts between the national league or circuit and international competitions.

With the school and youth sectors, avoid difficulties and dangers in practicing the sport that come from impractical equipment and inadequate playing surfaces. Determine the best age to pass from children's to normal equipment and strongly emphasize the correct use of equipment and proper attention to rules of the sport. Organize outdoor training and competition camps with boys and girls under 15 using specially designed equipment.

Restructuring Top-Level National Competitions

These competitions must be given the highest priority considering it is elite individual competitors and clubs that project the competitive image of the sport. It is necessary for competitors, full-time employees, and administrators to portray professional qualities, as well as the office and the organization itself. This section describes the types of actions that are recommended.

The national organization can offer training programs to improve individual technical skills and abilities. Use these opportunities to communicate that professionalism concerns not only competitors, but also full-time employees, administrators, and organizational methods.

Another possible action is to create professional leagues and individual sport event circuits under the auspices of the corresponding special section in the NF. Give them enough technical and administrative autonomy while still ensuring the oversight of the national sport organization and compliance with international regulations. You can counter independent professional leagues and sport circuits with as many competitions as possible under the authority of the NF.

Require professional administration of all clubs taking part in elite competitions. A professional attitude is indispensable in their responsibilities toward the sport at the national, continental, and international levels.

Sport organizations should engage a professional manager to take over sport marketing and fund-raising programs, as well as promotional and public relations activities. This marketing manager should

- promote the personalities of the sport's individuals so that these players and coaches will become national stars;

- secure at least one major sponsor for the national league and one for the national circuit of sport events;

- highlight the athletic, aesthetic, and fair play values of the different disciplines of the sport;

- institute a national media strategy giving priority to television interviews, press contacts, and press attendance at all kinds of sport events; and

- raise the competitive standard of middle-level clubs, individuals, and teams by promoting the participation of the best local or foreign athletes available.

Standardizing the Competition Calendar

Children's participation in competitive sport events at the national and international levels should follow national educational programs and guidelines in regard to the most suitable age for them to participate. The rest of the competition calendar should ensure a smooth transition and progression from one program to another.

The national organization of a specific sport must therefore carefully draw up its own competition calendar, paying special attention to certain important aspects. One such item is to take into account the international calendar and the role of the specific sport in regional, continental, and world competitions.

Ensure that national leagues or sport circuits take place during the same period every year for no more than six consecutive months. Reserve five months a year for the preparation of national teams or athletes and their participation in different championships, cups, national events, and international competitions, respecting their commitments and training programs. Foresee no less than one month's rest for the national teams or athletes taking part in long-lasting national pro leagues or sport circuits.

Improving Local Conditions for Sport

The major obstacles challenging local and national sport organizations are the poor sport infrastructure existing in their community or country and the insufficient availability of sport equipment and material for mass sport and even competitive activities. The following sections will give attention to actions to improve these conditions.

Competition Facilities   You must use the best available facilities for national and international events. If basic sport infrastructures do not exist in the country, those sport organizations requiring sport facilities should not forget that almost every sport is also practiced outdoors on a whole range of different surfaces, including open stadiums, public parks, and school facilities.

Whenever facilities are available, national sport organizations should always use the *best* sport facility for top national competitions, with a view to creating public awareness and linking the high class of the facility with the quality of the event.

Pay close attention to large local building projects for sport facilities, immediately contacting the promoters to ensure that all technical requirements for high-level competitions are integrated into the project, thus making such facilities eligible for international sport events. Volleyball, for instance, needs adequate lighting over the free zone along both sides of the playing court and over the warm-up courts. For basketball, solid anchors for the posts are necessary, as well as other specific requirements in the playing and warm-up courts.

National sport organizations should consult the technical personnel of the respective IF regarding the technical specifications or areas needed for a sport facility to host official competitions: the surface requirements, the ground consistency or material, and the specifications of such structures, particularly those concerning synthetic or special courts. Obtain information from specialized organizations (such as the International Association for the Construction of Sports Facilities) on the preparation and building of sport structures and playing courts.

Sport Materials and Equipment   Materials and equipment must be clearly distinguished. *Sport materials* are all articles necessary for the practice of the sport that are *not* personal items, such as goals, balls, basketball hoops, scoreboards, or arrival pads for swimming. *Homologated materials* are the articles that the official international bodies have approved as meeting the standards set by the rules of the sport.

Sport equipment (sportswear) consists of all personal items used in the practice of the sport, such as uniforms, shoes, padding, and knee and elbow protectors. *Homologated equipment* is the sportswear garments and shoes approved as being in accordance with the rules of the sport.

National sport organizations should initiate programs and promotional activities to raise funds to obtain material and equipment for competitions from local distributors at discount prices or in exchange for publicity during competitions. Continental branches of the IF might even supply equipment for competitions directly to national sport organizations within their continent, negotiating discount prices for certain events with distributors or manufacturers.

National sport organizations should consult the technical personnel of the respective IF for their assistance, as needed, on the following topics:

- Producing adequate sport materials and equipment in the country, ensuring their availability at all times, and producing low-cost sport materials and equipment locally
- Choosing the homologated materials and equipment available in your country. Other brands or types may be chosen only if homologated equipment is unavailable and the IF has confirmed such unavailability with the manufacturers. Normally, only homologated materials should be used for official international events, though there is no such obligation for sport involving two countries only.
- Obtaining homologated materials and equipment in sufficient quantities
- Obtaining from the manufacturers of homologated materials and equipment the list of their regional and national agents, distributors, or retailers with special prices for NF activities
- Determining with the manufacturers of homologated materials and equipment the best ways of making them available, on each continent, to the NFs

Improving the Competitive Level

Give special attention to the preparation and training of national teams and individual athletes by arranging, together with the national coaches, annual training and competition programs based on no less than five months of continuous activity. Avoid clashes between national events and the international calendar, leaving room for national sport competitions during a six-month period without interruption. Assure at least one month's rest for athletes.

It will also improve the athletes' ability to focus on competing if you can secure no less than one major sponsor for each national team or athlete that includes endorsements (sharing revenue with athletes), shirt publicity, and other benefits. Bring new young athletes into higher class national teams or competitions by including junior athletes in youth national meetings or competitions and youth in top national meetings or competitions.

Reach an agreement with educational authorities to create special high school sport classes for students selected for their athletic talents in a

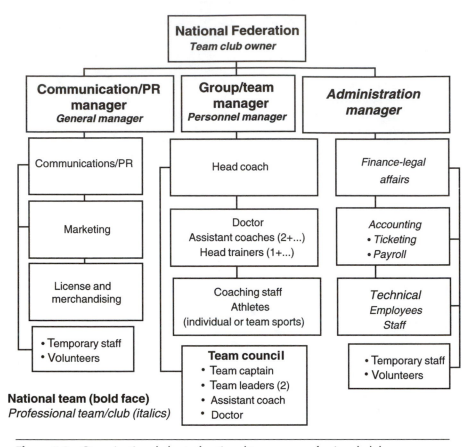

Figure 6.2 Organizational chart of national teams or professional clubs.

specific sport and to incorporate a bonus point system for access to universities or colleges. This allows for the regrouping, in the same school, of a region's young athletes with a view to their receiving more intensive and specific training by national coaches. Encourage high school sport events nationwide.

National teams and professional clubs may not succeed unless they have an adequate ongoing clerical structure that is able to relieve head coaches and trainers of time-consuming administrative matters that they normally do not understand. A national team having an organization of its own will be better able to be sold as a product and be ready for more productive fund-raising. See figure 6.2 for a useful model for professional teams.

Promoting the Image of a Competitive Sport

Not all competitive sport activities attract the media or public interest. Many take place in empty sport facilities in a depressing atmosphere for the competitors. Sport organizations are expected to take the necessary measures to create public awareness. This section will suggest some actions to help do this. For more specifics in carrying out these actions, see chapter 4 for detailed discussions on public and media relations.

Attract Media Interest Improving the sport organization's internal conditions (structure, working conditions, self-financing, and above all a competitive image) will heighten public awareness and attract the attention of the written press, radio, and television. This is because a more efficient organization will more effectively provide sport services and will have the necessary PR staff to promote its activities.

Specific actions to attract media attention include the following:

• Encourage national clubs to adopt a better organization and internal structure and thus set up a modern, professional administration. This will attract media attention indirectly through a better image and directly through professional PR staff and programs.

• Frequently contact local television channels to offer them technical and promotional videos to strengthen the identity of the sport on television, and arrange for the regular broadcasting of at least the finals of national meetings, tournaments, or championships in individual sport and national league matches in team sport.

• Establish, promote, and broaden relations with the entire national written or audio-visual press by regularly keeping them informed of the activities of the national sport events, league matches, and the main national championships.

• Keep the sport information flowing frequently enough in order to create public awareness for each competition using the best possible means, including pamphlets, leaflets, posters, and gadget and souvenir sales.

• Secure the distribution of information, decisions, recommendations, and programs of the international bodies to the clubs and all members of the NF, as well as media contacts.

• Convince one or more companies to take an interest in sponsoring the national league or circuit of sport events, provided that the latter is professionally managed and the events are presented with some kind of spectator entertainment.

• Create a real national league or circuit of sport events, with its own structure, management, and marketing programs, under the umbrella of the NF.

- Choose the best dates, halls, and cities for national events; invite only the best available teams or athletes (with written confirmation); and hire a profes-sional image communicator, a press coordinator, and the best possible marketing agency or promoter to organize the event (letting the professionals do the difficult part and only taking care of the technical conditions).

Give Television Priority   To improve both revenue and image, national and international sport organizations are strongly advised to negotiate, regardless of financial considerations, a single comprehensive four-year television contract for the regular TV broadcast of their top competitions or traditional international events. If you create a national professional league, circuit, or international competition with its own structure, management, and marketing program, allow it to negotiate its own television broadcasting.

This chapter has focused on planning in sport organizations: the planning process, long-term planning, and the creation of a medium-term national strategy. The detailed description of planning steps included a discussion of many action possibilities for improving sport, including some focusing on the sport image. Figure 6.2 graphically portrayed the organizational structure of a national team or professional club, showing the framework for the positions to carry out the programs described in this chapter. The role of PR and media contacts is such a significant one for sport organizations that the rest of the chapter will be devoted to the subject.

A National PR and Media Relations Plan*

It is a common error by national and new sport organizations to focus their actions exclusively on internal matters aimed at solving technical aspects or sport-related issues, such as the playing ground, competition rules, sport materials, technical officials and judges, etc. In so doing, they neglect the highly important activities that are externally oriented, particularly those geared to creating public awareness and promoting public interest for the sport, the athletes, or the events, or improving the public perception of their image and the benefits that the organization represents for the community.

Special attention and important resources should be dedicated to court government agencies, the media, major sport organizations, and corporations in order to obtain their support and understanding of the need to contribute financial or other means required for the organization to expand its benefit to the community. It is important to expend at least some time and resources to gain public confidence, or even to do like President Truman.

---

*Based on a proposal made by Mr. Andrew Napier, former IOC Public Relations Director.

For a modern and professional sport organization, the PR and media relations aimed at attracting spectators and media will always be at least of the same importance as the technical aspects. A dilemma can occur when the interests of media and spectators conflict with the technical aspects or with isolated interests of the athletes. However, the modern sport manager will know that a sport's future can only be ensured through support from the spectators and the media.

The more popular a sport, the more the media will be interested; and the more the media cover the sport, the more popular the sport can become. As well as looking after the technical aspects of staging events, sport organizations, and particularly national sport organizations, must also maximize spectator interest in their different sport events and take into account the interests of the media.

Some international sport organizations are undertaking a worldwide drive to make their sport events major spectator events. To do so, they have identified the need for a concerted effort at all levels—world, continental, national and regional, federation, league, event organizer, and club— to adopt a planned and proactive approach to PR and media relations. The same principles are valid for all Olympic sports.

Media and sponsors both target the general public as a market. Media attention and sponsorship are two signs of the interest drawn to a sport event by the general public. To capitalize on this, sport organizations must take the following kinds of action.

"Free" Coverage

Television and sponsors can help to finance a sport and make it popular, but both are more attracted to sports that are already popular. The challenge is to create this *virtuous circle!* Generally speaking, they are willing to pay more for sports that correspond to the profile of the target audience they are trying to reach. However, they also pay a premium for exclusivity or high visibility in a sport. Raising money through marketing the sport to television broadcasters and sponsors is the domain of marketing experts, but a good PR and media relations program can help to increase the "free" coverage given by broadcasters (television and radio) and the printed media, and thus bring each sport discipline to a wider public.

Promoting the Best Athletes and Teams

Unknown athletes or teams will never arouse the imagination of the public or the interest of the press. This problem may only be solved through a constant flow of stories or reports about feats and qualities of the most charismatic or skillful players and teams, as discussed in the following section.

Not only world-class teams and athletes can be famous and popular. A major part of PR and media relations should be devoted to promoting the images of the best athletes in each discipline. In sport, anonymous teams and athletes, no matter how technically excellent, rarely catch the public's imagination. It is important to be aware that the popularity of a sport is heavily dependent on the popularity of the sport's major athletes. Therefore, both the knowledgeable sport fan and the wider public should be given opportunities to know more about the teams and athletes, especially the best performers and the most charismatic—or maybe even the most beautiful or handsome—athletes. A NF does not need to have a world-class team to be able to develop athletes who can become famous and popular within the country.

Publicity efforts should focus on top-level competitors as role models for the sport, underlining that they are fit, healthy, skillful, committed to fair play, and showing respect for other competitors, the rules, and the officials responsible for controlling the competition.

In the absence of local stars, sell top foreign teams or athletes. A combination of a team's or athletes' heritage, reputation, and performance attracts people to events and makes them want to follow the events through the media and thus also attracts the interest of the media and sponsors. This, in turn, can bring their exploits to a wider public and attract greater interest, and so on. In major sport events like world and continental championships, it is frequently observed that only local athletes or the home team can attract the big crowd. In order to attract spectators to competitions or events where local teams or athletes are not really competitive, you need to make top foreign teams and athletes popular.

At all levels of the sport, make efforts to promote the best, make them better known within the sport, and make them known to a wider public. At the end of the day, it is the public who decides who their "stars" are, but sport administrators and promoters can help create the context in which the public makes their choices.

For the long-term benefit of the sport, national sport organizations should aim to have the media focus on the best athletes, the events, and the sport itself. The sport's administrators should be seen making decisions in the interest of the sport, its players, and spectators, but should otherwise be in the background, efficiently managing the sport.

Communications

Sport fans want to know instantly or as quickly as possible the results of competitions that matter to them. The main suppliers of such information are the news agencies, whose clients are the broadcasters and the print media. News agencies will provide instant results of events when they believe the events matter sufficiently to a large enough group of broadcasters, print media, and spectators to warrant the cost of providing such instant coverage. It is useful to think of the speed of information being available as reflecting its importance: If the media receive the competition results a day late, they will probably ignore them!

International bodies, continental and national branches, and organizers should take the following steps to improve communications:

- Create a wider understanding of each sport discipline, its rules, excitement, athleticism, and fair play.

- Help to turn the best athletes into stars and personalities. Cooperate with television, equipment manufacturers, sponsors, agents, managers, and others who also have an interest in promoting the best competitors.

- Provide factual information to the media and the television and radio commentators at times and in formats that make it easy for them to do their job.

- Enhance the image of the disciplines of the sport as high-level competition—clean, modern, and appealing to spectators of all age-groups.

- Turn the sport disciplines, be they swimming, archery, rowing, or any other, into spectator sports that will attract greater media interest.

NFs' Images

As part of a long-term plan, NFs are encouraged to become more "professional" in their work, to adopt and follow their own mission statements, and to pay more attention to the image of the sport in their country. NFs should promote their image as autonomous, able to operate according to professional and ethical standards, and as trustful guardians concerned with the good of the sport and its participants at all levels (from primary schools to professional leagues/circuits). NFs should always be positive, ambitious, dynamic, and unafraid of change. This will earn them the right to be considered respected and full-fledged partners of governmental sport authorities and the NOCs.

The Events

In regard to events, publicity efforts in each country should focus on presenting the highest level competition, preferably playing to "full houses" with enthusiastic, knowledgeable family spectators. Televised competitions held in venues with numerous empty seats are not good for the sport's image and will not ensure continued sponsorship, advertising, or television revenues.

In addition, publicize events of the different disciplines of the sport as being competitive at lower levels (including schools) and ideal recreational sport, in the context of "sport for all" programs.

Media and PR Priorities for NFs

National sport organizations and particularly NFs should develop PR and media relations plans as part of their long-term planning. International bodies are giving serious consideration to the following 20 initiatives and to the drafting of a set of media priorities appropriate for the development of their sport disciplines in each country.

Adequate Press Facilities   Adequate facilities, working conditions, and communications materials at events make it easy for the press, broadcasters, and photographers to give optimum coverage to the sport and its competitors. Media coverage of sport falls into five main categories:

1. Before the events: announcements, previews, team line-up, and athletes' list
2. During the events: instant results, coverage, and commentary (television/radio/electronic media)
3. After the events: reports, summaries, interviews, opinions about the performance, and statistics
4. Information about teams and athletes
5. Other news and features about the sport. There are many other ways of appearing in the media than just by winning competitions.

Importance of the Event   Publicity prior to events is particularly important since efficient pre-event publicity will attract the spectators and the media and create the virtuous circle. The main task of the PR before an event will be to make this event important. If the event does not appear to be important, there is no reason for the spectators or the media to attend. The PR must build up an atmosphere of expectation around the event by carefully planning the PR in the months, weeks, and days preceding the event.

Prepare a media strategy to select the right time and place for the announcement and release of "news." (Instead of releasing two important news items at the same time, the second can be saved for the following week in order to keep the interest of the public alive). The strategy of building up the atmosphere around the event can be compared to the fundamental PR strategy of a political candidate running for election:

- Don't miss the smallest possible opportunity to appear in the media.
- Don't lose momentum on the way.

- Don't go too fast.
- Don't slow down at the end.
- Don't give up if you lose!

Regular Contact   Keep the national and local media informed of developments in the sport, plans, and future events through regular, factual announcements. Sport editors and journalists generally prefer press releases to be straightforward and factual. Decisions, team or athlete selections, results, or events should be announced first; additional helpful information or background material may be added later.

Maximizing Spectator Interest   Sport events should be planned with a view to maximizing spectator interest, entertainment value, and media appeal. For example, the proximity of spectators to the competition area, how well they can see the sport actions (and be seen on television!), public address announcements, and programs can always increase excitement. Other ways of adding to the excitement and heightening interest in the sport actions and the competitors depend on the facilities available. For example, competitors can warm up away from the main competition area, having their entry to the main area announced individually over the public address system, along with essential aspects of the competition.

Needs of Commentators   During events, particular attention should be paid to the requirements of television and radio commentators and public address announcers. They should be given appropriate facilities and the best access to information regarding the sport, the event, and the competitors. Ask the latter for information about themselves as people, their interests, their education, and their family, as well as their physical details and sporting achievements.

Needs of Reporters and Photographers   Throughout the year, national sport organizations must also be sure to look after the interests of reporters and photographers from news agencies and the written press. They should be accessible; give the media appropriate facilities and regular information about the sport, the events, and the competitors; and arrange interview opportunities with competitors, especially the star athletes (in agreement with their managers). For more details on addressing needs of media representatives, see "Press Expectations," page 113.

Focusing on the Best   Draw attention to the best competitors and the most exciting moments of a competition, series, or championship. One method successfully used in many sports is to stage special awards or competitions, such as the following:

- After each competition you could present an award to the "best team or athlete," who is nominated by an "expert" (for example, a respected commentator or journalist, a former athlete, a sponsor, or other sport personality).

- Television viewers could have the opportunity to nominate the best sport action of the month, the championship, or the season, and those viewers whose choice matched that of the "panel of experts" could go into a prize drawing.

- You could nominate a "personality of the year" in the sport, perhaps with the involvement of the main television broadcaster.

- Commentators could also nominate the "best sport action of the day" or "magic/golden moment of the competition," and so on.

There are many variations, but the principles are the same: Create "news," recognize and give repeated coverage to the most exciting sport actions and athletes, and give fans the opportunity to agree with or talk about expert opinion. Such schemes can usually be sponsored or run in conjunction with a television or radio broadcaster, giving them further opportunities to promote their involvement in the sport or event.

Facing the Media Call a press conference for face-to-face contact with the media. Do this when an important announcement could interest many journalists who would certainly wish to have the opportunity to ask questions, or when it is considered important to give a large number of journalists the opportunity to interview the same person(s) at the same time. Call a press briefing to share information that isn't necessarily linked to any particular announcement with a smaller number of journalists. Anticipate questions and prepare answers in advance; write down key messages to convey and express them with confidence.

Developing Personalities Develop a few "star players." In addition to publicizing the best athletes at all levels, there are advantages for each country to have one or two real stars—a "sport personality of the year" with whom the sport is strongly identified. These stars are singled out for feature articles in magazines and newspapers, television and radio interviews, posters, training videos, books, regular columns in magazines, and so on. Depending on the popularity of the sport and the personality of the athlete(s), they could also become more widely known outside the sport (for example, through product endorsements, guest appearances, entertainment programs, and the like). The private lives of stars can be featured—for better or for worse—in "gossip" columns of newspapers and magazines.

Looking After Supporters   Although an athlete's main value to a team is through contributing to its sporting performance, the athlete's appeal to supporters can bring other benefits, both short-term and long-term. Supporters play a key role: They create reputations, their "word of mouth" publicity carries weight with their friends, they usually pay to watch their heroes, and they want information about heroes and instant knowledge about their performance and team or individual results. They also buy souvenirs, sport equipment, and other products that strengthen their identification with their favorite athletes; and they buy programs and often have their own magazines (fanzines). Nowadays they may even surf the Internet for information about their teams or athletes, contact supporters' clubs in other countries, or even set up their own "home page." Looking after the interests of supporters—or at least acting as facilitator—is probably one of the key requirements for success.

Showing Off Top-Level Values   It is recommended to take advantage of the excellent opportunities that international competitions or events offer to promote each country's best competitors and to show off the sport's disciplines as high-level competitive sport.

As soon as the international schedule is known, provide information to the country's main media (especially television and radio), so that they can plan accordingly. It must be ensured that they understand the significance of the competitions (as qualifications for Olympic Games, world or continental championships, or major world events).

There will be many opportunities to interest the media, including drawing lots for the participation of the teams and athletes in major competitions or championships (fans will want to know instantly). There will also be team or individual selection, team members or individual athletes getting together to start training, teams or athletes leaving or visiting, teams or athletes arriving, and information about opponents. During the competition, you can highlight the performance of other teams or competitors in the same group and championship (who may be past or future opponents), teams or athletes returning from a competition overseas, and so forth.

Using Unsold Tickets Wisely   A local atmosphere and a strong local interest are vital for international events, to ensure good spectator attendance and satisfactory media coverage. As already mentioned, an enthusiastic "full house" is advisable for televised events. Not only does it add atmosphere to the coverage but it may increase revenue for the event also. However, if there are likely to be unsold seats, it is advisable to consider giving them away through promotions or competitions and increased allocations for sponsors and other people whose involvement can be important.

233

Announcing Rankings Regularly   Interest in the sport and its best competitors can be nurtured by rankings at world level (the IF ranking), continent (confederation), country (NF), or league/circuit. For these rankings to be eagerly awaited by competitors and public alike, the announcements should be made at regular, predetermined times and run over a period of years. The announcement of the latest rankings (even if only by press release and on the Internet) becomes news, which will interest the media.

Developing a Win-Win Situation   Develop a good working relationship with other parties who also have an interest in the sport's becoming a major sport: competitors and officials, sponsors, sport equipment manufacturers, promoters, agents, and broadcasting rights-holders. In their different ways, all should be equally committed to the growth of the sport, even though the interests may sometimes conflict.

Agents and sponsors are particularly important when it comes to promoting star athletes. Agents will want to manage the stars, and sponsors will want to use them in their promotions, which in turn can further publicize the sport. Generally speaking, the sport and the athletes benefit most when all interested parties are able to work together.

Focusing on the "Fair Play" Attitude   Competitors at all levels can enhance their reputations by their attitude to the sport, other practitioners, officials, and supporters of all ages. Coolness and grace under pressure win more friends than angry retaliation, brusqueness, or off-handedness. A friendly smile to a young autograph-hunter can mean a lot.

Involving the Best Competitors   In school or club training programs, incorporating the appearance of a star athlete can build loyalty and enthusiasm, as well as ensure the future of the sport. The most popular characters or well-known personalities of the sport in the community, in the nation, or if possible worldwide will make a tremendous impact, not only on children but also their parents, if they personally give a speech or make a presentation or a short demonstration of their abilities in the school, training camp, or any kind of public event. Children, youngsters, in fact everybody, love to be close to, or touch, the winners and feel the glamour of fame and glory.

Considering Alternatives   You should always consider other ways of building up the sport's heritage. For example, some countries perpetuate a sport's heritage and the memory of the star athletes through a "hall of fame," and athletes' equipment and other memorabilia become sought-after and valuable commodities.

The appearance of star athletes can help build loyalty toward a sport. These children won't soon forget their brush with fame.
Courtesy of Nuova Immagine.

Keeping a Media Record New journalists assigned by their editors to cover the sport must be recognized and media lists kept up-to-date. Local sport organizations must compile and keep up-to-date a list of all local media, such as radio stations, television channels, magazines, daily newspapers, and all publications circulating in the community. National and world sport organizations are advised to act likewise in the expectation that the media will report on their activities and sport events.

Any new journalist recently assigned by his or her editor to cover the sport must be welcomed and his or her name, private and business telephone numbers, fax, address, and if possible hobbies and interests incorporated in the media list.

Learning From Others   In developing a national promotional program, a NF should try to adapt solutions that have worked elsewhere. Much can be learned from how the most popular sports manage their affairs in the same country, and—through the IF—how other countries manage the same sport affairs successfully in other parts of the world.

Focusing on Appropriate Names   Other people should not be allowed to give the sport different names than the one conceptually conceived as the name for the discipline: Athletics is the official name, not "track and field"; hockey is the name of the sport, not "grass hockey" or "field hockey"; table tennis is the name, not "ping-pong"; and volleyball is the sport's name, not "indoor volleyball."

In England, volleyball's main disciplines are currently known as "indoor" and "beach volleyball." Yet, the "indoor" version is played at some levels on beaches and is an excellent outdoor sport, and the "beach" version is also played indoors. For volleyball, after hearing various people concerned, the following changes are proposed:

> The term "indoor" should be dropped so that the two disciplines governed and managed by the FIVB, the Confederations, and NFs will henceforth be known as "volleyball" and "beach volleyball," depending on which set of rules is used. Both will be promoted as "team sport," so the terminology "team volleyball" for either discipline should be avoided. The term "beach volley" should only be used in spoken language: In writing, the term "beach volleyball" is preferred to reinforce the notion that the discipline is governed, managed, and promoted as a serious high-level competitive sport.

The essential message of this section is that public and media relations are in effect the most important tools for a sport organization desiring to recruit practitioners; construct loyalty among youngsters; create heroes; build up public recognition and heritage; attract media supporters; gain the respect of important organizations, corporations, and government officials; and in general establish and improve credibility, personality, and image.

CONCLUSION

Planning is the act of establishing objectives and goals, selecting actions required for the organization to achieve them, assigning tasks (labor division) in compatible administrative units, and arranging them in an organizational structure able to operate as a system. The selection of objectives is the most important part of the plan, and for this reason they must be clearly defined and unequivocally understood.

Administrative provisions are the backbone of a plan. They include securing financial, material, and human resources required for the completion of activities. The underlying problem in planning is how to establish a strategy to achieve the goals. The solution suggested here is to plan through participatory planning. This involves individuals representing the whole spectrum of the organization, working in group sessions, and including the most knowledgeable and experienced members, a process which is also known as team planning.

The mission statement or compelling vision determines what the organization wants to accomplish. It should contain the critical elements of the four environmental conditions: strengths, weaknesses, opportunities, and threats, together with the organization's objectives, all of which will identify the organization and differentiate it from others. While being realistic and achievable, the mission statement needs to be revised periodically (at least every five years) to keep operations in line with new environmental conditions (both internal and external).

If financial, material, or human resources are not available in the amounts required by the original strategic plan, you will need to prepare a contingency plan. This includes only those strategic actions for which the NF or organization concerned has already secured the three primary resources (human, material, and financial).

Keep objectives precise, clear, achievable, measurable, realistic, and interesting so that people responsible for actions to achieve them will find it easier to accomplish them. Among the goals and objectives to be pursued within an organization's medium-term plan, the following merit attention:

- To turn its sport's disciplines into competitive sport activities
- To transform the most important competitions into media events
- To make the sport organization financially self-sufficient and its administration professionally oriented
- To raise the competitive level of the national teams or competitors

Emerging or newly created sport organizations need to strive for the availability of the three basic material priorities: office space, office equipment, and personnel. For their part, major sport organizations should prepare themselves professionally to meet the new external demands of modern sport through the improvement of organizational and administrative structures; the managerial abilities of the leaders; and the competitive sport level of their affiliated clubs, teams, and individual competitors.

There is no major sport organization without a professional league or individual sport events circuits. One of the highest goals of the organization should be to support the incorporation or recognition of such leagues or circuits. They need sufficient technical and administrative autonomy, while simultaneously retaining the authority of the national sport organization and of the IF.

Appoint a professional manager to take over sport marketing and fundraising programs, as well as promotional and public relations activities. A modern and professional sport organization must always make PR and media relations a priority. The modern sport manager knows that the sport's future can only be ensured through support from the spectators and the media.

Publicity prior to events is particularly important since efficient pre-event publicity will attract the spectators and the media and create the virtuous circle. Plan sport events with a view to maximizing spectator interest, entertainment value, and media appeal. To attract spectators where local teams or athletes are not really competitive, publicize top foreign teams or athletes. A media strategy must be prepared to select the right time and place for the announcement and release of "news." The strategy of building up the atmosphere around the event can be compared to the fundamental PR strategy of a political candidate running for election:

1. Don't miss the smallest possible opportunity to appear in the media.
2. Don't lose momentum on the way.
3. Don't go too fast.
4. Don't slow down at the end.
5. Don't give up if you lose!

It is essential that athletes understand and embody the values of "fair play" and "attitude," as well as technical skills. At all levels they can enhance their reputations by their attitude to the sport, other practitioners, officials, and supporters of all ages. In the end, the goal of planning is to improve the organization and its services in every respect.

seven

CONTROLLING YOUR ORGANIZATION

Courtesy of Nuova Immagine.

> **Who controls the past controls the future: who controls the present controls the past.**
>
> *George Orwell,* **1984**

Chapters 1 and 2 of this book explained the social conditions that determine the sport setting, the national and international environments in which the sport organizations operate, and how they could contemplate a new start using different organizational concepts. Chapters 3 and 4 described the many concepts that pave the road to success. These are the necessary tools to build efficient, responsible, and financially powerful sport organizations. Chapters 5 and 6 developed the main concepts relating to management and ways to tackle planning in the short, medium, and long term. These are meaningful only when used with sound fiscal management and adequate control of the organizational programs and the people in charge of each area of the organization.

The final chapter of this book will open with various basic budgeting concepts, including pre-controls, administrative and management controls, resource allocation, and financing and budgeting operations. In addition, my colleague Timo Santalainen has made a contribution on how sport organizations could prepare results-oriented budgets. Finally, I will address how national and international organizations will need self-control to enforce modern administrative principles of leadership and management for survival in the 21st century.

Fundamentals of Budgeting*

Budgets are the numerical expression of plans and its unraveling in parts following the organizational structure. They provide a useful tool to coordinate planning and a means to delegate authority.

J. Gomez Morfin, Modern Administration
and Systems of Information

Budgeting is an administrative activity required in any size of organization, whether an emerging or competitive sport organization. The bigger the organization, the more complex budgeting will become. Whatever the case, budgeting is an effective method of control and evaluation.

To fulfill their functions properly, budgets need broad acceptance and participation, goals accessibility, and flexibility in their preparation. Par-

---

*This section is based on a contribution from Mr. Timo Santalainen.

ticipation of operational managers and workers leads to motivation and positive attitudes in the process of budget planning and control. Operational managers should play an active role in the preparation and supervision of their budgets, and operational personnel should be allowed to take part freely and spontaneously in any of the specific aspects.

When preparing budgets, managers should be realistic and base their predictions on past experiences and previous budgets, all of which could be taken as the starting point for new budgets. Prepare principles to deal with discrepancies, and carefully analyze significant deviations. Take corrective actions immediately, incorporating adjustments or budget amendments where possible.

Budget structure and handling will determine the flexibility of a budget. Structural flexibility is the possible automatic adjustment of the components of the budget in regard to changing conditions. Handling flexibility consists in the possibility of making an interpretation of the allocated amounts, representing an approximate rather than a rigid approach.

Preparing Your Budget

Budget preparation is based on obtaining accounting information, tracking expenses and revenues, drawing up a general financial statement of the organization, and carrying out audit controls.

Every sport organization operates with an eye on the future. Its actions are in the present but are directed toward the achievement of future goals. It is important to foresee changes, obstacles, and deviations and their economic impact on the organization during the budget's preparation phase.

The budget of an organization is the numeric representation of the plans and their breakdown into programs. It represents an important tool for coordinated planning and delegation of authority throughout the different levels of the organizational structure. If a budget is the numerical expression of an organization's operation and represents economic standards to measure results, then the following are important before a budget is prepared:

- Adequately plan operations with clearly determined objectives.
- Adequately distribute functions and responsibilities.
- Determine authority.
- Efficiently manage operations.
- Consciously and ethically manage behavior.

The president and sport manager are responsible for the decision to base an operational system on a budget, even though the actual design, implementation, and coordination of the budget may be delegated to the treasurer or an executive member of the organization. Whatever the case, the authority or decision-making power for the budget's final approval must remain the exclusive prerogative of the organization's highest authority.

Budgeting in Major Sport Organizations

Each department of a sport organization, such as public relations, marketing, specific events, administration, and competitions, must prepare its own budget as a standard to measure its particular efficiency. Subsidiary budgets need to be based on planning premises so that they may be consolidated. These premises are principles previously issued by the organization for its annual budget.

To help managers in coordinating operations, each budget should include specific programs. Every budget is a prognosis of how the financial accounts should appear at a future date. This prognosis could fall short of reality or surpass it because of influences beyond the organization's control. For this reason, it is important to be able to readjust budgets if necessary, using appropriate means.

Allocating Resources

Resource allocation budgets are normally made once a year. Managers should verify the validity of each request, compare its respective cost, and assess its relative weight in the achievement of long-term objectives. Then they must decide whether all the requests received from the departments can be satisfied with the financial resources available and finally determine the amounts to assign on the basis of duly confirmed revenue, setting aside a small reserve.

Budgets of sport organizations normally include the following:

- **Fixed assets:** land, buildings, machinery, and equipment
- **Scientific research:** new events, PR activities, new promotions, and new rules and techniques
- **Institutional publicity:** news releases, press interviews, presentations, and conferences
- **Personnel training:** teaching employees better use of computers and office equipment
- **Market development:** new activities to recruit new members and increase the number of volunteers and people practicing the sport and supporting or watching events

Even if expenditure included in such budgets is essential to the achievement of long-term objectives and goals, the organization can increase, decrease, or even cancel allocated amounts that do not affect the daily operations of the organization. However, sport managers should not authorize any purchases or leases unless the specific amounts have been approved in the resource allocation budget.

Controls As Measurement

Controlling is not spying but ensuring that actual results or activities conform to the planning and organizational structure previously established. It is also advisable to have control of the use of resources, not only financial but also material and human, bearing in mind what Don Marquis (1878-1937), an American journalist, once said: "Honesty is a good thing but it is not profitable to its possessor unless it is kept under control."

Through administrative controls, the sport manager ascertains—but through budget controls he or she can verify—whether the budget satisfies the needs of each program, whether the departmental structure corresponds to the objectives of the organization, whether foreseen resources can achieve goals and objectives, and whether the right person was hired for the job.

Just like any other enterprise, society, or business unit, a sport organization needs to operate on the basis of a budget conceived as a system of control and balance. Every control is carried out in three phases:

1. Consider organizational standards for efficiency.
2. Compare actual results with expected efficiency. (Experts analyze the evaluation and correct as necessary.)
3. Select measures to correct deviations.

The elements to control are as follows:

- **Cost.** Every cost item must be under control, including services, equipment, operation, and personnel.
- **Quality.** Professional quality must characterize every person, material utensil, form, letter format, contract, attitude, behavior, protocol, and standard, whether in competition venues or meeting rooms.
- **Investment.** All fixed assets, each piece of office material and equipment, together with the financial investments, must be under control.

To achieve efficient control based on budgeting standards, evaluate results, and correct deviations, the sport organization must make a certain number of prior decisions:

- When and where should they measure work efficiency?
- Who should measure or evaluate it?

- Which standards will be used to qualify results?
- Who should be informed of the evaluation results?
- How should the evaluation process be completed quickly, fairly, and at a reasonable cost?

The response given to each and all of these questions may lead the manager to establish flexible routines for adequate and cost-effective evaluations for timely corrections.

Controls As Accountability

Managers are more able to be accountable when the organization has established adequate controls based on effective checks and balances. These should be carried out in three phases:

1. **Pre-controls** are related to effective staff selection, accurate budgeting, and clear identification of financial resources.

2. **Operational controls** are the daily monitoring of the operations.

3. **Administrative and management controls** are routine audits including performance evaluation of employees and profit levels according to financial statements. Administrative audits can measure whether more people are practicing the sport, more journalists are attending events, and more effective and long-lasting television broadcasts (including sport news, competition highlights, or event broadcasting) have been carried out.

Pre-Controls

This type of control is made at the beginning of the organizational cycle of activities and concerns mainly the control of human resources, the quality of material produced, and the adequacy of financial planning.

Controlling Human Resources
Effective job descriptions, thorough market research, and the selection of the right person for the job are critical preliminary controls of human resources. Research each post thoroughly to ensure that key job components are included, together with appropriate job expectations and employee responsibilities. This is essential to match a candidate with the job responsibilities and manager's expectations. Consider other sport organizations as a reliable source of information, and request information from them regarding their own job descriptions.

Current employees could describe their own tasks to enable the manager to determine the real job components. Documenting *job descriptions* can help to clarify employee responsibilities and facilitate job performance. A job description should include the following:

- The job title (specific name)
- Job responsibilities (duties, performance, and expectations)
- Job requirements (experience and educational background)
- Additional job information (recommendations, salary range, starting date, and to whom and where to send the job application and accompanying material)

Another area of consideration is recruitment. Identify appropriate recruiting services and then publicize the position internally and externally. You may submit job announcements to newspapers, newsletters, or magazines. An internal search might boost employee morale and motivate internal competitiveness. Promoting an insider avoids training a newcomer to the organization, but external recruiting brings in "new blood" with new ideas, energy, and potential leadership. Interviews are critical since the person hired must clearly understand the goals and expectations for the job.

Controlling Material Quality
Quality control is typical of a manufacturing organization and is made through sampling the finished products. A 3% defect rate in material is normal; more means poor parts and less means greater efficiency.

Sport organizations should control not only the quality of their work in organizing competitions, seminars, courses, congresses, and any other sport activities but also the physical and mental qualities of the national team, individual athletes, coaches, and officials. Only consider top-class athletes, coaches, and team management staff for national teams. In addition, the organization of sport events should be of the highest quality (world-class).

Controlling Financial Planning
This pre-control method focuses on the budgeting process. Top-level management should prepare programs and operating budgets every year. Industrial companies develop *line-item budgets,* meaning that each specific item is described by specifying its cost. Top-level management of sport organizations should prepare *sport program budgets* along with *operation and management budgets.*

Like any other enterprise, sport organizations and particularly NFs should estimate yearly costs per department and event on the one hand, and identify sources of revenue on the other. Every program or activity entails expenditure, and the organization should indicate how much time it will take to pay for such expenditure and how it intends to do so. Significant financial commitments must be strictly under top management control, especially purchases over $1,000.

Operational Controls

This is a duty assigned to low-level managers overseeing day-to-day operations. Upper-level managers should maintain an open-door policy to be able to consult with employees where necessary. Operational controls include the following:

- **Critical incident reports** are short statements documenting the time and date of positive and negative employee performance. Such reports are kept in the employee file and used in yearly evaluation sessions or to assist in promotion or dismissal.

- **5-15 reporting** consists of a series of reports by groups, which allows employees to voice their feelings periodically about their job, department, and overall working conditions.

- **Weekly or monthly meetings,** though any meeting must be justified and include an agenda. Topics should be job training, new programs, or special events.

- **Monitoring floor operations,** which is not a spying system but rather a way of expressing concern and interest in employee affairs. Personal contacts and short exchanges of opinion help monitor employees and contribute to better employee relations at the same time.

Administrative and Management Controls

Controls of this nature examine the actual performance of employees, the quality of results or of work performed, operational and financial budgets, progress toward short- and medium-term objectives, and organizational structure.

Performance Appraisal   No one likes to be critical of someone else's performance, but the organization must assess the productivity of its employees. With appropriate methods, all parties can view performance evaluation as a positive experience and an opportunity to improve.

Evaluate employees with positive comments and subtle statements concerning areas for improvement, and provide an opportunity for employee feedback.

The job of management is to nurture and facilitate employee growth and development, not destroy careers. Evaluation should work two ways: from the management and employees' point of view, in order to avoid prejudices and subjective judgment. Direct supervision or managerial evaluation should be possible.

Evaluation should contain specific desired work performance (bar-rating is the most effective and consists of assigning levels of performance in every field to be evaluated, such as *poor, low, intermediate,* and *high*). Avoid any of the following during evaluations:

- **Halo effect** happens when an employee's behavior pleases and is given high rating in all aspects; the most recent behavior is wrongly taken to reflect the yearly performance.

- **Central tendency** involves poor managers who look for little more than middle-rate performance in every field.

- **Harshness or leniency errors** involves managers who are either too hard or too lenient; they rate employees the lowest or the highest in all fields of performance.

Quality Control of Results   This control is aimed at measuring the number of errors made by the organization. Most consumer goods manufacturers have no more than 3% defects, which is a normal rate of efficiency considering the number of activities involved. Sport organizations should be attentive to the quality of letters and faxes, the accuracy of texts, and respect for administrative policies and procedures. This affects the organization's image, credibility, and legal status.

Management Audits   These audits meticulously scrutinize all policies, procedures, and phases of the control techniques adopted by the organization. They assess pre-controls, together with operational and administrative control measures, to find out if the organization's efficiency is rated low or high. These audits are made by outsiders and can be used to measure the performance of a national, continental, or even international sport organization. Management audits are costly but convenient to assess productivity, efficiency, and achievements.

Budget Control   This is the analysis of the organization's revenue and balance sheets to assure concordance between the initial budget and year-end assets and liabilities. It includes expenditure, profit or loss, and long- and short-term debts on a yearly basis. It must show investments (over or under), profits (up or down), and inventory (low or high). It is the profile of the economic success or failure of an organization.

An advantage of budget control is that it makes it easier to compare and summarize the situation of the organization, considering that costs and results are both reflected in cash. Budget control has three facets:

1. The expression in cash of the plans for a future period. This control is made in accordance with the accounting system of the organization and should show the amounts representing full implementation of plans.

2. The coordination of partial budgets (by department and project) to balance the global budget of the organization. Carefully coordinate each different administrative unit's account. Assess its compatibility and ensure that its operation and plans are on sound financial footing. Several readjustments may be necessary during the budgeting period.

3. The comparison of the actual results with the budget. Expect to take corrective measures.

Controlling Organizational Structure

A sport organization must have a structure that enables it to meet its goals and objectives, with a minimum of interference and with a substantial economy of effort. A good organization requires structure, strategy, an operational system, style, and personnel, as well as short-term goals and long-term objectives. The specific needs of each organization are the best indicator when selecting the type of organizational structure. This must be adapted both to the needs of the organization and to the personality of its leaders.

Good structures can greatly facilitate the management of a sport organization; deficient structures can prevent the programs from operating or being executed. The functions of supervision, communication, efficient operation, reception of information, and feedback require clear, coherent, and flexible organization.

Every sport organization needs a structure founded on regional or local criteria, given the multiplicity of activities that must be undertaken at the local, city, provincial, and national levels. The structure must also enable the organization to keep in permanent contact with schools, universities, governmental and military authorities, and companies. For more information on structural organization, see "Choosing a Type of Organization," pages 64-75.

Controlling Management

Management control includes controlling administrative policies and procedures. A *procedure* is the expression of how to perform an activity without any sense of permanence. *Administrative policies* outline a field of action to guide management on a longer-term basis. Prepare them with the participation of all those concerned or responsible for their application, development, and preparation. The efficiency of a sport organization largely depends on the degree of coordination between individuals and departments, which will be possible only through a personal and collective understanding of clear-cut administrative policies.

Every sport organization should have its own administrative policies in accordance with its own level of complexity. A very simple association should have a general concept, and a major organization running professional events should have a more elaborate concept. Administrative policies should be formulated in accordance with the following principles:

- Keep the wording positive and clear to facilitate common understanding within the organization.
- Each unit of the organization should be able to implement them through procedures corresponding to its own practices and peculiarities.
- They should have a sense of permanence, while remaining flexible.
- They should contain foreseeable conditions, without purporting to be comprehensive.
- They should respect economic principles, applicable laws, and the general interest of the community at large.

A sport organization should consider administrative policies in the following areas:

- Aspects related to sport in general: the competition area, sport materials and technical equipment, purchasing and supplies, event inspection, organizational standards, participation, promotion, marketing mix, and media and public relations
- Internal relations: personnel administration (recruiting, salaries, incentives, training and personnel development, working conditions, vacations, and budgeting).

Financing and Budgeting Operations

The organizational structure of major sport organizations will not function unless it includes a unit or department responsible for finance and administration. The responsibilities of finance and administration cover no less than four different areas: accounting and investment control, budgeting and cost control, services and administrative procedures, and human relations.

Accounting and investment control consists of establishing an accounts system for an efficient and quick registration of economic movements together with risk-free handling and control of funds. *Budgeting and cost control* structures the rational use of financial, human, and material resources. It also controls their allocation through entries assigned to top-priority programs, project management, and operational expenses of the organization.

General services and administrative procedures is the efficient and timely supply of material resources, services, and working facilities (office equipment) that the organizational units require for their normal operation.

Personnel or human relations is the recruitment of employees in accordance with the required physical, intellectual, and moral conditions and experience that are outlined by the responsible authority of each unit of the organization.

These are the objectives of finance and administration:

- Secure an effective, efficiently coordinated, and rational use of financial, material, and human resources.
- Identify and collect resources, as well as budget, and rationalize expenses for the implementation of the organizational units' plans and projects.
- Unify budgeting and cost-control systems.
- Create manuals for purchasing and payment procedures.
- Revise, analyze, and adjust budgets in accordance with the organization's plans and projects.
- Seek personnel recruitment sources.
- Identify and comply with the organization's legal financial regulations and principles.

The sport manager must clearly understand the finance and administration unit's functions. These are research, planning, action, and integration. *Research* is the study that identifies sources for finances and recruitment and secures costs controls. *Planning* is the preparation of budgeting procedures and systems, office working routines and accounting, and purchasing and payment procedures. Planning involves preparing internal working regulations and manuals of procedures and operational routines.

Action involves implementing the inventory controls and procedures for purchasing, hiring personnel, and mailing and services, together with the supply of material elements, services, or personnel requested by the units of the organization. It also involves collecting resources in accordance with registered contracts, sales, contributions, and services provided and, finally, preparing official forms for accounting; budgeting; engaging personnel; and for use of materials, equipment, and services. *Integration* involves the preparation of financial reports related to the use or disposition of entries, whether budgeted or not, and reports on the availability of financial resources, materials, and equipment.

Results-Oriented Budgeting

Sport organizations need concrete and efficient resources to operate not only specific events and day-to-day activities but to pursue the objectives outlined in the compelling vision. The following concepts may provide a better understanding of the budgeting principles and their proper use in final budget preparation.

A *budget* is a comprehensive, formal plan, expressed in quantitative terms, describing the expected operations of an organization over a certain period of time. The most typical unit of time for budgets of permanent sport organizations such as national sport organizations (NFs), leagues, or clubs is one year. Major sport events and tournaments also call for systematic quantitative planning.

Planning and *control* are the two basic functions of budgeting. Planning encompasses the entire process of translating goals and actions into quantitative plans for the use of resources over the specified period of time. Careful planning provides the framework for control. Control is the comparison of actual results with budgeted data, evaluation of the differences, and making adjustments for differences when necessary. The comparison of budget projection and actual data can occur only after the budgeting period—typically one year—is over and actual accounting data are available. However, it may be wise to monitor performance in smaller increments of time such as three or four months. These principles of control also apply to projects that have their own budget. For example, in team sport, there may be three or even more administrative units or organizations with their own budget: the NF, the league or circuit, and the national team(s).

Benefits of Budgeting in Sport

Budgets offer a variety of benefits to sport organizations. It is important to note, however, that successful budgeting is not possible without professional, results-oriented, strategic, and annual planning of operations and activities. Among other common benefits, budgeting

- compels managers of sport organizations to plan the future operation of the organization in concrete and specific terms;
- fosters cooperation, coordination, and communication among key persons responsible for the results of the organization;
- forces the administrative units and their heads to quantify their proposals, which in the best of cases includes the balancing of income and expenditure;
- provides a framework to evaluate performance;
- creates cost-consciousness;
- satisfies legal and contractual requirements; and
- orients the activities of a sport organization toward common goals and objectives.

Making Results-Oriented Budgeting Effective

The great majority of businesses, governmental units, and sport organizations already spend a huge amount of time and money on budgeting. Unfortunately, not everyone achieves the same return for the time and resources invested in budgeting. Effective, results-oriented budgeting should be based on the following guidelines:

- Budgets should help focus on resource use in accomplishing the organization's main goals and objectives.

- Budgets must realistically quantify action plans and not just be wishful thinking.

- Budget control phases must effectively provide a framework for performance evaluation and improvement of activities at the next budget planning stage.

- Major sport organizations should use participative budgeting to generate a sense of collaboration, commitment, and team spirit.

- Budgeting should, on the one hand, force members of the organization to justify fully any resource request. On the other hand, it should push managers to meet appropriate human or material resource requests and not simply use budgets as an excuse for denying what is amply justified.

- There should be a fair balance between responsibilities and powers to undertake actions within the approved budget.

- The president, general secretary, or manager of a sport organization should use the budgeting process as an excellent vehicle for modifying the behavior of employees, including volunteers, in order to achieve the common goals and objectives.

Developing Your Budget

Regardless of the size or type of organization, most budgets can be divided into two categories: the operating budget and the financial budget. The *operating budget* consists of plans for all those activities that make up the normal repetitive operations of a sport organization and includes both income and expenditure. The *financial budget* includes all of the plans for financing the activities described in the operating budget, plus plans for major new projects, as well as income and expenditure.

It is common knowledge that budgeting practices vary widely in different parts of the world. For this reason, this information will only deal with common principles that apply everywhere. The contents of an operating budget vary greatly depending on the range of activities of the sport organization. Some typical components may include the following:

Income

Services or operations

Fund-raising activities

Marketing contracts (sponsorship)

Television contracts (broadcasting rights)

Contributions and other income

Expenditure

Personnel expenses (wages, social security contributions)

Administrative expenses

Management expenses

Competition and promotion expenses

Public relations and marketing

Other expenses

The financial budget is more simple to explain, because it typically includes only four major components. These are the

1. Capital expenditure budget
2. Cash budget
3. Budgeted statement of financial position (balance sheet)
4. Budgeted statement of cash-flows

A large part of a financial budget is determined by the operating budget. This is important for any organization and particularly for sport organizations wishing to balance their budget. Furthermore, if an annual budget results in a positive balance, it is recommended to make a reserve for future years. Sometimes major investments in activities such as world-class tournaments may create a slight imbalance. In this regard, a realistic plan for future budgetary balance should exist. The creation of future viability is a major responsibility of any sport manager.

There is no magic formula for successful budgeting. But a responsible sport manager will set priorities, constantly monitor progress, avoid surprises, know well the sport activities of the organization, and keep the lines of communication open with the key stakeholders when managing a budget.

Controlling Deviations

It cannot but happen . . . that those will survive whose functions happen to be most nearly in equilibrium with the modified aggregate of external forces. . . . This survival of the fittest implies multiplication of the fittest.

H. Spencer, "Principles of Biology"

Sport organizations in general, even the most successful, are subject to internal and external pressures that force adjustment of their working conditions or modus operandi. The personal cultural level, financial status, and political inclination of the sport leader will strongly influence the actual conditions and environment of the organization. Equally, the average cultural level, financial status, and political inclinations of the group of persons leading the organization will play a significant role in the modification of those conditions and environment. This environment is demonstrated on the international sport scene by the International Olympic Committee (IOC), International Federations (IFs), and National Olympic Committees (NOCs), which often voice, through their leaders, their strong unity within the Olympic movement. Former IOC President Juan Antonio Samaranch Marqués de Samaranch skillfully and wisely managed to prevent their differences from surfacing and softened the commercial approach that the NOCs were constantly trying to impose against the technical authority of the IFs through the promotion of changes to the Olympic Charter.

However, the IOC, IFs, and NOCs operate on unequal cultural and financial grounds. Such inequalities undermine the autonomy and free will of many IFs. Also, many NOCs have become docile instruments of personal ambitions and a fertile ground for unwelcome or chauvinistic attitudes of group leaders. These prevent free and healthy discussions from taking place inside the Olympic movement and facilitate sectarian proposals being approved through personal influence or pressures. This has even led to disrespectful comments about the ability of sport organizations to continue playing their part in the Olympic Games.

In most countries, national governing bodies of sport (NFs) are being left out of the development of professional sport. Most of the IFs seem to be unwilling or unable to tackle the new professional sport environment, thus losing ground to private professional organizations that are mushrooming worldwide and gaining the upper hand over the NFs and NOCs.

The Challenges in Sport Today

The commercialization of the Olympic Games, the merger of NOCs and governmental sport bodies, the constant meddling in NFs' affairs by the latter and other multisport organizations, the professional drive of athletes, the use of advertising for commercial purposes, the fierce local advertising of OCOGs during Olympic Games—all these issues will likely be hotly debated in the years to come. These debates, both private and public, will arouse impassioned turmoil over the essential principles of the Olympic Charter. If these principles are eventually replaced by subjective or unilateral considerations emanating from an alignment based on individual or group interests, it will be a tragic outcome for sport in general.

Services Needed for Sport Today

It is of the utmost importance to prepare national sport organizations to fulfill their duties efficiently so that they can provide the kind and quality of services that youth, press, television, and sponsors alike expect from them. It is also a priority to satisfy the claims of sport practitioners for professional opportunities in sport. To attempt the latter, national sport organizations could enter into joint ventures or partnerships with professional promoters and marketing agencies, leaving in their hands marketing, fund-raising, and image communication. However, they should take great care to retain control over the technical and managerial issues of sport.

Need to Evaluate Results

Unfortunately, most of the sport organizations and NOCs—unlike other professional organizations such as sport promoters, marketing agencies, and entrepreneurs—are not measured according to the results they achieve. Yet this is precisely the criterion that should be used to determine whether or not their leaders should stay in business.

Organizational Problems

Today, national sport organizations are bogged down in internal politics, and they suffer from a range of ills including organizational complexities, self-serving ambitions of a few key influential members, and the unfortunate and systematic interference of NOCs and governmental authorities in their affairs. The latter particularly afflicts emerging countries, although certain developed countries are also concerned.

Such internal turmoil constitutes a heavy burden for national sport organizations. It seriously hinders their ability to direct energy toward other worthwhile pursuits, such as coordinating their sport activities under a comprehensive plan to achieve a better national sport system, greater technical development, and higher international performances of their athletes.

Another problem with today's sport organizations lies in the fact that they are too divided to follow a set course, a situation that is largely due to recently imposed legal constraints preventing their leaders from being re-elected in accordance with the needs of the organization. This lack of leadership continuity gives a substantial edge to sport promoters and professional leagues who through continued action can build up public interest in their professional sport events, which then constitute the spawning ground for the development of national sport heroes.

It is the local sport heroes who arouse and catch the imagination of fans. They are a catalyst for bringing people, sponsors, and media into action. National stars ensure that major sport events retain public favor and become a deterrent to imported idols.

Rising to New Challenges

The world of sport today evolves in a challenging environment, forcing sport organizations to adopt a free-enterprise approach to the administration of sport activities in their community.

Roles of Sport and Sport Organizations

Sport's role in society made almost a full turn by the end of the last millenium. For most of the second half of the 20th century, sport constituted a great social catalyst and an excellent educational tool; it has now become a major professional entertainment for the masses and represents an important segment of economic activity.

Despite this change of orientation, sport still plays an important political role in strengthening national identity and educational and social values, but it seems in general that the dream of sport developed under the Olympic ideals has faded in favor of professionalism and its accompanying partner, commercialism. We also witness today a general trend toward the practice of more freely personalized, informal, and self-serving sport activity.

Since the late 1970s, sport has attracted outside elements, groups, and "parallel organizations," which seek by hazardous methods to control the sport movement for their own benefit and profit. They have grown from the inertia of the sport organizations themselves, which were (and many still are) not ready to operate in a businesslike fashion and in many cases do not even know the meaning of professional management for sport.

Faced with the dangers of these hazards and trends, traditional sport organizations continue to neglect the challenges facing them in the world sport arena. The most serious of these have to do with sport's relationship to television, commercialization, the media, and marketing. Before dealing with the other challenges, it is important to give special attention to the dangers of over-commercialization of sport. On the path toward bigger audiences, overly commercial marketing often transforms a sport event into a "circus" or fake competition. As they use sport marketing methods, these traditional sport organizations should never forget that their prime responsibility toward sport is to safeguard its moral, educational, and social values.

Need for Change

It is obvious that sport organizations need to stop living in the past and wake up to the actual needs of the world's sporting environment. They will need to change their attitude, behavior, and strategy, even if this entails changing their structure, organization, and management principles.

Even so, the main goals of sport organizations in the 21st century remain the same. These goals include satisfying the needs of the millions of sport practitioners, as well as those of the top athletes, through the national governing bodies and meeting their responsibility in safeguarding the public image, credibility, and reliance on the organization and in the quality of their sport events. They also include fulfilling the needs of the written and electronic media by providing adequate facilities, services, information, and working material and satisfying the spectators' and athletes' expectations. While facing those challenges, sport organizations must preserve a clean image, creating the correct environment where the athletes and officials are ready to provide the kind of sport entertainment that everyone expects from them. These ingredients are also needed to keep the sport venues crowded!

New Approach

The sport environment today is characterized by persistent movement toward professional sport, which means not only sport being played by professionals, but also the tendency for sport to be managed and organized in a professional way.

This new approach requires close cooperation and mutual understanding between all the actors involved in the sport movement, and television is clearly one of the most important. Sport organizations can help television and the media better serve public needs by providing the most exciting, entertaining, and competitive sport performances possible.

To face properly all sorts of dangers, internal shortcomings, and external challenges, sport managers need a new approach to the operation of sport organizations in the third millennium. They must prevent "parallel" promoters from exerting influence, not only on the athletes themselves through tempting offers they do not intend to deliver but also on the operation of sport organizations at the local, national, or world level. Sport bodies and managers must be aware that the only aim of these "parallel" organizations is to take over sport. They prey on inexperienced sport organizations or associations whose leaders are not prepared to face their responsibilities.

In the long run such parallel organizations tend to dictate their cause to athletes and to the sport movement, quickly abandoning their faked friendly attitude. But more damaging still is the fact that most of the time they do not have legal status, recognition, or registration in any country. In this way they take advantage of the situation to their own benefit and to the detriment of athletes or organizations that entrusted them with their sport events or careers.

Serving the Sport Organization's Clients

Sport organizations establish a relationship with individuals performing different activities within the world of sport. Each group of individuals has its own needs and the organization should be willing and ready to satisfy such needs.

National sport bodies should guarantee that clubs and leagues, even at the local level, have operating units to organize daily or weekly practices.
Courtesy of Nuova Immagine.

National sport organizations and managers are today required to provide professional and personalized support to their clients in many ways, including technical advice, entertainment, and the many other services expected by each group of clients: participants, spectators, media, or sponsors.

These clients are not only target markets, they should also be considered as individuals involved in the practice of sport. They have specific requirements as spectators or media representatives, and even companies or products expect to satisfy certain marketing needs through the sport they envisage as an ideal marketing tool in itself.

Sport Practitioners

Sport practitioners must be provided with technical services and given every reason to see national sport bodies as reliable organization. This includes a professional administration and management that perform duties in an orderly and timely manner to gain their loyalty.

With this aim, competitors, clubs, and members need to be guaranteed

- competitive sport opportunities at all levels;
- clear-cut rules for sport practice and participation in competitions;

- operating units organized for the daily or weekly practice of the sport (clubs and leagues established at local, city, provincial, and national levels);
- competitions or events at all levels (international if possible) in a regular annual calendar;
- regular official information to all members; and
- regular access to the latest technical advances and new rules, including a constant updating of their technical manpower.

Spectators

To determine and satisfy their needs, it is important to do a segmented study of spectators, analyzing them as regular television viewers, occasional viewers, or regular or occasional spectators.

They should also be the subject of a segmented study from these areas:

- **The geographic point of view.** Region, size of community, climatic area, and population density.
- **The demographic point of view.** Race, sex, occupation, education, national origin, annual income, religion, family life cycle, and age.
- **Their behavior in sport.** Introductory stage or frequency of practice.
- **Their attitude toward the sport.** Benefits sought through the practice of that sport, loyalty to it, frequency of attendance as a spectator.
- **Their social and economic status.** Social class, lifestyle, and personality.

Media

Knowledge, skill, and competence to work with the media are essential for sport managers who must begin by acknowledging their personal responsibilities toward the media and an understanding of the media duties toward the public. This is an indispensable step prior to developing and nurturing a professional relationship with the press, television, and radio. Sport organizations should understand that the media is required to report news and facts in an unbiased fashion, and such news must be adequate to suit public needs and expectations.

Corporate Sponsors

As sport organizations develop important sport activities they should look at their sponsors not only as clients of the organization, but as partners as well. Their sponsorship is to achieve specific marketing objectives by taking advantage of the quality of the sport image and popularity of its events. In exchange they provide the organization with financial support.

The manager should make every effort to satisfy the companies' marketing objectives and allow them to enjoy promotional flexibility and the opportunity to address different objectives. The elements of promotion (advertising, publicity, personal selling, and sales promotion) must also be protected to favor the objectives the company wishes to achieve.

Better Management and Committed Leadership

A good manager must demonstrate good management and leadership. People who are responsible for organizations must use the best of their abilities, improve their capabilities, and dedicate themselves to excellent leadership.

Managers' Needs

To implement plans and programs, managers need organized and efficient departments, people motivated sufficiently to perform their best, and adequate information to make decisions. They also need definite leadership skills. Leadership, which is intertwined with the entire array of management functions, requires the ability to influence others and to hold a leading position. Leadership implies reliance and determination.

To this end, successful leaders should master two managerial attitudes: understanding the needs stemming from a given situation and examining the wishes expressed by employees. These will enable them to use one of the two following leadership concepts as appropriate: *participatory leadership,* which is recommended when dealing with complicated tasks involving experienced employees, and *autocratic leadership,* required in situations where simple tasks are executed by new employees.

Managers should hire the right person for the right job, establish a shared vision of how to accomplish job goals, and understand that every work situation and each individual employee will require a reassessment of their leadership style.

Managers' Leadership

Good leaders are neither tyrants nor despots out to exercise power in an aggressive manner with a view to imposing their personal will on others. A leader is clearly distinguished by personal qualities, inborn or acquired, that make people want to follow him or her with faith and enthusiasm.

Sport managers are expected to provide leadership, courage, and maturity to people working for their sport. They set the example that will either increase or dampen the enthusiasm, optimism, and efforts of their followers. Leaders should demonstrate that they

- know where to go and how to get there;
- have determination, courage, and a tenacious character;
- are credible and enjoy the confidence of followers because their deeds always match their principles, and they never trade such principles for personal profit;
- clearly evaluate the importance of the tasks needed to accomplish the objectives and goals that have been set; and
- can communicate self-confidence to their followers to accomplish the tasks they are assigned.

Sport managers should never compromise with a second-class result or the mediocre outcome of a project. It is their responsibility to strive for the best in any aspect related to the organization, its structure, operation, or image.

Not only are managers full-time paid employees responsible for the smooth running of the sport organization, they are also high-ranking honorary officers who take on managerial duties when they assume responsibility for planning, organizing, coordinating, controlling, and making decisions within their assigned functions. They regularly intervene, on a full- or part-time basis, in activities that have an important impact on the progress and results of the sport organization in general.

Need for Skills and Knowledge

In order to lead an organization to success, a manager should master both the professional skills and the necessary knowledge to hire competent staff and secure appropriate administrative facilities, equipment, organizational structure, and working environment, and the best material conditions for the athletes and the events. Managers also need to be able to carry out timely planning of sport events, coordinate and supervise day-to-day operations, plan the most appealing grassroots events, and plan the most competitive, entertaining, and interesting sport events for spectators and the media (television, press, and radio). See chapter 5 for more information on the role of the sport manager.

Each one of these responsibilities demands that managers be professionally knowledgeable in subjects other than sport technicalities. This fundamental fact is mostly forgotten by government authorities and decision makers in countries searching for a solution to their low competitive level of sport, the lack of national sport structure, and need for sport promotion.

Such countries call on prize- or medal-winning athletes to lead their national sport organization or end up by leaving sport activities to unemployed politicians. They then learn the hard way that nothing can be achieved through former famous athletes or politicians if they do not have the necessary organizational, administrative, and management skills and knowledge.

The Future of the Organization

Colin Coulson-Thomas offers a good view of the situation of organizations today and what should be expected of them in the future. You can get a better understanding of his ideas by reading his book.* However, an excerpt from chapter 14 is reproduced here that pertains specifically to the situation of sport organizations:

> **Innovations are occurring in many areas that collectively have the potential to radically transform the nature of our lives. However, many social institutions, corporate mind-sets and certain social values are inhibiting rather than enabling beneficial change. We are lagging farther behind where we need to be if we are to fully embrace the opportunities open to us and secure the advantages they promise. We are defensive where we should be bold.**

> **We need the courage to formulate our own philosophies of business and develop our own tools and approaches. Inspiration should be sought from what is simple yet fundamental, and from within rather than from what is trendy.**

> **We are surrounded by opportunities to re-engineer supply chains, create learning environments and liberate potential, establish new markets and introduce new services. As information, communications and learning technologies come to be taken for granted and integrated into the physical and social fabric, greater priority should be given to our social needs.**

> **People should be encouraged to work and learn in whatever ways suit their circumstances and preferences, match their aptitudes and otherwise allow them to give of their best. Social creatures thrive on trust, and the interaction and interdependence that allow individuals to create and negotiate roles that enable them to contribute while being true to themselves.**

> **Management must focus primarily on people, whether customers, suppliers, employees or partners, and on their anxieties and dreams**

---

*Adapted, by permission, from C. Coulson-Thomas, 1997, *The Future of the Organization* (London: Kogan Page), 400-403. © Kogan Page.

as well as their needs and requirements. **The emphasis should be on values and relationships; roles, competencies and behaviors rather than procedures and structures; flexibility and intuition rather than prescriptive and mechanical approaches; the fostering of diversity and creativity rather than the enforcement of standards; learning rather than control.**

Choices have to be made. There are new visions, values and priorities to agree. We must focus on what is important, such as end customers in supply chains. Self-awareness is demanded, and honesty with ourselves and with others. Focusing on what we are particularly good at rather than striving to "improve everything" makes it easier for us to work cooperatively with others who have complementary capabilities.

The options, examples and opportunities we have examined suggest that, given a shared sense of purpose, supportive learning and transformation partners, and an appropriate mix of change elements, renewal and transformation can be achieved.

Such is the future foreseen for private enterprises. I do not see much difference for the future of national and international sport organizations in the 21st century.

Understanding and Cooperation—the Only Way

Sport organizations in the 21st century need to readjust concepts, identify sources of power, and define a new profile for sport leaders. There is no doubt that national and international sport organizations urgently need to take a close and hard look at the environmental conditions of today's sport. They will need to be involved in sport in a new way. In particular, they will need to do the following:

• Adopt mutual understanding and cooperation as the modus vivendi, readjusting concepts and establishing new rules to live together.

• Define the relationship sport has with television, commercialism, the media, and marketing.

• Improve management and require committed leadership.

• Revise and readjust their operations to fit with high-tech communications and the new global political and economic order.

• Identify genuine sources of authority and flag bearers, to dispel conflicts relating to their own roles, the sharing of Olympic sponsorship revenue, and individual antagonism.

• Define the profile of new leaders as ones who are in their position regardless of personal fortune and have a sincere and honest sense of mission and a commitment to guarantee the preservation of ethical, legal, and democratic values.

Readjusting Concepts

New sport concepts involve governmental agencies in the running of sport affairs, including the need to guarantee the civil rights of individual members of sport associations, clubs, and leagues. Respecting the particular interests of each NF, governmental agencies must coordinate efforts with them, preserving their freedom of action in the face of the overt commercial ambitions of NOCs that might jeopardize the NFs' financial feasibility.

The Olympic movement should decide whether to maintain a separate identity, focused on the staging of Olympic Games every four years as conceived by Pierre de Coubertin, or adopt the new trend of multisport and youth games. This latter direction, following in the footsteps of several NOCs, presents a hazardous course of overlapping Olympic responsibilities with other national activities as well as international programs.

IFs and NOCs need to find better ways of supporting the activities of NFs so that the latter can more easily fulfill their essential duties and harmonize the calendar of sport activities in their respective countries. IFs and NOCs should try to understand each other better and come to realize that their functions will be more effective and important when based on successful, smooth coordination of NF activities. Both should acknowledge that they are neither autocrats nor the only source of authority, as some of them seem to believe. They are no more and no less than the representatives of the interests of athletes grouped in NFs, and their power takes on its real value only when it is delegated by a sovereign assembly.

Establishing New Rules

IFs and the IOC need to redefine the rules related to the technical operation of the Olympic Games and coordinate efficiently their respective responsibilities. This will facilitate a smoother flow of operations related to the Olympic competitions, taking into account the permanent authority vested in each IF by the athletes' representatives.

There is also a need for an open discussion on commercialism within the Olympic Games. This should no longer be left to lobbying or private negotiations but instead become the subject of serious planning in which all parties concerned would participate. It could begin with a brainstorming session enabling each party to express its own standpoint, devoid of bitterness or ambiguity. After this brainstorming session, a reduced number of elected people, including representatives of the IOC, major NOCs, and IFs (giving preference to NOCs and IFs having successful marketing programs underway) would establish the basis on which to share the Olympic proceeds—which could hopefully be made on the basis of each party's contribution to the staging of the Olympic Games.

The other alternative would be to leave things as they stand. Nothing will happen at the next Olympic Games, of course, but sooner or later organizations will feel an inevitable uneasiness, nurtured by the need for an appropriate sharing rather than fixed allocations. The balance of power currently depends on the relations of individuals, and such relations could easily change and provoke a major upheaval.

New Sport Leaders for New Challenges

New sport leaders will be facing different social conditions from those prevailing today as the sport environment becomes even more professional. The structure, administration, and management of sport organizations will hopefully be adequately prepared and equipped to cope with these new conditions. However, if the strength of leaders is based solely on their political ties or personal fortune, sport organizations will not succeed in their attempts to overcome the hardships in the new challenges stemming from conflicts with professional sport.

Youth, already attentive to their own financial and material interests, will need guidance and supervision to uphold the legal, ethical, and democratic values inherent in sport. Such guidance will be more effective the day youth observe that democratic and fair play principles are the basis for all decisions in any field, be they sport decisions, sport conflict rulings, or sport financial allocations.

These values and principles cannot be applied in this century by a leader who does not share them, who has no sense of commitment, and who fails to understand the need for a better use of the power inherent in sport. From here on, sport leaders will need to serve youth sport with the loyal conviction that "there is always a better way for a better human" and with actions that lead the way.

CONCLUSION

Every sport organization performs actions that are directed toward the achievement of future goals and objectives. It is important to foresee changes, obstacles, and deviations, along with their economic impact on the organization. Consider these aspects as you plan your organization's budget.

While preparing resource allocation budgets, managers should verify the validity of each request made, compare respective cost, and assess its relative weight in the achievement of long-term objectives. They then need to decide whether all requests can be satisfied with the financial resources available and determine the total amount to assign on the basis of confirmed revenue, setting aside a small reserve.

Controls help the organization and the sport manager to ascertain whether the budget satisfies the needs of each program, whether the departmental structure matches the organizational objectives, whether goals and objectives can be achieved with foreseen resources, and whether the right person was hired for the job. Most importantly, when the organization has established adequate controls based on effective checks and balances, it will increase the accountability of managers.

Assign operational controls to low-level managers overseeing day-to-day operations. Upper-level managers should not neglect contacts but maintain an "open door" policy to be able to consult with employees when necessary. Administrative and management controls examine the performance of employees, the quality of results, reports from management audits, and control of operational and financial budgets.

Budgeting for sport organizations is preparing a comprehensive, formal plan, expressed in quantitative terms that describe the expected operations of an organization over a certain period of time. The most typical unit of time for budgets of permanent sport organizations such as NFs, leagues, or clubs is one year. Major sport events and tournaments also call for systematic quantitative planning.

> **Management must focus primarily upon people, whether customers, suppliers, employees or partners, and on their anxieties and dreams as well as their needs and requirements. The emphasis should be upon values and relationships; roles, competencies and behaviors rather than procedures and structures; flexibility and intuition rather than prescriptive and mechanical approaches; the fostering of diversity and creativity rather than the enforcement of standards; learning rather than control (Coulson-Thomas, 1997).**

National and international sport organizations are already compelled to take a close and hard look at the environmental conditions of today's sport. Undoubtedly their involvement in sport is under scrutiny from not only the media but also sponsors and governments. It will be in their best interests, and in the best interests of sport as a whole, to take adequate action and adopt mutual understanding and cooperation as the basis of new rules to live together. At the same time, they should improve management and require committed leadership, which will help them to define the relationship sport has with television, commercialism, the media, and marketing. It is a must for international organizations to revise and readjust their operations to fit with high-tech communications, but at the top of the agenda they need to identify genuine sources of authority and flag bearers, to dispel conflicts relating to their own roles and individual antagonism.

The structure, administration, and management of sport organizations will hopefully be adequately prepared and equipped to cope with the new conditions. However, if the strength of leaders is based solely on their political ties or personal fortune, sport organizations will not succeed in their attempts to overcome the hardships of the new challenges stemming from conflicts with professional sport.

These values and principles cannot be applied in this century by a leader who does not share them, who has no sense of commitment, and who fails to understand the need for a better use of the power inherent in sport. From here on, sport leaders will need to serve youth sport with the loyal conviction that "there is always a better way for a better human" and with actions that lead the way.

GLOSSARY

accountability matrix: This matrix is a record of responsibilities; time frames, costs, goals, actions, and resources needed to achieve each objective and shall contain the assignment of the critical issues among the competent members of the NF attending the planning process, as per their choice. It must mention the nature of the project; final and intermediate objectives; the schedule and phases of the activities; personnel, materials, and facilities needed for its implementation; the amount of money needed to pay for each part of the plan; where the funds will come from; any specific financial arrangements; specific managers responsible for the various projects; and the general management responsible for the completion of the whole action plan. In short, the accountability matrix tells you who is going to do what, how, when, and through the use of which resources.

accounting and investment control: Consists of establishing an accounts system for a quick and efficient registration of economic movements, together with risk-free handling and control of funds.

administration: The timely allocation of human, material, and financial resources needed to maintain the smooth running of an organization and implement its strategic actions.

administrative policies and operational procedures: Management control includes the control of administrative policies and procedures. A procedure is the expression of how to perform an activity without any sense of permanence. Administrative policies outline a field of action used to guide management on a longer-term basis.

advertising: This is a paid message using any communication means or media vehicle, whether via newspapers, magazines, television commercials, billboards, or brochures. A more general definition is to announce, through presentation to the public, the actual or future existence of services, goods, or things (including a person, a group as a whole, or a fact).

antidoping tests: A method, practice, or examination procedure established by the competent sport organizations to ascertain the presence or the absence of forbidden substances in sport practitioners.

authority: Refers to the supervisory role of managers through which they possess the legal right to give instructions to or make demands of others on a certain behavior.

autocratic leadership: Less educated and inexperienced employees, as well as those who are not internally motivated, require a more *autocratic* style of leadership. Autocratic leadership or unrestricted authority without compromise is also required in situations involving new employees executing simple tasks.

barriers to communication: Barriers can affect or prevent the receiver's proper understanding of a message. The most common barriers include sexual, political, and racial differences; prejudices and biases; enmity; social, religious, and age differences; superstitions; circumstances; multiple meanings of words; words taken out of context; poor timing; poor choice of communication means; lack of clarity; distance; and pride.

budgeting and cost control: Budgeting and cost control structures the rational use of financial, human, and material resources. It also controls their allocation through entries assigned to top-priority programs, project management, and operational expenses of the organization.

bureaucratic organization: *Bureaucratic* indicates a more formal model of organization under hierarchical principles and in which regular activities required for the achievement of the organizational objectives are listed as official fixed duties; operational activities are governed by a system of abstract rules applied to individual cases; top-level managers operate with impersonal formality; and employment within the organization is based on technical aptitude and is less subject to arbitrary or selfish decisions.

business portfolios or units of the plan: This is what private enterprises call the set of activities pursuing a given target or objective. In a sport organization, these correspond to the different programs. Each program should contain the actions required to achieve a certain objective or goal, in relation to growth, development, social penetration, or diversification of activities.

central tendency: This pertains to poor managers who, when evaluating employees, look for little more than middle-rate performance in every field.

centralized organization: An organization subject to central planning, in which, in a linear command-like manner, one person concentrates on both authority and responsibility, whilst the others must follow suit. A major disadvantage is that the clubs, practitioners, and people involved in the sport have no say in regard to the implementation of programs or events and so cannot engage in any competitive activity without prior approval and support of the central authority. When such centralization means that a governmental authority concentrates authority and responsibility, the organization enjoys the advantages offered by full governmental financing. However, in such cases effectiveness depends on the government scale of priorities and whether or not sport is considered to be part of national policy, be it under educational or health programs.

chair the meeting: To preside over the meeting and direct the debates to ensure that the meeting runs smoothly. The president is responsible for chairing the meeting.

channels of communication: The channels of communication follow the hierarchy of the staff members. They are vertical channels when following the chain of command, starting at the top level with parallel communication to subordinates. When the message is discussed among peers (managers or employees), the channels of communication are horizontal. When communication is made from management to specific departments of lower levels concerned with a given plan, they become the diagonal channels.

citius, altius, fortius: Olympic motto that expresses the message with which the IOC addresses all who belong to the Olympic movement, inviting them to excel in accordance with the Olympic spirit.

close discussion: Close the discussion of each item, once the members have expressed their opinions. After closing the discussion, a brief summary must be made and then conclusions and/or proposals may be drafted.

coercive power: Causes fear and panic in others and normally becomes abusive within the organization.

collective planning: The objectives outlined in a long-term plan require collective participation in their preparation. All individuals who are deeply involved in a sport, in whatever capacity, as athletes, team owners, promoters, coaches, associations, members, employees, or volunteers, should have similar concerns.

compelling vision: The expression of an organization's, department's, or individual's strategic activities, in relation to the objectives to be achieved through such activities. The vision can be organizational, departmental, or sectional in relation to their specific tasks.

competitive sport: Sport activity characterized by the urge to compete or the rivalry between two or more opposing practitioners.

constituency development: The planned programs and activities to be implemented in a community in order to identify and retain those people already taking part in the sport, those who are favorable to it, and to incorporate into the sport other groups belonging to the community but not yet involved in the organization.

constitutional bodies: The bodies created by the constituent assembly in a sport organization to be the organization's most representative body, subject to the constitution.

contingency plan: A contingency plan includes only those strategic actions for which an organization has already secured the necessary human, material, and financial resources, and which consists of shorter, more realistic projects.

corporate sponsorship: This is a sport marketing approach from a corporate standpoint, which involves the use of athletes, sport events, or programs in the marketing activities and publicity of a company.

de Coubertin, Pierre: French baron; founder of the Modern Olympic Games and of the Olympic movement.

decentralized organization: This type of organization consists of having, in different regions, states, or provinces, a local committee with identical or similar functions to those of the central committee.

decision-making bodies: These are the main bodies responsible for making decisions in a sport organization; they are the board of administration and the general assembly of affiliated members, also called the Congress.

decision-making level: The body in charge of supervising the management tasks entrusted to the executive committee and to the president is called the general assembly. It confers all power and is thus vested with the highest function of decision making and must meet regularly to see that its decisions have been applied.

delegation of authority: Managers can delegate to their subordinates only specific tasks and responsibilities but not overall responsibility. Delegation is only effective when it goes hand in hand with the authority to accomplish the task properly. If this is not the case, the result can be a power vacuum and, ultimately, anarchy.

delegation of responsibilities: Delegation of responsibilities encourages decision making on the part of employees, which can lead to job satisfaction. It also helps create a productive working environment by increasing employee efforts and freeing managers of some tasks, thus allowing them to take on other responsibilities.

disciplinary powers: The right granted to an association to reinstate the validity of its rules when they are infringed by a member. These powers require that the constituents themselves establish the penalties and that they be applied in full respect of individual rights.

disciplinary sanctions: Corrections imposed by judges or referees on the participants concerned in order to balance disadvantages created in a sport competition through the infringement of the rules.

division of power: Every sport organization should establish a clear-cut division of power in three major bodies and one operational structure. This division of power has the effect of providing the best (or least damaging) harmonization of behavior and understanding and a balance between social and individual rights. These three bodies are as follows: 1) A legislative body consists of the members' delegated or elected representatives. It reflects the members' interests and has authority to make binding principles and decisions to enable the achievement of organizational objectives. 2) An executive body is in charge of abiding by and enforcing those principles and decisions. It acts as a guarantor of the organization's independence and sovereign powers. 3) A jurisdictional body is entrusted with legal powers to solve sport conflicts. It protects an individual's rights, including those of self-defense and due process, consisting of defense, audience, and procedure.

educational sports: Sports practiced with the purpose of providing individuals with a series of attitudes, principles, or exercises aimed at adjusting physical deviations or providing guidance for a better moral, intellectual, or physical formation in life.

eligibility code, criteria: This code establishes the general principles that an athlete must fulfill before he or she can participate in the Olympic Games. It essentially declares that, "To be eligible for participation in the Olympic Games, a competitor must comply with the Olympic Charter as well as with the rules of the IF concerned, as approved by the IOC, and must be entered by his NOC."

Eligibility criteria are the specific standards of each sport pertaining to the Olympic Games program established by the corresponding IF and which an athlete must adhere to in order for that athlete to be declared eligible, qualified, and ready to be entered by his or her NOC.

event marketing: These are activities undertaken by the event organizers, marketing agencies, or sport organizations themselves, with the purpose of identifying specific groups of corporations, in order to offer them the opportunity of joining the image of a sport event to the image of their products or services, in exchange for cash or value-in-kind.

executive body: An executive body is in charge of the administration and coordination of activities, the attainment of objectives laid down in the constitution, and of enforcing and abiding by the principles and decisions made by the general assembly. It acts as a guarantor of the organization's independence and sovereign powers.

executive committee: The body responsible for the administration and coordination of activities, the attainment of objectives laid down in the constitution, and the implementation of general assembly decisions is generally called the executive committee. It meets to plan strategies for reaching goals, oversees the administrator, sets up the operational structure, and maintains necessary contact with the various governmental groups. When not in session, the executive committee acts through the intermediary of its president, who is entrusted with the management and administration power for daily tasks.

executive performance: A manager is measured by his or her personal work and decision-making ability, as well as his or her manner of planning, organizing, coordinating, and controlling.

expert power: Influences people by dispensing or withholding information from those who would benefit from such expertise.

extended command: This is a command given by a manager of superior level to an employee involved in a particular project, who is placed one or more levels below the manager.

feature stories: Prominent stories published in newspapers concerning an athlete, sport organization, or event that is not related to news information but to interesting aspects or situations that set apart the person who is the subject of the story.

feedback loop: Recipients of a message should confirm that a message was properly received and understood. Such response will complete the feedback loop.

filter debate: The so-called diagnosis or filter debate takes place when you analyze each idea in relation to the definitions and either put it on a new list or drop it if it does not fit the definitions determined by consensus (never by vote). It is necessary to ensure that the group discusses and evaluates all ideas before either discarding them or considering them for the final list of critical elements.

financial budget: Includes all of the plans for financing the activities described in the operating budget, plus plans for major new projects, as well as income and expenditure.

forbidden substance: A substance declared forbidden by the international sport institutions (IOC, IFs) or national law to athletes taking part in official sport competitions (local, national, or international).

freedom of consent: A competitive sport is chosen by individuals or groups who freely give their consent to practice a specific sport together with other individuals or groups. This practice will take place in accordance with the rules that regulate competition in that specific sport, including rules of conduct, restrictions, and disciplinary measures. Rights, duties, and responsibilities are also part of the freely chosen sport.

free-time sports: Sports usually practiced after working hours or after school, without the formalities of an official competition but in full compliance with the rules.

functional organization: This type of organization is based on the division of labor and requires a careful analysis of the functions needed to carry out the tasks of the organization so that those functions may be grouped by department with clearly defined levels of authority and responsibility. Orders may emanate from different levels of the organization.

fund-raising: To solicit donations from individuals, businesses, or organizations, which requires a specific plan with a defined strategy for reaching a reasonable goal. Fund-raising must be supported by promotional activities and can help the NF promote specific programs, such as the national team (junior, youth, or senior), athletes' training, participation in international competition, or courses for coaches or officials.

games under the patronage of the IOC: These are multisport events organized in conformity with the rules of the Olympic Charter, recognized by the IOC, and held in accordance with the rules of their corresponding IF.

general assembly: The general assembly is the gathering of the constituent members and is normally held periodically (every year or two), with the constitution stipulating clearly who can attend and what business should be discussed.

give the floor: Authorize the use of the microphone or grant the right to speak to those wishing to discuss items in the order listed on the agenda.

governmental organizations, governmental sport programs: Organizations created by the government for the purpose of facilitating government support to sport activities or to supervise private sport organizations or government sport involvement. Governmental sport programs are the sport activities that are arranged to take place at a scheduled time and under the authority of these organizations.

governmental sport institution: An organization created by the government for the purpose of facilitating government support to sport activities or supervising private sport organizations or government sport involvement.

Glossary

halo effect: This happens when an employee's behavior is pleasing to his or her manager and he or she is consequently given high ratings in all aspects; the most recent behavior is wrongly taken to reflect the yearly performance.

homologated equipment: Uniforms, shoes, etc., approved by the IF of the corresponding sport as being in accordance with the rules of the sport and thus declared to be in compliance with its international standards.

homologated materials: Sport materials declared by the IF of the corresponding sport as being in accordance with the rules of the sport and thus declared to be in compliance with its international standards.

identity prism: Values inherent in each sport can be projected to potential customers (athletes, spectators, sponsors, and the media) from six different facets, all of which may be viewed together as the identity prism of the sport (cf. Professors Kapferer and Bernard Catry).

IFs: International nongovernmental organizations administering one or several sports at the world level and encompassing organizations administering such sports at the national level (cf. Olympic Charter, 1997, page 46).

illicit sport practices: The use of any forbidden method or the taking of forbidden substances to enhance athletes' performance for an official sport competition.

immediate command: This is the direct command from a supervisor to people placed under his or her personal supervision.

interferences in communication: Interferences distort the meaning of a message and represent obstacles that prevent the sender and receiver from having the same understanding.

International Court of Arbitration for Sport: The highest jurisdictional institution recognized by the IOC and all members of the Olympic movement to arbitrate, in the last instance, any and all disputes concerning antidoping sanctions against athletes.

IOC: Founded in Paris on 23 June 1894 following the ideas conceived by Pierre de Coubertin, the IOC leads the organization of the Olympic Games and the promotion of the Olympic movement under humanitarian principles. Its first president from 1894 to 1896 was Demetrius Vikelas (1835-1908, Greek), followed from 1896-1925 by Pierre de Coubertin (1863-1937, French baron), from 1925-1942 by Henri de Baillet-Latour (1876-1942, Belgian count), from 1942-1952 by J. Sigfrid Edström (1870-1964, Swedish founder and president of IAAF), from 1952-1972 by Avery Brundage (1887-1975, American Olympian and businessman), from 1972-1980 by Lord Killanin (1914-1999, Irish businessman and journalist), from 1980-2001 by Juan Antonio Samaranch (Spanish marquis and banker). Finally in July 2001, the IOC elected Dr. Jacques Rogge (Belgian Olympian and surgeon) as its new president.

job description: A list of specific duties and responsibilities of the position. The employee is directly responsible for each one of the tasks and cannot delegate that responsibility. The responsibilities assigned to the person should include the definition of the demands, particularities, experience, and abilities needed for the position.

jurisdictional body: This body is entrusted with legal powers to solve sport conflicts. It protects the rights of the individual, including those of self-defense and due process consisting of defense, audience, and procedure.

league: An association of sporting clubs with the aim of organizing matches between member sports teams who are of a similar standard or level.

legislative body: A legislative body is composed of the delegated or elected representatives. It reflects the members' interests and has authority to make binding principles and decisions, in order to achieve organizational objectives.

lineal organization: Lineal organizations are under lineal command, which means that authority and responsibility are centralized in one person (i.e. the manager or president). Orders emanate from that person, with everyone below following those orders.

line-item budget: Each individual component of the budget, as per the accounting plan.

management: The executive ability to create, maintain, and control a coherent system of decision-making procedures and to motivate people to identify themselves with and strive toward the accomplishment of an organization's strategic plan. Management requires an adequate flow of information; the determination of objectives and goals; the selection of activities required to pursue those objectives; and the motivation of members, employees, and volunteers to work together toward those goals.

management by objectives (MBO): To implement programs, ensure that departments are organized efficiently and operate effectively toward the achievement of objectives, and lead everyone in line with the ultimate objectives of the organization.

managerial skills: The proficient ability to perform management duties and managers' responsibilities.

market penetration: Involves action(s) directed toward the groups of people (children, students, or workers) already involved in a given sport.

marketing: The activities undertaken with the purpose of identifying specific groups of people in an effort to buy from or to sell them a given product.

mass communication: Mass communication involves conveying messages with the purpose of informing or educating individuals in general, creating impressions, reinforcing or exchanging opinions held by others, influencing behavior, reinforcing habits, exchanging fashions or trends, developing allegiances, or establishing attitudes. This communication implies the use of publicity and the media.

material or physical resources: These are operational, marketing, and other manipulable resources, such as office space, data processing or duplicating equipment, transportation, and communications equipment.

media: The communication means able to reach a large number of people through the press, television, radio or, nowadays, the Internet.

media relations: Dealing with the media is only effective through PR activities aimed at creating a good impression among media representatives, especially journalists and TV and radio commentators. This requires that you have a good understanding of media needs and foster close relationships with the media, thus eliminating anything that gets in the way, because developing and nurturing a truly professional relationship with the media needs to be a NF's top priority.

medium-term objectives: Objectives must be precise, clear, achievable, measurable, realistic, and interesting. When objectives are achievable over a three- or four-year period, they are called medium-term objectives.

mind-setting: The effect that sport stars have on their fans, who live in the aura that the stars project while performing during a sport event.

mission statement: This is a collective statement or declaration of the organization, also known as compelling vision. It corresponds to the definition of what is to be accomplished and should usually contain the critical elements of the four environmental conditions identified during the SWOT analysis. This statement should be realistic and achievable.

multisport organizations: Sport organizations governing or coordinating activities of more than one type of sport.

narrow span of control: Less time for supervising people or controlling the proper direction of the job or less people under supervision.

national governing body (NGB) of a specific sport: A national federation (sport organization) gains the title of "national governing body of (its) sport" when it is legally recognized by its governmental instances as the only national organization with legal authority over that specific sport within its territory and which, with such recognition, becomes an affiliated member of the IF that administers the corresponding sport worldwide.

newsworthy situations: Circumstances considered to contain valuable information of interest to the press and the general public.

NOCs, NOC members: Sport organizations with mainly NFs as their members, established in accordance with the Olympic Charter, linked to the role of the International Olympic Committee, and recognized by the latter as National Olympic Committees in their respective countries.

numerical principle: Authority and responsibility must have uninterrupted direct flow from the highest to the lowest executive level, whereby managers are given a number. This principle simply establishes the organization as a hierarchy and follows the "chain of command." The highest manager is number 1, the next is 2, and so forth.

objectives: The aims or ultimate goals of an individual's or organization's endeavors.

OCOGs: Organizing committees of the Olympic Games.

Olympiad: The four-year period between two Olympic Games.

Olympic Charter: The codification of the fundamental principles, rules, and by-laws adopted by the IOC. It governs the organization and stipulates the conditions for the celebration of the Olympic Games.

Olympic ideals: The ethical values that the Olympic movement seeks to attain.

Olympic movement: The group of people and organizations recognized by the IOC who share the Olympic ideals, as stated in the Olympic Charter, and respect the principles contained therein.

Olympic spirit: The ideals and principles considered, as a whole, to be the life-giving force of the Olympic Games.

Olympic sport: A sport included by the IOC in the official program of the Olympic Games.

open the debate: To ask the members to take the floor on each subject, once all of them clearly understand the topic of discussion.

operating budget: Means the allocation of financial, human, and material resources to each department of the organization and in accordance with the programs under way.

operation and management budget: The contents of an operating budget vary greatly depending on the range of activities of the sport organization. Normally, they should include the different item budgets of the accounting plan, under the concepts of income and expenditure. The management of the budget should be under the responsibility of a sport manager who is able to set priorities, constantly monitor progress, avoid surprises, sufficiently understand the sport activities of the organization, and keep the lines of communication open with the key stakeholders.

operational bodies: They are responsible for implementing the programs, actions, and decisions throughout the organizational structure by means of adequate administration and professional management. They are the administrative units composed of the people directly working for the organization.

operational level: Constituted by the group of people, volunteers, or employees who are responsible for the administration of programs; implementation of decisions; execution of policies; and the actual performance of the day-to-day activities of the organization.

operational meetings: Meetings at the operational level are held inside sections, departments, and administrative units to assess priorities, define work routines, and eventually discuss small discrepancies or distribute tasks. These meetings must be called and conducted in a friendly atmosphere by the unit head. Meetings are also held between heads of administrative units, departments, or sections to coordinate action on a project, receive information on new projects, or evaluate current ones and agree on sensitive issues affecting all their units.

operational planning: The operating plan determines the day-to-day activities and responsibilities of the different units of the organization that are adequate to ensure that the NF serves the expectations of the sport's practitioners and club members, as well as those of the sport's fans and spectators.

operational structure: A good organization requires an operational structure, consisting of a system in which the units move toward common objectives that can be achieved in a timely manner and where everyone operates under policies aimed at maximizing efficiency, productivity, and employee performance and establishing a good relationship between all units, all of which makes the operational structure work.

organizational chart: An organizational chart provides the description of the organization's internal working conditions and represents the units structured as a system.

organizational communication: Is a manager's important tool for achieving organizational objectives through a good communication system. Organizational communication keeps the members informed, motivated, and confident (see Francis, 1987).

organizational structure: The pattern established for the placing and arrangement of interdependent units and elements of an organization with the aim of maintaining an easy flow of information and keeping their interdependency unobstructed.

participatory leadership: Participatory leadership is achieved through coordination and supervision, making final decisions only after having obtained input from people reporting to you. The participatory leadership style is recommended when dealing with complicated tasks that are entrusted to experienced employees.

participatory planning: This planning requires the participation of a group of members from various important areas and levels of the organization. Some of them should be able to contribute technical know-how, others administrative skills, decision-making ability, or problem-solving talents. They will generate plenty of ideas, each one of them to be filtered through lengthy discussions, adopting or rejecting them by consensus and leaving only those acceptable by consensus for the purposes of planning. The process first requires a freewheeling brainstorming of ideas without discussing their validity or quality. Only at a later stage are the ideas analyzed, criticized, and put in order as the actual suggestions for planning.

participatory strategic planning: This is a method of planning with the participation of competent people representing the different layers of the organization who, in one or several sessions, follow a process that starts with a brainstorming session of ideas and concludes with the establishment of an accountability matrix, in which critical situations, actions, objectives, people responsible, delays, budgets, positions, communication lines, and organizational structure are foreseen.

policies: Outline a field of action used to guide management on a long-term basis.

positioning: Positioning the sport means to place the image of the sport organization, the sport itself, or the event in the minds of its customers and to influence the perception they have of the organization and its products (disciplines and events). Positioning the sport requires the prior identification of the needs and wants of its potential customers at a given moment and an awareness of the position of other sports, as well as their strategic actions in the customers' minds.

power: This is the effective ability or capacity used to force or influence others to fully implement a task or adopt a certain behavior.

power delegation: The effective ability to influence others cannot be delegated, even if power delegation is understood to be the legal delegation of the authority used to give instructions to or to demand of others a certain behavior.

power to judge on site: The power vested in referees and officials to judge on site the conduct and actions of participants in the light of the rules governing the sport and, at the same time, to instantly apply the sanctions as foreseen in the rules when they are infringed.

pre-controls: This type of control is made at the beginning of the organizational cycle of activities and mainly concerns the control of human resources, the quality of material produced, and the adequacy of financial planning.

press agency: A public or private enterprise engaged in the business of news distribution at the national level (national agency) or international level (international press agency).

press chief: This is the person to whom the organizers of a sport event give the responsibility of nurturing good media relations, keeping the press informed about the event, and providing adequate press facilities.

press clippings: These are press cuttings and documents kept in a folder/file or in an envelope containing press releases, reports, photos, and specific information, which is deemed essential.

press officer: This NF or IF official is designated by the international organization in charge as the person responsible (jointly with the press chief appointed by the organizer of an event) for taking care of the journalists and other reporters attending events, coordinating the organization of press conferences, following up the press accreditation process, and supervising the press information flow before the event and the smooth running of the media center during the event.

principle of authority: Corresponds to the power that the organs representing the organization have over its constituency, and the principle of inviolability of its administrative and disciplinary powers and procedures.

procedure: The expression of how to perform a frequent or routine activity without any sense of permanence.

product endorsement: Endorsement occurs when the use of a product is recommended by athletes, teams, event organizers, and sport organizations (such as the National Basketball Association, National Football League, etc.).

professional circuits: A series of sport events held, within a comprehensive concept, in different places and on different dates every year, in which top-level or professional athletes perform a specific sport activity to the best of their ability.

promotion (of sport), promotion campaigns: Activities designed to increase the number of people practicing a sport or the duration or the frequency of that practice. A series of coordinated activities designed to achieve a social status, commercial result, or consideration of the sport by a certain sector of the public, media, or corporations.

promotion: Activities based on public relations principles that are aimed at creating public awareness or making people clearly understand the importance of the sport, its program, or its events in order to motivate and obtain their participation and, eventually, their financial support.

public relations: Public relations is one of the most important activities, the purpose of which is to influence, modify, or improve the attitude and behavior of the public, spectators, media, sponsors, sport leaders, governmental authorities, and others toward the sport, the sport organization, its leaders, members, constituency, etc. It involves adequate communication to enhance the image of a given sport, sport program, organization, sport event, or the people involved with it. The aim is to create an honest, valuable, and credible image of the sport, organization, sport program, or sport event and of the people involved, making all of them worthy of public sympathy and support.

publicity: Publicity is the methodical and systematic notice to the public of services, goods, or things (including a person or group as a whole or a fact). The objective of publicity is to make the information available frequently and in a variety of media so that the sport program remains in the public eye, contrary to news, which only remains in the public eye for a limited time span.

qualifying events: Sport competitions involving athletes or teams not yet authorized to enter the final stage of a competition, which will be held during the Olympic Games or a World Championship.

referent power: Is the power of role models and heroes over people willing to emulate them.

reflex: Or reflection, synthesizes the idea of sport fans who either practice the sport or take part in it as spectators and for whom the sport seems to have been made. Reflex also synthesizes the idea of the sport sponsor and the media, who decide whether the sport is suitable or not to reach their marketing objectives or satisfy their needs. The target of the brand (sport) is the objective description of the practitioners or spectators of the sport, and the reflection (reflex) is the image that sport produces of them as spectators or practitioners, thereby creating an "identification model" and generating a spirit of a community inasmuch as their own image is also reflected in other spectators or practitioners.

regional sport organization: Group of people or countries located in a geographical region and organized into a form of association in order to promote sport practice or competitions.

resource allocation: Sufficient material, human, and financial resources must be allocated in participatory strategic planning to each of the actions foreseen and be used during the whole period required for the implementation of the plan.

reward power: Is used to reward others for behaving or acting in a certain way.

rights of the athletes: Sport rights of the athletes must be guaranteed by the statutes, rules, and regulations of the respective NFs and IFs. This means that in order to apply sanctions, NFs and IFs must carefully comply with strict procedural rules, which include the right of audience, security, defense, etc.

sample-taking procedures: The step-by-step order of activities followed by authorized medical institutions for the taking of samples (urine or blood) from the athletes during a sport event (i.e., antidoping test).

short-term objectives: These objectives are to be achieved over a one- or two-year period (i.e., short term).

social profile: The social profile of a sport organization corresponds to the individuals or groups that could be interested in the sport and the other groups and individuals who could be targeted in an effort to enroll them in the sport.

sport associations: Group of people sharing interest for the same sport-related activities.

sport club: An association of people with sports or a specific sport as a common interest.

sport commercialization: To exploit, for profit, athletic events, athletes' performances, or their names, fame, or charisma; or to have profit as a main aim of sport activities.

sport diversification: Diversification occurs when you offer a new activity, service, or event to the new group of people being targeted. This requires more personnel and more money and time for publicity, public relations, and services, as well as new strategies for advertising, promoting, and organizing events.

sport environment: Is constituted by the attitudes, as well as the economic, political, and social conditions that the community offers for sport participation in a country.

sport equipment (sportswear):   Consists of all sportswear garments and personal items used in the practice of a sport, such as uniforms, shoes, padding, knee and elbow protectors, etc.

sport event sponsorship: The patronage of a sport event by which a person, organization, or corporation provides human, material, or financial means to facilitate the preparation or development of the event, in exchange for a certain public exposure of the corporate image of their products or services during that event.

sport identity: Consists of the values inherent in each sport that can be projected to potential customers (athletes, spectators, sponsors, and the media).

sport image: The way in which potential customers perceive the brand (sport) or the state of mind created in them when they perceive the sport, as presented to them by the sport's distributors (managers of associations, event organizers, sport clubs, leagues, and regions).

sport market development: Addressing your action to the specific new groups of people whom you want to incorporate into sport activities, services, or events.

sport marketing, sport event marketing, marketing of sport events: To buy or sell the image of a sport event, a sport organization, or an athlete in order to finance the event, the organization, the athlete, or other sport activities in exchange for promoting a sound image of the sponsor or of the sponsor's products.

sport materials: These are all the articles necessary for the practice of the sport but that are not deemed to be personal items, such as balls, nets, poles, starting gate, starting blocks, scoreboards, etc.

sport program budget: This is the allocation of funds to specific programs or projects undertaken by the organization.

sport show: The presentation of athletes' performance, displaying sport abilities at their best.

static publicity: Advertising bills posted in strategic places in full view of spectators or TV cameras that broadcast a sport event.

strategic actions: The series of activities or movements foreseen by the organization or an individual, aimed at achieving predetermined objectives or goals under the best possible conditions.

strategic diagnosis or SWOT analysis: This is a method designed to analyze both internal factors (strengths and weaknesses) and external factors (opportunities and threats). The analysis will show the "gaps and gains" of the organization and provide a planning platform of critical elements for overcoming gaps and taking advantage of gains.

strategic planning: Strategic planning is the blueprint of an organization. Through such a plan, the organization decides what type of actions will be undertaken and which internal operations are needed to deliver desired results to the constituents of the organization and to achieve the organization's objectives and mission statement.

strategy: A particular method of tackling specific situations in a long-term plan.

system: A group of assembled, interrelated, and interactive units responding to the same stimulus and forming a collective entity.

target groups or individuals: These are the people who will be the object of marketing activities and who are normally identified through a process called market segmentation.

team planning: Team planning consists of preparing a plan with the participation of individuals who represent the whole spectrum of the organization and include the most knowledgeable and experienced members working in small group sessions.

technical complaint: A formal protest against a violation of the rules governing the practice of a sport during a competition.

technical control: Overseeing, directing, and ruling the conditions under which sport events are organized.

territorial organization: Territorial organization offers improved coordination and control of each zone considered a territory, with adequate administration of its own and of delegated authority. However, the danger is that people in each different geographic zone gradually tend to identify only with their region and consequently neglect the general interests of the organization.

unity of command: Means that each member of the organization reports to just one supervisor.

virtuous circle: Consists of attracting TV and sponsors in order to achieve popularity for a sport, without forgetting that the more popular a sport is, the more interested TV and sponsors will be.

wide span of control: Means more people under the supervision of one manager or more time for supervising duties of employees.

BIBLIOGRAPHY

Barnard, C.I. 1938. *The functions of the executive.* Cambridge, MA: Harvard University Press.

Black, S. 1995. *The practice of public relations.* Oxford, UK: Butterworth-Heinemann.

Brody, R., and M. Goodman. 1988. *Fund-raising events: Strategies and programs for success.* New York: Human Sciences Press.

Coch, L., and J.R.P. French Jr. 1948. Overcoming resistance to change. *Human Relations* 1 (4): 512-532.

Coulson-Thomas, C. 1997. *The future of the organization.* London: Kogan Page.

Cutlip, S.M., A.H. Center, and G.M. Broom. 1999. *Effective public relation.* 8th ed. Englewood Cliffs, NJ: Prentice Hall.

Davis, K.A. 1994. *Sport management.* Madison, WI: Brown & Benchmark.

Drücker, P. 1954. *The practice of management.* New York: Harper & Row.

Francis, D. 1987. *Unblocking organizational communication.* London: Gower.

Freeman, D. 1987. Ethical considerations in fund-raising. *Fund-Raising Management,* 18 June.

Goldhaber, G. 1990. *Organizational communication.* Dubuque, IA: Brown & Benchmark.

Herzberg, F. 1959. *The motivation to work.* Urbana, IL: Division of Microfilms, University of Illinois.

Kepner, Ch., and B. Tregoe. 1970. *El directivo racional.* Naucalpan de Juárez, Mexico: Libros McGraw Hill de México.

Knowles, M., and H. Knowles. 1965. *Cómo adiestrar mejores dirigentes.* Buenos Aires: Editorial Bibliográfica Argentina.

Koontz, H. 1976. *Making strategic planning work.* New York: McGraw-Hill.

Koontz, H., and C. O'Donnell. 1955. *Principles of management.* New York: McGraw-Hill.

Lazzaro, V. 1968. *Systems and procedures.* Englewood Cliffs, NJ: Prentice Hall.

LeBreton, P.P., and D.A. Henning. 1961. *Planning theory.* Englewood Cliffs, NJ: Prentice Hall.

March, J.G., and H.A. Simon. 1962. *Teoría de la organización.* Barcelona: Ediciones Ariel S.A.

Margulies, N., and A.P. Raia. 1979. *Desarrollo organizacional.* Mexico 12, D.F.: Editorial Diana.

Maslow, A.H. 1954. *Motivation and personality.* New York: Harper & Row.

Massie, J.L. 1986. *Essentials of management*. Englewood Cliffs, NJ: Prentice Hall.

McCormack, M. 1984. *What they don't teach you at Harvard Business School*. New York: Bantam Books.

Milo, O.F. 1989. *How to run a successful meeting in half the time*. New York: Simon & Schuster.

Mintzberg, H. 1998. *The manager's job: Folklore and fact*. New York: Harper & Row.

Newman, W.H., and C.E. Summer. 1962. *The process of management*. Englewood Cliffs, NJ: Prentice Hall.

Oxley, H. 1989. *The principles of public relations*. London: Kogan Page.

Raia, A.P. 1974. *Managing by objectives*. Glenview, IL: Foresman.

Schoderbek, P., C. Schoderbek, and A. Kefalas. 1990. *Management systems*. (4th ed.) Plano, TX: Business Publications.

Stevens, D. 1988. *Participatory business planning*. Brighton, Australia: Wrightbooks.

Stier, W.F. Jr. 1994. *Successful sport fund-raising*. Dubuque, IA: Brown & Benchmark.

Tannenbaum, R., and W. Schmidt. 1973. How to choose a leadership pattern. *Harvard Business Review* 51 (3): 162-164.

Tannenbaum, R., F. Weschler, and I.R. Massarik. 1961. *Liderazgo y organización*. Buenos Aires: Editorial Troquel.

INDEX

Graham, P.J. 138
grassroots programs 220

H
halo effect 247
Herzberg, F. 169
Herzberg's motivation theory 171
homologated equipment 222, 223
human relations, internal
    goal of 116
    levels of organization and 117
    organizational pride and 117-118
    positive work environment and 118-119
human resources. *See also* staff
    controlling 244-245
    description of 201, 215

I
identity and image
    brand identity 41
    defined 41
    establishing 48-49
    identity versus image 47
    public image of sport 124-125
    sport's identity 42-44
    volleyball's 44-46, 47-48, 50t
international federations (IFs)
    defined 12
    Olympic Games and 12-18
    Olympic movement and 8, 9t
    recognition of 12-13
    role of 13-14
International Olympic Committee (IOC)
    antidoping tests and 38-40
    historical responsibility of 6
    relationships within Olympic movement and 8-9t
    role of 10-11
international sport environment 8

J
job analysis 178-179
job descriptions 203, 244-245
Johnson, E.L. 4

K
Kapferer, Professor viii, 41, 48

L
leaders, good
    Lundborg Laws for 175

ABOUT THE AUTHOR

Dr. Rubén Acosta is president of the International Volleyball Federation (FIVB). During his tenure, the volleyball association grew from a $100,000 operation into a powerful $200,000,000 organization, making it one of the most successful marketing efforts in modern sport. Beach volleyball has also been recognized as an official Olympic medal event, while the FIVB has been under his guidance.

Dr. Acosta is currently serving on the International Olympic Committee. In the past, he served as the CEO of three major world championships in Mexico, the secretary general of the Mexican All Sports Confederation, and an executive member of the Mexican National Olympic Committee.

Dr. Acosta has received the Cross of the Chevalier of the Legion of Honour, the highest distinction of the French government. He has also been inducted into the International Scholar-Athlete Hall of Fame. Dr. Acosta resides in Mexico but spends a great deal of his time in Switzerland. In his spare time, he enjoys swimming, playing golf, and listening to opera and classical music.